The Right to Literacy in Secondary Schools

The Right to Literacy in Secondary Schools

CREATING A CULTURE OF THINKING

Edited by Suzanne Plaut

Foreword by Theodore R. Sizer

TEACHERS
COLLEGE
PRESS

Teachers College, Columbia University
New York and London

pe┼bc

**Public Education &
Business Coalition**

INTERNATIONAL
Reading Association
800 Barksdale Road, PO Box 8139
Newark, DE 19714-8139, USA (302) 731-1600
www.reading.org

Published simultaneously by Teachers College Press, 1234 Amsterdam Avenue, New York, NY 10027, the Public Education & Business Coalition, 1244 Grant Street, Denver, CO 80203, and the International Reading Association, 800 Barksdale Road, Newark, DE 19714-8139

Library of Congress Cataloging-in-Publication Data

The right to literacy in secondary schools : creating a culture of thinking / Suzanne Plaut, editor ; foreword by Theodore R. Sizer.
    p.   cm.
    Includes bibliographical references and index.
    ISBN 978-0-8077-4918-0 (pbk : alk. paper) — ISBN 978-0-8077-4919-7 (cloth : alk. paper)
  1. Language arts (Secondary) 2. Thought and thinking—Study and teaching (Secondary)
3. Language arts—Correlation with content subjects. I. Plaut, Suzanne.

LB1631.R537 2008
428.0071'2—dc22
IRA Inventory Number 9307
                                                      2008027895

ISBN 978-0-8077-4918-0 (paper)
ISBN 978-0-8077-4919-7 (cloth)

Printed on acid-free paper
Manufactured in the United States of America

16 15 14 13 12 11 10 09   8 7 6 5 4 3 2

To Matt
Here's to a place of bright peace and a world of yes!

Contents

Foreword

Civil rights and literacy are two rarely connected concepts. Both, however, are embedded in the American system of education and of government.

"Literacy" assumes curiosity.

I want to be able to understand something that intrigues me. As others in the past have likely been as intrigued as I am now, what did they learn? Why does this cake mix produce soggy cakes and that one airy, spongy cakes? Why do Arabs and Jews in Israel, peoples who live in close quarters, so suspect each other? In fact, what is suspicion? Why did Hamlet hesitate, pondering whether to be or not to be?

Many—indeed, most—school-age children have questions, from the mundane, and, for parents, infuriating ("Why do I have to turn off the TV now?"), to the more engaging questions of adolescents ("How high should I throw this Hail Mary pass against this particular opposing team?").

Literacy—generally meaning the ability to read and write—depends on words, words that well (or ill) serve a particular situation. Hitler's Reich (usually in the pen of Josef Goebbels) used words carefully; the appalling mass murder of Jews, Gypsies, and other minorities was all too quietly called "the Final Solution," implying (Hitler and Goebbels hoped) the end of something people wanted finished.

Literacy lies at the heart of free democracies as well. Franklin D. Roosevelt built an entire political program around two familiar words, New Deal, and an international plan that called for Four Freedoms that every citizen and community in the world deserved. More recently we read of an Axis of Evil and No Child Left Behind.

Words count. The ability to decipher those words is called literacy. This is what this book is about.

The use of language—at least of language that is understood by most people nearby—must be elicited, taught toward, and thereby learned. Language involves both a speaker/writer and a hearer/reader. The advertising industry understands this well. Words and images, carefully reinforcing each other, are its staple instruments. It works.

Using language effectively is hard work. You and I—readers and writers, at least—struggle hard to find the "right"—meaning the most apt and telling—words. We surround ourselves with dictionaries and thesauruses to assist us with this process.

Teachers forward this process. It is demanding work. No two students (even twins) are totally identical, and no one student is predictably ready to learn, day after day in the same manner. Literacy is a collaborative process. There is the teller/writer and there is the listener/reader. The same words, or formations of words into metaphors, arguments, speeches, and stories, have different meanings for various students in various places.

Literacy is thus a collaboration, a dialogue. As Jennifer Kirmes claims (Chapter 11), literacy is an act of collaboration, a joint effort of speaker/writer and hearer/reader. She points out that such collaboration—"literacy"—is an expression of power. The one who controls the conversation, whether by demand ("Order in the Court") or by tacit personal agreement ("Let's talk") is in command. The managers of political campaigns (such as those of George W. Bush and Albert Gore) and the industry that exists to help people "sell" their "products" (whether Fritos or Fords, Democrats or Republicans) understand these distinctions well.

There is nothing at all wrong with this. Without it we citizens would not be informed, even gulled, or infuriated.

Marjorie Larner reminds us that literacy needs to be tied to our students' desire for a good life (Chapter 4). This reminder should cause us to ponder. "Goodness," if it is to be shared by a couple or a national population or everyone in between, has to be defined, for each person in each situation; and such pondering is useful only if it finds expression in words, in clusters of words, that have meaning for each of us and for those with whom we share the ideas described by those words, the sinews of deep understanding.

Finally, and obviously, the gaining of the power of literacy is hard work. No citizen of a modern society should be allowed to dodge it; literacy is a sort of moral imperative. We Americans and others like us should note how the rising nations of Africa and Asia start their massive growth with a broader and deepening use of language. They understand that without the ability to communicate, and to evaluate what is being communicated, we are sheep, easily manipulated by those who want our participation on their terms. Literacy, in sum, is the fuel for freedom. It is, indeed, a right.

As the authors of this valuable book demonstrate, literacy is a necessity in a democracy that is healthy and respectful of its citizens. We count on it.

—Theodore R. Sizer

Acknowledgments

Thank you to all those who shepherded and supported this work.

To the established authors at the Public Education & Business Coalition (PEBC): You paved the way, providing proof positive that this "next generation" of PEBC authors could and should be writing.

To PEBC staff developers, lab teachers, and clients, all of whom share a collective belief in students' ability and right to think: That belief pulses through every page of this volume.

To those who joined the study group for this loosely defined project, yet whose work ultimately was not included: Thank you for embracing this professional development opportunity.

To those whose work is represented in this volume: Kudos! I appreciate your insight, stamina, and patience with me as we all learned how to see both the forest and the trees in order to make an edited volume work. And thanks to Marjorie for early research on literacy.

To the PEBC Advisory Board for this project: Lori Conrad, Brooke O'Drobinak, Annie Patterson, Karen Lowenstein, Ellin Keene, Stevi Quate, and Rosann Ward. You helped formulate this volume's vision and helped carry me and the authors over the finish line.

Special thanks to Ellin, godmother (*not* grandmother) of this project, and to Cris: catalyst, touchstone, and advocate for PEBC's adolescent literacy work.

To members of the National Adolescent Literacy Coalition: PEBC is honored to be part of this network. Specifically, thanks to Melvina Phillips (National Association of Secondary School Principals) and Cynthia Mata-Aguilar (Education Development Center, Inc.) for feedback on the early thinking that grew into this volume.

To Rosann Ward, PEBC President: Your belief in students, teachers, school leaders, and staff make you a joy to work with and for. Thanks for seeing how PEBC can keep pushing the national conversation and for allocating resources to this end. And to Judy Hendricks, for gracefully managing our ongoing work in schools.

To Natalie Newton, PEBC Executive Assistant: References, release forms, resources—you handled it all, for 16 authors, with grace, efficiency, and impeccable execution.

To Cris Tovani, Anne Goudvis, Ellin Keene, Stevi Quate, and Sally Nathenson-Mejía: You generously read drafts of this manuscript, serving as essential and incisive "critical friends."

To two "PEBC principals": Garrett Phelan and Diane Lauer. As leaders you have made literacy matter for your teachers and students; we hope that your writing in this volume will do the same for readers nationwide.

To our Teachers College Press team. To Brian Ellerbeck, for believing this book was possible, and for your "persnickety questions" as you helped me move this project from a loosely formed idea to a tightly crafted text. To Meg Lemke: you are the type of editor every author dreams of having—responsive, exacting, and incredibly clear about what matters. To Wendy Schwartz, development editor, for your eye for detail and incredible efficiency! To Adee Braun for ongoing support, Lyn Grossman, and all the others behind the scenes at TC Press.

Personally, I would like to thank my students and colleagues at Colorado Academy, who sparked my passion for teaching. And thanks to those at the Harvard Graduate School of Education—professors, colleagues at the *Harvard Educational Review*, and Annie Howell and Sarah Birkeland—who taught me to think and write in community, balancing clarity and compassion. Thanks, too, to my longtime circle of friends, who have helped me evolve as a thinker, professional, and human being. And to my parents, Frank and Linda Plaut: two of my first, and still two of my best, editors. And to my husband, Matt: official and unofficial editor, and constant sounding board. You help me see the big picture. I cherish your respect for my professional life, your strong commitment to social justice, and your deep kindness.

Collectively, we would like to thank all of the students, teachers, school leaders, colleagues, and coaches who have informed our work in schools. In particular, I would like to acknowledge the dedicated teachers and school leaders from the Harbor School in Boston (1998–2002) and the César Chávez Charter School in Washington, D.C. (2005–2008). Your voices, successes, needs, and students drove my work with colleagues to craft this volume. May this text serve you, and your national colleagues and their students, well.

Introduction

Suzanne Plaut

> An informed and literate public is the foundation of democracy.
> —National Adolescent Literacy Coalition

The authors of this book seek to spark a social movement to ensure that our education system empowers every student to become fully literate.

Every young person in the United States has a constitutional right to education (see *Brown v. Board of Education*, 1954). Yet that student's education is meaningless if it does not actually increase the student's ability to use his or her intelligence to make sense of and engage with the world. John Dewey argued that "the only freedom that is of enduring importance is freedom of intelligence, that is to say, freedom of observation and of judgment exercised in behalf of purposes that are intrinsically worthwhile" (1938, p. 61). Teacher Baynard Woods elaborates on this point in Chapter 1 of this volume.

Our youth are truly free only when they are fully literate—when they are able to not only observe but comprehend, and not only comprehend but evaluate, or take a critical stance; when they can ask about the author's or source's bias and viewpoints, note which voices are silenced or discounted, examine issues from alternative perspectives, and take action on the basis of what they have learned (McLaughlin & DeVoogd, 2004). Then they can analyze, evaluate, critique, and question text.

Adolescents have a right to such literacy. They have a right to schooling conditions that empower them to achieve it. And they have a right to what that literacy makes possible for them within and beyond school.

The vision of adolescent literacy we offer encompasses far more than the five components—phonemic awareness, phonics, decoding, fluency, and comprehension—named in the No Child Left Behind Act (NCLB, 2001) and set forth in *Put Reading First* by the National Reading Panel (2001). Rather, we embrace the following definition, which includes Dewey's concept of judgment and purpose as essential aspects of exercising one's intelligence fully: "Literacy may be viewed as adaptation to societal expectations [or] power to realize one's aspirations and effect social change" (Sylvia Scribner, quoted in Harris & Hodges, 1995, p. 140).

Only when we give all students the skills to access learning and to access power in society (Delpit, 1995) will they experience what Patrick Finn (1999) describes as a "liberating education," in which work is challenging, knowledge is relevant to students' lives, and analysis is essential (p. 198). This kind of education contrasts with what Finn calls a "domesticating education" that gives students just enough information to make them useful while remaining dependent.

Literacy is not just a desirable ideal; it is a social imperative. This literacy—and the freedom it offers—is a necessary precondition for students to be able to access and exercise their other civil rights, such as freedom of speech and the right to vote.

This cause is one around which secondary educators must rally. Such literacy enables students to have a voice, take a stand, and make a difference. In other words, it gives them power.

LITERACY AS A CIVIL RIGHT

The contributors to this book believe that literacy is a civil right. Increasingly, scholars are embracing this belief, as evidenced by the rich recent volume *Literacy as a Civil Right* (Greene, 2008), which examines the sociopolitical context of schooling, with a particular focus on the ways in which students of color have been denied equitable educational opportunities and outcomes. Maisha Fisher (2008), writing in *English Education*, asserts that "for Black and Latino youth who typically attend public schools with the fewest resources, the need for critical reading, writing, speaking and thinking can mean the difference between life and 'civic death'" (p. 96). Renowned researcher Sonia Nieto (2006) notes that "social justice is about understanding education and access to literacy as *civil rights*" (quoted in Greene, 2008, p. 4; emphasis in original). Just as voting is a "gateway" right that lets citizens access their other rights, literacy is a "gateway"—to learning, leading, and active citizenship. All students have the right to learn in a culture of thinking, one that empowers them to participate in, lead, and transform society.

Literacy has not been found to be a civil right in the strict legal sense, as defined as an enforceable "right or privilege, which, if interfered with by another, gives rise to an action for injury" (Cornell University Law School, 2005). But for the right to education to have any meaning, the definition of *education* must include literacy. Thus our position that literacy is a civil right is more a moral than a legal one. As secondary educators, we must face the ways we have not yet fulfilled our moral obligation to all students. Lipman (2004) nails a central premise of our volume when she asserts that all students have a right to an "intellectually powerful education" (quoted in Greene, 2008, p. 81). The contributors to this volume strive to show some of what this vision looks like in practice.

We believe that there are six components of this new civil right. Students have the right to schooling conditions that empower students to achieve literacy:

- Active *engagement* with content worthy of sustained attention
- Thorough *thinking* about that content

They also have the right to what literacy makes possible for students within school:

- Deep *understanding* of key concepts in core content
- Increased *independence* through skills they can use to make meaning of current and future content and contexts

And finally, they have the right to what literacy makes possible beyond school:

- *Access* to relevant knowledge
- *Power* to participate in a democracy—to interact with, influence, and transform their world

Such literacy both depends on and generates a meaningful education, which in turn is central to freedom of intelligence.

Every secondary teacher plays a role in developing students who can think well and are literate at high levels. Every middle and high school can and must make this work central to its mission.

A VISION OF A SCHOOL THAT CREATES A CULTURE OF LITERACY

Two years ago, when a colleague and I held a daylong retreat with the administrators of a small (three schools) urban charter school system, we asked, "What would a culture of literacy look like—for students, for teachers, for school leaders—at your school?" These passionate school leaders gave the following answers:

Students would read for pleasure, pass and share books, read a variety of texts, use the reading strategies naturally across contexts, and use writing to create change. As one principal said, "books and ideas would be in students' heads and hands."

Teachers would view themselves as readers in their discipline, teach literacy explicitly using common language, stock and assign rich and varied texts, teach inquiry and questioning, encourage debate, and help students see how literacy is empowering. They would encourage and inspire literate youth; as one administrator said, they would "model literate lives" to their students.

School leaders would be explicit with students, teachers, and parents that literacy is central. They would invest in accessible texts for every content area, fund staff positions to support literacy, provide training and ongoing professional development for teachers, and protect time for teachers to learn about literacy in their disciplines. They would keep learning about literacy, and would create schoolwide literacy traditions (i.e., book readings, poetry slams). They would, as their chief academic officer said, "use literacy to define our school culture."

This school system—despite its ongoing struggles—has done all this and more. They have trained "mentor teachers" in the four core content areas: mentors teach half-time and spend the rest of their time coaching colleagues on curriculum design and literacy integration. Teachers collaborate weekly to share best practices and regularly observe each other in "literacy labs." Student investment, and achievement, is rising.

Sadly, this system's intentional focus on promoting literacy is the exception. Too many secondary schools suffer from what a colleague of mine calls the "fast food" syndrome. We feed our students junk thinking—quick, easy, but lacking much nutritional value. We pay teachers low wages, making it difficult for us to recruit or retain the best. We let the government's incentives—the educational equivalent of farm subsidies—drive us to make narrow-minded or short-term decisions. And we often minimize the long-term impact: an impending crisis in adolescent literacy and thinking at least as destructive as the burgeoning epidemics of childhood obesity and diabetes.

In this volume we do not have room to tackle all of the comprehensive issues related to professional development, secondary school reform, or national and state educational policy. Instead, we offer a starting point: the teaching and learning that takes place in our classrooms. We seek to help individual teachers and entire school faculties develop the perspectives and skills to foster literacy learning that is integrally tied to clear and effective student thinking.

We wrote this book for teachers of all students in Grades 6–12, and across all content areas. By "all students," we mean students representing the full range of linguistic, cultural, academic, and economic diversity. We hope that leaders in reform-oriented schools and districts will use this text with school-based study groups or professional learning communities, as a practical way to guide whole-school inquiry about adolescent learning, thinking, and literacy.

WHY SECONDARY TEACHERS SHOULD CARE

Secondary teachers, typically more than their counterparts in elementary schools, tend to be intensely dedicated to helping students master content. Ask what they teach, they are more likely to name the content ("I teach biology") than the student ("I teach 10th graders"). Since many of their students have not yet mastered literacy, the teachers face an apparent trade-off: "Either I cover the curriculum or I teach literacy." Yet strong literacy skills and deep content understanding are interdependent and mutually reinforcing. Together they make up the DNA of learning—a sustaining double helix, each strand essential to the other. Nearly half of all incoming ninth graders in U.S. comprehensive public high schools cannot understand the texts teachers give them in order to complete class assignments (Carnegie Foundation Report, cited in Strickland & Alvermann, 2004, p. 3). Students need to learn and understand challenging content; and they need literacy in order to do so.

In this country, concern is growing that students in middle and high school are not able to read, write, listen, speak, and think at the levels needed to succeed as college students, as members of the workforce, and as fully participating citizens. On the 2007 National Assessment of Educational Progress (NAEP), just 31% of eighth graders performed at or above the "proficient" level in reading; for students of color or from lower socioeconomic status, these percentages are even lower (National Assessment of Educational Progress, 2007).

Given economic trends, the current U.S. educational system is not developing students with the skills to compete or contribute globally. According to the report "Tough Choices or Tough Times,"

> [Job] candidates will have to be comfortable with ideas and abstractions, good at both analysis and synthesis, creative and innovative, self-disciplined and well organized, able to learn very quickly and . . . have the flexibility to adapt quickly to frequent changes in the labor market. (Tucker, 2007, pp. xviii–xix)

Students do not just "learn to read" in elementary school and then "read to learn" in secondary school. To cultivate truly literate students, we must give them the tools they can use to take apart, reformulate, examine, critique, retain, and claim ideas. This type of literacy, often referred to as *critical literacy*, focuses on helping students name, demonstrate, and monitor their own progress as thinkers (McLaughlin & DeVoogd, 2004).

Therefore, teachers must design curriculum and instruction that engage students in real thinking, which requires reading, writing, and discussion. As high school literacy teacher and well-known author of *I Read It, But I Don't Get It* (2000) Cris Tovani has said, we all may not be "reading teachers," but we are all "teachers of readers" of our particular subject matter.

WHAT IS THE PUBLIC EDUCATION & BUSINESS COALITION (PEBC)?

The Public Education & Business Coalition (PEBC), where I work and where this book began, is a partnership of business and education leaders working together to improve K–12 public education. Driving our work is the goal that all students graduate from high school with the skills and knowledge to succeed in the twenty-first century.

Our work is organized around two central areas of focus: professional development, and policy and business engagement around educational issues.

The mission of the PEBC's policy work is to build public awareness and understanding of fundamental education issues, advocate for effective education policies, and mobilize the business community to support student achievement and positive, sustainable change in our schools.

The mission the PEBC's professional development work is to grow thinkers and improve student achievement by inspiring and developing educators' instructional and leadership practices through inquiry, application, and scholarly discourse.

We provide high-quality professional development that guides and supports K–12 teachers, school leaders, and district personnel as they implement research-based best practices that lead to student achievement. Typically, a school or district contracts with PEBC for multiple years; a staff developer and leadership coach work on site to train and coach teachers, teams, and whole staffs as they implement the type of instruction described in this volume.

Our organization is nationally recognized for its professional development in literacy and instruction and for over a dozen publications that have emanated from our work, including Ellin Keene and Susan Zimmerman's *Mosaic of Thought* (2007) and Cris Tovani's *Do I Really Have to Teach Reading?* (2004).

HOW THIS BOOK CAME TO BE

This book emerged from a PEBC study group. Once a month, a group of teachers and staff developers gathered, munchies in hand, to discuss what we most wanted for students. We began putting our passion to paper, pushing each other with the ever-important questions: "To what end" for the students? "In what ways" for the school staff? These conversations, and the writing that emerged, diminished our sense of isolation in our work with students, teachers, and school leaders. What a relief to take a collective stand! And what an exciting prospect that our writing might buoy up other educators and propel them on the crucial journey of helping evolve into intelligent, literate, *thinking* young adults. Several years later, after more iterations than any of us would care to count, this volume was born.

About half the chapters are based in literacy/humanities classrooms; the other half are based in other content-area classrooms. We hope this mix of chapters gives history, math, and science teachers an entry point into the text. We also hope it helps teams or an entire faculty see connections and build bridges across content and contexts.

The chapter authors give equal attention to middle and high school classrooms, since teachers in Grades 6–12 have a shared responsibility to ensure that all students graduate equipped as resourceful learners and active citizens. We hope these chapters help the two groups view each other as resources, not impediments, in addressing the challenge of adolescent literacy.

About half of the chapters are written by PEBC staff developers. The other half are written by classroom teachers who are a part of the PEBC network. All PEBC staff developers are former classroom teachers, teacher trainers, and principals who not only have extensive teaching experience and knowledge of instructional best practices, but also have advanced education and training in adult learning strategies and coaching practices.

Some of the teachers who wrote chapters are PEBC "lab hosts." These teachers, who have benefited from years of PEBC professional development, regularly open their classroom doors to national visitors who attend a PEBC "national lab," in which participants observe and reflect on exemplary instruction and the outcomes for students. This writing has challenged these lab hosts to reflect on their own instruction in ways they have found energizing. One author even shared all of her rounds of revisions with her students, showing them what real writers do when they craft, rethink, and respond to critique. She said that these students have become her strongest writers in years, largely because they now get in their guts what it takes to write (and rewrite, and rewrite!) for a real audience and purpose.

The other teacher authors are PEBC clients—teachers who have been coached by a PEBC staff developer to implement the frameworks and strategies we describe. They dove into this writing challenge with courage and conviction, eager to share their own steps on this journey.

The mix of teacher and staff developer voices offers readers both the "outsider" consultant view and the "insider" view of how real teachers think about and do this work.

Throughout the volume, all student names are pseudonyms, unless otherwise noted. We use the actual names of most teachers, with their permission, unless otherwise noted. In most instances, the school demographics reported in these chapters are for the 2005–2006 school year.

OVERVIEW OF THE CONTENT

The book is organized in three parts, each of which begins with an introduction to the part's content and intended purposes, and ends with a "Reflecting" section containing discussion questions for study groups and reflections and thought-provoking questions from two school principals. Each chapter also contains guides for the reader, beginning with a summary and list of key points, and ending with four brief sections on how to begin teaching the material, lingering questions, principals' perspectives, and related readings.

In Part I the authors describe what it means to claim literacy as a new civil right. They show the quality of thinking we strive to foster in students, and explain that literacy matters both within and beyond school because it enables students to understand essential content, develop independence as learners, and gain access and power in society. Part I puts forth a vision, showing why all secondary educators should care about adolescent literacy. The first three chapters in Part I move from broad to narrow—from thinking, to thinking about thinking, to thinking in content areas—while the fourth chapter considers how literacy empowers students.

In Chapter 1 Baynard Woods lays out the central argument of this volume: that students have the right to think, that thinking and literacy are intricately connected, and that secondary teachers have the responsibility to honor and develop students' literacy skills.

In Chapter 2 Jennifer Swinehart delves into the role that metacognition plays in giving students the literacy skills they need to tackle difficult text, and to "own" their own learning. She explains how she teaches metacognitive strategies, and how this benefits all students, particularly her English Language Learners.

In Chapter 3 Angela Zehner then articulates the role of content-area teachers in this crucial work, asserting that literacy is a means to every content teacher's ends. She also shares how and why literacy has become so central to her instruction as a math teacher.

In Chapter 4 Marjorie Larner addresses the age-old student question "Why do I need this?" and the companion teacher question "Why should I spend time on this?" by emphasizing how literacy gives students access and power in their lives now, not just in some distant future of college, work, or citizenship.

Part II shows how our belief that literacy is a civil right is embodied in actual classroom practice. The authors describe how they help students apply high-level literacy skills to acquire and use content knowledge, as well as how students master key concepts, make meaning of difficult texts, and develop independence in core content areas. The authors show how literacy manifests in service of the core cognitive work in each content area (e.g., reasoning in math, crafting argument in social studies). And they show how these teachers' underlying beliefs guide their daily work with students.

In Chapter 5 Paula Miller and Dagmar Koesling make a strong case that we are *all* literacy teachers: We teach the literacy needed for content area understanding, and we teach whole students whose literacy skills are our shared responsibility. They describe how Koesling helps students grapple with complex math content by having them read word problems in specific ways to build mathematical reasoning skills.

In Chapter 6 Moker Klaus-Quinlan and Jeff Cazier argue that the inquiry and framing of a task (not the literacy) is what ignites students' curiosity in science class. The literacy strategies allow students to think through a problem, argue based on evidence, and synthesize their own discoveries with what the standards require them to learn.

In Chapter 7 Joanna Leeds presents the work of Gerardo Muñoz, who teaches at an alternative high school in Denver. Leeds shows how oral argument serves as both a rehearsal and a scaffold as students learn to construct clear arguments that are supported with relevant text.

In Chapter 8 Lesli Cochran explains how she teaches eighth-grade Language Arts students to use their own standardized testing literacy scores to self-assess and guide their own literacy learning. She emphasizes that students have a right to understand and "own" their data, and that honoring this right helps foster engaged, self-directed, and masterful learners.

In Part III we provide common concepts and frameworks to help an entire teaching faculty implement the type of instruction described in Part II. Each author focuses on one central goal for students (engagement, understanding, independence, or thinking) and gives readers a simple framework for how to get started. They explain to teachers in all content areas how to begin using some basic practices to make the kinds of shifts in teaching and learning that we advocate.

In Chapter 9 Michelle Morris Jones describes three necessary preconditions for getting students to think: belonging, rigor, and support. We must know our students, challenge them, and give them a safety net as they take intellectual and emotional risks.

In Chapter 10 Wendy Ward Hoffer helps readers see how to design instruction that leads not only to engagement but to genuine understanding. She provides a model for how teachers can reevaluate their goals, tasks, teaching, and assessment to get there.

In Chapter 11 Jennifer Kirmes shares how she longed for her students to be independent learners, but struggled to get them there. She shares what she has learned about using the Gradual Release of Responsibility framework (Pearson & Gallagher, 1983) to help her plan instruction that promotes student independence.

In Chapter 12, Samantha Bennett describes the "Workshop": a system, structure, ritual, and routine that lets teachers put student thinking at the center. Bennett synthesizes many of the themes of this volume, showing how literacy expert Cris Tovani uses the workshop structure in service of our goals for students.

HOW TO READ THIS BOOK

Teachers can read this text in several ways. Ideally, a full faculty will read this together: Everyone would read Part I, smaller groups would select relevant chapters from Part II, and everyone would read Part III. But an individual, department, or grade-level team also could read this book to help develop a shared, heightened understanding of the issues and promising practices.

Throughout the volume, we address how to support English language learners (ELLs). One in five students in our K–12 public schools is a child of immigrants, according to the U.S. Census of Population and Housing. This number is growing dramatically: in secondary schools, the percentage of students with Limited English Proficiency doubled from 1980 to 2000 (Capps et al., 2006). In our experience, anything a teacher does to serve ELL students well—whether specific strategies, broader frameworks, or the beliefs on which both are grounded—serves *all* learners well.

Finally, as noted above, the "Reflecting" sections provide specific discussion questions, and all the chapters include various aids for structuring further reflection and exploration. We hope that groups of colleagues will use the information and the discussion tools herein as a catalyst for rich conversation and collective action.

HOW THIS BOOK IS DIFFERENT

This book differs from other texts about adolescent literacy in two ways. First, many other texts tell teachers *what* to do in terms of "integrating literacy instruction," yet do not state forcefully *why* it matters. Others state *why*, but not *how*. Secondary teachers need not only the skills to teach students to truly think, but also the will—individually and collectively—to make that happen. We offer teachers more than just new tips or tricks to use in tomorrow's lesson.

Second, we simultaneously provide an entire staff with shared language and instructional practices and show how teachers of each content area play a unique role in fulfilling each student's literacy rights.

Irasema Salcido, founder and CEO of the César Chávez Charter Schools in Washington, D.C., and a PEBC client, praised her teachers for having "a fire in the belly"—an intense commitment to ensure that students are learning the literacy skills needed to be active citizens and agents of change. We hope that this book helps all educators feel that fire and use it for the benefit of each of our students and for all of our futures.

Literacy is more than "useful": it is a civil right. Let the movement begin!

Vision and Value: What Literacy Looks Like and Why It Matters

As secondary educators, many of us face a sea of students every day, students who are perhaps underprepared, disengaged, or unconvinced that the tasks we are asking them to do in school will serve them well in the world beyond. We may struggle to remember the brilliance and potential inside of each of these young people.

In Part I of this volume, authors seek to remind us all what it means for our students to think hard and well about the content we are teaching them:

- What does it look and sound like for middle and high school students to think and be literate at high levels?
- How might we embrace the belief that adolescents' literacy rights matter?

Ideally, your entire school staff would read all four chapters in Part I to develop this collective vision; alternatively, an individual teacher, department, team, study group, or professional learning community, might read and discuss these chapters.

A second purpose for Part I is to remind us of the value: "To what end" are we doing this hard job and asking students to do this hard thinking? What does literacy, this gateway skill, give students? These authors show how literacy enables students to understand essential content and develop independence as learners, and how that in turn gives students access and power beyond school.

We hope that as your faculty reads these chapters, you will develop a shared definition of *thinking* and *literacy* and a shared commitment to this work. We encourage you to consider why it is important that every teacher play a role in helping students develop both the literacy specific to their academic content and the ability to reflect on and refine their own thinking. And we encourage you to consider what this hard work gives you as a teacher, and what it gives your students, now and later, within school and beyond.

CHAPTER 1

The Right to Think: Giving Adolescents the Skills to Make Sense of the World

Baynard Woods

IN THIS CHAPTER: Baynard Woods, a teacher of history and politics, explains the relationship between thinking, literacy, and students' rights. He argues that since rights are based on reason, thinking is the first right or the only freedom.

KEY POINTS

- Students have the right to think.
- Teachers can teach thinking by empowering students to see the role thinking plays in the world, giving students material worth thinking about, and giving them time to practice skills and reflect on their own work.
- Thinking requires the same skills as literacy.
- Teachers need to teach content through text, not around it.
- Student success in school and beyond depends on their ability to think.
- Our democracy depends on our ability to empower adolescents to think.

A scraggly-looking 17-year-old dressed in baggy clothes hid behind the hair hanging in front of his eyes. It was January and he was new to the school, expelled from a different school; and he sat, sunken and sulky in his plastic chair, until he heard the names Byron and Shelley. This student aspired to be a poet, and flipping through an older friend's textbook, he had accidentally discovered the romantic poets. He started to pay attention. The teacher in the grape-colored dress praised Byron's originality. She even seemed to praise him for drinking from a skull.

Maybe things would be better here, the student thought, as he scanned the book while the teacher talked and his classmates nodded, uncomprehending. The bell rang and the teacher asked the new, and now almost enthusiastic, kid to come back to see her after school.

"You wanted to see me?" he said when he returned at the end of the day. The teacher looked up from grading papers with a big red marker. Her chair rolled back as she straightened her legs. She stood up and looked at him, eye to eye.

"I don't know where you came from, or why you are here," she said. "But you are at River Wood now and you need to start behaving, dressing, and thinking like everyone else here." She did not emphasize any of the words. It was as if they were all the same. I stood there in a stunned silence, angry and bitter.

That confirmed it. I was right. School was not a place where thinking was encouraged. It was the site of indoctrination. It seemed to me that my teachers were interested in obedience to the exclusion of thinking and independence.

Later, as a college philosophy teacher, I hit the same problem from the other end. I wanted my students to think about the things they were reading. I wanted them to probe, challenge, push, and question. I wanted them to care. They didn't seem very interested in disagreeing with Descartes or Plato. They wanted me to tell them what these strange texts meant. They wanted to know what was on the test.

I saw a connection between these experiences and I started to ask, How can we encourage and inspire students to think? The question led me back to high school as a history teacher, at César Chávez Charter High School in southeast Washington, D.C. A majority (68%) of our students are African American, 30% are Latino, and 26% of the Latinos are English language learners; 68% are eligible for free or reduced-price lunch. I found a school that faced many of the same problems that inner-city schools have traditionally faced. Our students showed a great many talents and a great deal of character, but most of them did not come to us with well-developed literacy skills.

After 3 years at Chávez, I still ask the same questions that brought me here. How can we turn schools into the kinds of places where students are encouraged to think in the ways that they will need in order to be successful and independent actors in the world? And how we can teach them to think so that they may go beyond us and continue to develop our academic disciplines, our democracy, and the world of which they are a part?

If we do not answer these questions, then we have not only failed each individual student, but we have failed our disciplines and our society, all of which desperately need thinkers. If we do not create classes, lessons, and school cultures that promote and encourage thinking, then we are indoctrinating rather than educating.

Students have a right to think, and teachers have an ethical obligation to teach them to think and to provide them with meaningful content to think about. Schools and districts are responsible for creating cultures of thought that will empower students to engage in academic disciplines and American democracy.

THE RIGHT TO THINK

The U.S. Department of Education's Civil Rights Office exists in order to "ensure equal access to education" and to "promote educational excellence" (U.S. Department of Education, 2007). The right to an education places an ethical responsibility on educators to empower adolescents to be excellent. In order to fulfill this mission we must teach them to think so that they can achieve both understanding and independence.

When we deprive students of the space and time to think through problems, we are denying them more than the right to an education. All other rights depend upon the right to think. The enlightenment concept of the rational individual is the foundation of the concept of rights, which was "self-evident" to the rational mind. Thus all rights are dependent upon the capacity to think. The development of this capacity is the development of the individual and the fruition of freedom.

The capacity to think guarantees the right to an education, but it also provides its content. In other words, no matter how much our students know, they don't "get" math or science or history until they start to question and evaluate those disciplines, that is, until they think about them actively.

Knowledge is necessary but not sufficient to help adolescents reach independence. As the work of E. D. Hirsch (2004) suggests, students need to develop a strong base of factual knowledge in order to be successful students and full participants in our democratic society. But they also need to understand the "facts" they learn.

In *Understanding by Design* (1998) curriculum specialists Wiggins and McTighe define *understanding* as "a mental construct, an abstraction made by the human mind to make sense of many distinct pieces of knowledge" (p. 37). They go on to describe understanding as being about "the ability to transfer what we have learned to new and sometimes confusing settings" (p. 40). Such an ability to transfer is essential to success.

David T. Conley's *College Knowledge* (2005), a book based on extensive interviews with students, staff, and faculty, presents a picture of what happens when students graduate without the ability to transfer or to think, and "enter college expecting assignments and tests with clear right and wrong answers that do not require much interpretation or even thinking" (p. 75). This study makes it clear that high schools need to teach students how to think in order to make them ready for college and the world.

WHAT DOES THINKING LOOK LIKE?

In 2005, when I started teaching a philosophy elective at Chávez, I told the 20 juniors and seniors—most of whom were reading below grade level—that they were going to learn how to think. One of the students said, "Well then, I'm going to get an A, because I be thinking all the time!" The student laughed, but he was serious. We engaged the question.

"What did I mean by 'thinking' when I said that? What kind of thinking can you learn?" I asked.

"Yeah," another student said. "How can I learn to think if I have to know how to think first, before I can learn?"

"You're doing it now," I replied.

"What? Thinking? I know. That's what I'm saying." The class laughed.

"What is the difference between 'seeing' and 'watching'?" I continued.

Several students leaned in, some interested, others confused.

"You can't help but see," one ventured.

"If your eyes be open."

"And how is it different to watch?" I probed.

"If I'm looking at something, I'm paying attention to it. But if I see it I just see it. It just be there."

"But you have to have something to watch."

"Like what, Ralf?" I asked.

"Well, you aren't gonna be just watching the wall. You watch TV or a movie or a game," Ralf replied.

"Or girls," another boy said.

"Those are all things you look at but you just like see cars going by and whatever," Jackie added.

"You only start to watch it, right, when you pay attention to it because something catches your eye," Ralf added again.

"That's a big part of my job," I said, "to give you things to watch with your mind. Things that will catch your mind's eye. And to help you learn to really watch the world." Though I had thought about this before, it struck me now as if for the first time.

We continued to push on the idea of watching as seeing plus attention, and we discovered several key attributes that thinking shares with watching:

- Thinking is active; it is not something that happens, but an activity that makes meaning.
- Thinking is strategic; it is not automatic, inspired, or random, but learned.
- Thinking highlights what is important; it does not treat all material equally.
- Thinking is focused; it creates a foreground and background.

Adolescents are conscious in the same way that they see. But they must learn both to think and to watch.

HOW CAN WE TEACH THINKING?

If these are some qualities of thinking, how do we teach it? If Montaigne (1580/1965) claims that "my conceptions and my judgment move only by groping, staggering, stumbling, and blundering" (p. 107), can we expect something more fluid from our students? Nevertheless, watching students struggle with thinking is often too much for teachers to bear. There is always the temptation to give in, to break the silence, to give the answer, to tell them what to think. When we tell our students what to think, we inadvertently teach them that thinking is not important. We take shortcuts to knowledge at the expense of understanding.

Instead of telling our students what to think, it is our responsibility to

- Empower students to think by helping them see the role that thinking plays in the world
- Provide them with material worth thinking about
- Give them the time and space to practice the skills required to think about the material
- Give them time and opportunities to reflect on their own work and their own thinking, and reassess their positions

These components help create a thoughtful classroom. But thinking is often slow. It is also risky and full of the possibility for error. But it is worth it. If students don't think through the material, then they do not learn it; and they will not remember it because they won't care about it.

Most of our students have not been trained to value thinking, and so it is sometimes difficult to make them care about their own thought processes. In order to change these attitudes and preconceptions, school leaders must take broad actions to create cultures of thinking. But it is the individual teacher who has the most power to create a culture that values thought, for the thoughtful classroom is the model of the culture of thinking that must be extended to include whole schools and districts.

CULTURES OF THINKING

In my 2007 classical civilization elective (in which over a third of the students were English language learners), I kept typed minutes of a student seminar—a formal conversation that is "leaderless" and text-based—and posted the results on our class Web page. I printed out the transcript and gave it to the students in the class the next day. Immediately, they began to read the text, avidly underlining their own words and correcting my omissions. We had a second seminar on their discussion and it provided the students with a chance to recognize and refine their own thinking.

Initially, the students focused on their own comments, scanning the transcript for their own name. But eventually, as they began to look at the conversation and the dynamic of the group, they focused on the following exchange:

> TAYLOR: Can I introduce a new idea? I thought that Achilles refused them because in his speech on page 171 around line 325 where he says "if I stay here and fight I will never return home," he knew that whether or not he fought in the war death would happen.
>
> JONESSA: In my mind, he is conceited.
>
> STEVEN: He is a big powerful person, the most powerful of all time.
>
> JONESSA: But he is conceited.
>
> RONALD: Why does he have to humble himself?
>
> JONESSA: Yeah, he's powerful but he doesn't have to brag and be like "y'all wouldn't have got this far without me."
>
> RONALD: It's the truth.
>
> JOSÉ: Didn't you say if he lives that he wouldn't have the same glory if he dies?
>
> JONESSA: When he goes back home, everyone will be like "he did such a great job, because he's conceited."
>
> KEISHA: But he'd have the chance to live out his life.
>
> RONALD: He went out to the war and killed all them people and now he just don't care no more and so he's a cold gangster.
>
> JOSÉ: What's your definition of gangster?
>
> RONALD: The product of his environment. Product of the ghetto. Third world community. If you are the product of a third world community. They are a product of their community.

JONESSA: They live in a world full of pride. This is what happens when you have too much pride.

When the students reread this passage from their discussion the previous day, they were even more engaged than they were in the initial discussion.

Jonessa said, "I thought the *Iliad* was, I mean not stupid but I kind of like couldn't get it, but what Ronald said. I mean we had talked about pride or whatever but I just didn't make the connection."

"Yeah. I got it too. But," Ronald added. "I didn't know that I got it when we were talking. I only got that now, when we talked about us talking. That's weird isn't it? I didn't notice what Jonessa said. I was just talking. But it's right. That was their environment."

My students used this text and conversation as a way to reconsider their own thinking. Discourse served as a step toward a thoughtful relationship with a difficult text. My students read themselves in order to read Homer. And they read Homer to read themselves. And it was one of those rare occasions where I could see a change happening right then, in the moment. The students were interested in their own thinking. They had moved toward independence. The strategic engagement with text is not only important as a tool for understanding, but one of the most important factors in developing independence.

As my students started to think actively about the *Iliad*, they surprised themselves with what they comprehended. They started to see that they could learn to read the world by reading texts and learn to read texts by reading the world. They were using the strategies I had been teaching in an organic way. They were understanding.

THINKING AND READING

Reading is thinking. The most detrimental and perhaps the most common misconception about reading is that it is a physical activity. "He can read fine," a mother once told me. "He just has trouble with comprehension." This mother was worried about her son. And yet she separated reading from the act of understanding the words. Her son checked out when he read, perhaps because, like his mother, he did not make the connection between reading and thinking.

As a result of our work with the Public Education & Business Coalition, and in our effort to honor our subject areas and our students, César Chávez Charter School adopted eight thinking strategies, shown in Figure 1.1. These are based on the research of D. Pearson and M. Gallagher (1983), who articulated specific cognitive moves proficient readers make as they read. These are the same strategies thinkers use to make sense of the world. When students use these strategies, they are actively engaged in the action of understanding. We should create lessons that teach students about both the world and themselves. Whatever else we teach our students, we should always work to help them understand what it means to know. Knowing what it is to know enables students to assess themselves and to become engaged with their own learning; knowing what it is to know is the key to learning how to learn.

Figure 1.1. Thinking Strategies

- *Checking for understanding.* Readers can tell when they are understanding a text and when they are confused and have "lost the meaning."

- *Problem solving.* Readers use a variety of strategies to understand a text once their ability to easily grasp the meaning as they read has broken down.

- *Making connections.* Readers connect what they are reading to their own background knowledge, to other texts, and to their own experiences. They use these connections to help them understand a text.

- *Asking questions.* Readers ask questions of the text as they read. Sometimes readers ask clarifying questions, and sometimes they ask speculative or "pondering" questions.

- *Creating sensory images (visualizing).* Readers create images and emotions while they read. They use the text to "make a movie in their heads."

- *Drawing inferences.* Readers draw conclusions about the text by combining evidence in the text with their own knowledge and experience. Inferences help them predict and also generalize.

- *Determining importance.* Readers identify key ideas, themes, and information as they read. They distinguish between important and unimportant information. A reader's purpose plays an important role in determining importance.

- *Synthesizing.* Readers recognize how important information and ideas from different texts combine to create overall understandings of a topic or field. Synthesis involves summarizing a text and relating it to other texts or to general ideas.

Source: Pearson & Gallagher, 1983.

It is, however, essential to recognize that students need high-quality materials worth thinking about. If we simply tell them to think, they will drift along daydreaming in the stream of consciousness or find themselves swimming in frustration against its current. Strategies function only when applied to meaningful content.

Text is the most important way for students to think about the thinking of others—and thus learn how to think about their own. When students recognize the thinking inherent in writing, they start to recognize their own thinking and then the thinking that invests the world around them with meaning. When they recognize that the human world is made of thought, they realize that the world can be changed.

This transfer happens only when students start to think about text strategically, only when they start to watch it instead of simply seeing it. Some secondary teachers resist explicit literacy strategy instruction in order to save their "content." But literacy strategies are precisely those ways of thinking that we mean when we say "knowing."

If we wish to save our content areas, we must encourage our students to engage directly with the texts of our disciplines.

TEACHING THROUGH THE TEXT, NOT AROUND IT

Many teachers dealing with students of especially low literacy levels are able to avoid the temptation to tell students what to think, while still using a variety of tools to achieve understanding, such as role-play, video, and art. These teachers are striving to bring their students to understanding, though they often deprive students of the independence that comes from engagement with discipline-specific texts.

It is hard to watch our students struggle with reading. We know how many positive qualities they have. We don't want to think about their reading levels. As a result, we tend to want to tell our students what texts mean. My colleague Jody Peltason put it well, saying that in such situations we teach "around the text" rather than "through the text."

As long as we tell our students what texts mean without first demonstrating how we came to make that meaning and later working with them to make it for themselves, then we encourage them to see meaning as magic. Our students will not be independent until they realize that meaning is *made*. They can't realize this until they have made meaning for themselves. When adolescents see that meaning is made, they see that they can make meaning and become independent actors in the world. They realize this by repeated engagement with text accompanied by metacognitive reflection.

When we teach around the text, we inadvertently teach our students that thinking is not important. We also teach them that their thoughts are not important, because we do not provide the time or space for them to develop. We rush over the students for the sake of material and as a result what they really learn is that right answers are given, not created. Thus we fail to enrich the minds of our students and the material with which we want them to engage. When we value *what* we teach more than *whom* we teach, we devalue both.

When we teach students to engage with text, we help them learn to think and we provide them with the content to think about. But we can't stop there. If we want our students to work toward understanding and independence, we must teach them not only to read discipline-specific texts, but also to read their own work as evidence of their own thinking.

STUDENT WORK, STUDENT THINKING

My classical civilization seminar helped me see the role that student work can play in student thinking. One of the most significant things we can do to encourage student thinking is to help adolescents learn to see their work as a reflection of their thinking that they can use to learn about themselves.

Researchers from the Academy for Educational Development, the Coalition of Essential Schools, and Project Zero at the Harvard Graduate School for Education, have all concluded that the collaborative inquiry of teachers into student work is an essential component of successful teaching (Weinbaum et al., 2004).

There is little research, however, into the collaborative inquiry of students into their own work. Yet, if it is valuable for teachers to come together around the products of student thinking, would it not be at least as valuable for students to come together in a similar way around their own thinking? If we want students to achieve independence, it is necessary for us to help them see their work as a way to see themselves.

When my students saw their own speech transcribed, they saw themselves differently. It was not a sudden shift from boredom to engagement. But they were transformed. Their comments demonstrated that they had learned something about themselves.

I now know that I need to find more ways to help them look at their other work just as avidly. If we can use student work correctly, the simplest five-paragraph essays can help students come to see themselves like Joan Didion (1976), who says she writes "entirely to find out what I am thinking."

When students look critically at their own work and revise their previous thinking, they take another step toward internalizing the thinking strategies and content-specific knowledge that they are trying to understand. Such internalization of both content knowledge and strategies creates a disposition of thinking.

Ron Ritchhart (2002), of Harvard's Project Zero, discusses the role of dispositions toward thinking in the development of intellectual character. Ritchhart draws from both Aristotle and Dewey to define disposition as "the volitional, acquired and overarching patterns of behavior" (p. 20). This means that a disposition must be developed and cultivated. Over time, individual thoughts create patterns. Future thoughts occur in the context of those patterns. The development of such dispositional patterns of behavior, however, requires more time for practice than is often available to an individual teacher in the day.

TIME FOR THINKING

Although individual teachers can use class time differently, no one can make more time. Systemic change is required to provide more time, not for additional instruction but for guided and supported practice. Institutional action is required to create the kind of time required for the development of the dispositions of thinking.

When Chávez decided to extend the school day, groups of teachers gathered to research and create different plans for how to use this additional time. Most teachers agreed that students did not need time for additional instruction; our students struggled most with academic skills that no amount of instruction could help them develop. Lack of homework completion was the biggest factor in failing grades. Thus the plans for which teachers expressed the strongest support were those that provided additional time for students to actually work. And since many of us had

had rather negative experience with the chaos and lack of productivity that can come with unstructured periods for study hall or independent reading, we found this option unacceptable.

When the faculty voted on the plans that had been presented, the majority chose the Course-Specific Workshop, a program intended to provide students with supervised time to practice thinking and working in each of the academic disciplines. During two rotating 40-minute periods each day, students engage in silent, discipline-specific work while the teacher observes, listens to, and confers with individual students. It is important that students and teachers have very clear expectations regarding how this time is used. Teachers may be tempted to use the time to finish up a lesson that went a little too long or catch up on instruction. The students may try to use the time to catch up on work for another class. (They may even try to catch up on sleep.) Teachers in course-specific workshops must guard against both of these.

Ideally, the class preceding a workshop will prepare the student for a period of independent work, much like the work that would ordinarily be done as homework. One powerful thing about workshop is what teachers can learn from watching their students perform the tasks we normally ask them to perform elsewhere, thus breaking open the black box of "what happened with the homework," and providing the teacher with valuable insights into habits and dispositions.

While workshops offer the teacher an invaluable glance at student skills, the work done in that time must maintain a strong ground in the content about which we want the students to think. For instance, after a week studying the Russian revolutions and civil war (in which students read a biographical sketch of Lenin and a textbook chapter, and watched a documentary), students use the workshop period to start working on an essay from the perspective of a specific person representing a particular class or group within Russian society. The students argue from that perspective either that Lenin was a terrorist or a revolutionary. The teacher circulates and confers with individual students about specific features of that student's work, such as a thesis statement or the introduction of textual evidence (for more on conferring, see Chapter 9). During workshop the following week, the teacher may return that essay and have the students read over their work and make targeted corrections. The work teaches the students about thesis statements, perspective, and many other things, but it also allows them to think about the Russian revolutions.

Thinking is the essence of education. It must be integrated into the school day. Our course-specific workshop aims to provide students with additional time to develop dispositions of thinking—internalizations of the strategies that we have been teaching and the ability to apply them in new settings.

I began this chapter by arguing that thinking is the first right, or the only freedom. Thinking brings together the two goals of education: understanding and independence. These are the qualities that a student needs to be successful. But they are also the qualities that a democracy needs its citizens to posses. When we give adolescents the skills to make sense of the world, to understand and claim their rights, we not only improve these individuals and their potential for action in the world, we also improve the potential of the world and increase the power and the promise of democracy itself.

HOW TO BEGIN

- Talk with students about the kind of thinking required to arrive at content knowledge, so that they understand that chemistry or algebra were discovered and created by people like them.
- Provide time and space for students to reflect on content-rich material and then on their own work. Allow for revision and reconsideration.
- Avoid the temptation to "teach around the text." Provide students with ample opportunities to engage with meaningful and authentic discipline-specific texts.

LINGERING QUESTIONS

- How can teachers teach through (not around) the text in a class whose reading levels are greatly divergent? Can students arrive at the same thinking through different, leveled texts?
- How can we overcome the tremendous social and economic pressures that often keep our students from the thoughtful engagement with texts? How can we help our students believe that they can change a world whose power structures seem so impersonal, distant, and often cruel?

LEADERSHIP PERSPECTIVES

From Diane Lauer, former principal of Conrad Ball Middle School:

- *Vision for teaching and learning.* As a faculty, discuss the difference between seeing and watching; between telling and teaching; between listening and learning.
- *Instruction.* Woods says that thinking is "active, strategic, and focused." How might a faculty work together to make their *teaching* more active, strategic, and focused as well?

From Garrett Phelan, principal of César Chávez Charter School (Capitol Hill campus):

- *Tools for thinking.* Literacy is the carpenter's toolbox for thinking. It gives adolescents an authentic place at the learning table. Without literacy, students are just being served scraps enough to survive for the benefit of others.
- *Homework success.* How disempowering to allow students to go home alone and try to make sense of difficult content without the tools to help them make sense of it and grow as readers and people! How might students' homework performance improve if teachers were to actually give them tools for thinking?

RELATED READINGS

Hannah Arendt's essay "The Crisis in Education" (Arendt, 1961) takes a philosophical look at the history and purposes of education in a democratic society. She highlights the tension between the dissemination of tradition and the discovery of the new.

David Conley's book *College Knowledge* (Conley, 2005), based on extensive research, shows the kinds of thinking that are required to succeed in English, math, science, social studies, and second languages. Conley also provides specific steps that educators in each of these fields may take to prepare their students for college.

Ron Ritchhart's book *Intellectual Character* (Ritchhart, 2002) builds on Aristotle's *Ethics*, offering a compelling argument for the role of habituation and practice in the development of the disposition of thinking. He provides numerous classroom examples that help teachers know how to create cultures of thought within their classrooms.

CHAPTER 2

Metacognition: How Thinking About Their Thinking Empowers Students

Jennifer Swinehart

IN THIS CHAPTER: Jennifer Swinehart describes how she and her colleague taught their eighth-grade students to be metacognitive thinkers: to use and reflect on the comprehension strategies that good readers use when they read. She shows how she helps students actively make meaning of, with, and through text, and how they become increasingly independent readers, writers, and thinkers. Swinehart emphasizes that students must become metacognitive thinkers if they are to become literate members of society.

KEY POINTS

- Students must learn the metacognitive strategies used by proficient readers if they are to take charge of their own learning.
- Metacognition can help students successfully make meaning of difficult texts.
- Students learn metacognition when teachers think about their own thinking and model that thinking for students.
- Students have the right to have access not just to content but to thinking about that content.

As the bell rings, I enter our language arts classroom, herding the last stragglers through the door. Surprised by the sight of 14 extra adults in our room, the 32 kids are mildly distracted but quickly move into work mode with their daily writing. These eighth graders attend Bruce Randolph Middle School, one of the most highly impacted middle schools in Colorado: of our 650 students, 94% qualify for free or reduced-price lunch, 54% are English language learners. On state standardized tests for the 2003–04 school year, our students had the second lowest overall score in Colorado: only 12% of them scored proficient in reading, 7% in writing, and 4% in math.

Test scores aside, my students are amazing individuals. I had the good fortune to teach 20 of them for 2 years, "looping" with them from seventh to eighth grade. About two thirds of the students in this class are native Spanish speakers;

LOW
PROF
⟨→⟩
SP. ED?

half of those are formally enrolled in our district's English Language Acquisition program. Since almost a quarter of this class qualifies for special education services, I team-teach with Jill Dreier, the eighth-grade special education teacher.

Today we have guests from the Public Education & Business Coalition: 14 teachers from around the country who are here as a part of the National Lab Project. They are in our classroom observing; later in this chapter I will discuss their insights and questions about our instruction.

WHOA

After students write in their notebooks, I transition to the focus lesson. "Today we are going to continue reading *Fahrenheit 451* [Bradbury, 1953]. We are still practicing our metacognitive strategies. Who can remind us what *metacognitive* means?"

"It means thinking about your thinking!" Donald shouts out.

"Thank you, Donald," I say. "Remember, we have a collection of tools to help us be metacognitive."

Jill picks up here. "So while you read, write your thinking on sticky notes and then discuss the text page by page. Use your partner as a resource; share your thoughts and try to help each another make sense of the text. You might even ask your partner for clarification if you are confused about a part of the text."

"You will probably find yourself using several different strategies today," I continue. "For example, when I read page 3 yesterday I thought, 'Why is this fireman *burning* books rather than putting out the fire? My schema tells me this is the opposite of what should be happening; I infer that it's important to the story, but right now I'm confused!'"

I remind students that they should pay attention to the strategies as they read, and be prepared to share with me, Ms. Dreier, and their peers when we get to our discussion.

"Are there any questions?" No hands pop up. Eyes looking impatiently around the room indicate that they are ready to begin reading. "Okay, let's get started!"

METACOGNITIVE STRATEGIES

If you asked the average proficient reader what she does when reading, she might simply say, "I read." But upon further investigation, she would find that she unconsciously processes and problem-solves as she reads, almost like a reflex. We teach our brains to adjust to the different demands of various types of texts, which helps us read an income tax form just as successfully as we read a novel. We may not enjoy both texts equally, but we can read each effectively and strategically.

HOW
CAN
THEY
IF THEY
DK.
ENG?

Metacognitive awareness is important for everyone, but especially for students who are learning English as a second language (ESL). In most schools, ESL or ELL students are required to read content-area texts at grade level in English. If these students have learned strategies for breaking apart a text and building upon their own understandings, they will be more successful in eventually comprehending that text. As "Wenden (1985) was among the first to assert . . . learner strategies are the key to learner autonomy, and . . . one of the most important goals of language teaching should be the facilitation of that autonomy" (Brown, 2000, p. 130). Students' ability to independently self-monitor and think promotes language development and lets students advocate for themselves as readers.

English language learners need even more explicit support with using and applying metacognitive strategies. Because they are reading texts in their nonnative language, additional modeling and examples help them successfully use strategies. Teacher or peer modeling shows them how to focus on key aspects of a text and make choices about the strategies they apply to each content text. In their article, "Think-Aloud Strategy: Metacognitive development and monitoring comprehension in the middle school second-language classroom," McKeown and Gentilucci (2007) cited research by Bereiter and Bird (1985) that found that "students whose teachers modeled think-aloud strategies for recognizing comprehension problems and selecting repair stratagems scored significantly higher on tests of comprehension than those whose teachers did not. [Bereiter and Bird] stressed the importance of following an instructional pattern that included (in this sequence) teacher modeling, direct instruction and explanation, and individual practice" (p. 137). This means that we as teachers need to be diligent in guiding students through the process of metacognition and must intentionally work toward their gradual independence as reflective thinkers.

The thinking strategies that Jill and I use in our classroom are the bedrock of PEBC's work with teachers and students and are based on research by Pearson, Roehler, Dole, and Duffy (1992). They assert that proficient readers identify connections, access schema about text models, recognize when they stop understanding and take steps to repair meaning, discriminate between more and less important ideas when reading, synthesize information within and across different text types and reading purposes, infer to go deeper with textual analysis, and ask questions as they read. We also explicitly include visualization as another way to focus students on text and their thinking.

In our classroom, I name specific techniques students can use as they begin to try to make sense of a difficult text or work through difficult passages when they are confused. These techniques help make students' thinking transparent, which in turn gives them a certain power over their own learning process. A child can monitor what he thinks and how he understands *any* type of text; he can make connections between his science textbook and a movie he saw last spring. He can create a specific question about a math problem instead of groaning, "I don't get this!" I am also purposeful in making think-alouds an ongoing part of our instruction; I believe it is essential for each student to verbalize his thinking about text with peers and to collaborate with others in the quest for comprehension. The narrow focus of these active reading strategies gives him the ability to make meaning from *each* text he encounters.

When I first learned about metacognition, I wanted to experience what it meant. I practiced using thinking strategies when I read and would share passages from the text to show the students my questions, connections, or predictions. "So you can see here," I might point out, "that I was more focused on what this word meant and this person's background. Later on, I wondered more about the long-term effects of this incident and how I might react to the same situation."

I began to realize that although it is important for students to be metacognitive (i.e., consciously aware of their own thinking process), I also needed to emphasize how various strategies were beneficial when reading different texts. By talking to students about the application of their metacognition, they could start identifying which strategies might be more helpful when reading a social studies textbook versus a magazine.

I discovered through this journey that I was going beyond simply being a language arts teacher. I recognized that I could teach students strategies they could apply to texts in their other classes. I could teach them a life skill, an educational right, that would allow them to control their learning.

Every child deserves to know how he or she thinks and learns. This goes beyond whether they are visual or auditory learners to a deeper relationship between literacy and their rights as citizens. Students need support as they move into an application phase, a phase in which it becomes clear how and why literacy is an essential civil right for any thinking person. To ensure these rights, I consistently approach my teaching from a metacognitive point of view and consider two focus questions in my preparation to teach:

- What do my students deserve to know about their own thinking?
- What is it my obligation to teach them so that they can monitor their own thinking before, during, and after they read?

ENCOURAGING METACOGNITION

Between spurts of silent reading and hushed discussion, Jill and I circulate to pairs of students throughout the room. When I am not talking with a group, I eavesdrop on their conversation; I hear lots of questions being asked, main ideas being identified, and connections being made to the book. Today one discussion that I hear repeatedly centers on a single word in a passage from *Fahrenheit 451*, which initially might seem insignificant in the scope of the novel:

> He opened the bedroom door.
>
> It was like coming into the cold marbled room of a *mausoleum* after the moon has set. Complete darkness, not a hint of the silver world outside, the windows tightly shut, the chamber a tomb world where no sound from the great city could penetrate. The room was not empty. (Bradbury, 1953, p. 11; emphasis added)

During our closing meeting that day, we spent a lot of time talking about the word *mausoleum*.

"One place that I really struggled today was when I got to the word *mausoleum*," shares an ELL student, Allyson.

"How many of you had difficulty when you got to *mausoleum*?" asks Jill.

Hands shoot up all around the room, coupled with shouts of "I did!" and "Me too!"

I ask, "Who would like to share what their group thought it meant? Right now don't worry if you are right or wrong, just share what you discussed and your thinking behind your answer." Immediately four or five pairs look at each other and raise their hands.

"We thought it was like a museum because *mausoleum* kind of sounds like *museum* and we were visualizing a big marble room like in a museum we've visited," Katie, an ELL student, says. One reason Jill and I explicitly teach visualization as a metacognitive strategy is that we have found it especially beneficial for many ELL students, since it scaffolds other strategy usages.

"Great job!" praises Jill. "It was smart thinking to picture the word based on other descriptions Ray Bradbury shares with us. You also visualized and connected your schema to the word to help you figure out what you thought it meant. Who else would like to share?"

Another student adds, "Antonio and I thought of a place where people died because we saw the word *tomb* later in the paragraph. But we still don't know—is it like a cemetery or a hospital?"

"I think a cemetery because it makes more sense," Larry replies.

"Tell us more—what do you mean 'it makes more sense?'" I probe.

"Well, the next part of the story is about how Montag's wife has overdosed on sleeping pills. It doesn't sound like she is in a hospital when she overdoses, it sounds more like she is in a place full of death. I think Ray Bradbury says she is in the bedroom later, and that made me think it just sounded like a cemetery with this dead body in it."

"Nice explanation, Larry. Any other definitions that your group discussed that you'd like to share?" I ask the class.

Jill and I never revealed a "dictionary definition." But as we facilitated the class discussion, we affirmed our students' inferences.

EXPLAIN ⟷ METACOGNITION

TEACHING STUDENTS THE TOOLS OF THINKING

In our debriefing with the PEBC national visitors, we analyzed our instructional choices and the thinking behind them. Each guest teacher shared observations of our classroom work that day, and when we opened the floor for questions, someone pushed: "So what you're saying is that you don't care whether or not the students know what the word *mausoleum* means?"

I thought for a moment. "I think from today's conversation they have an understanding of what *mausoleum* means," I answered, "and they were able to determine that based on their toolbox of strategies. Sometimes I worry that if we focus on simply defining vocabulary, our opportunities to reinforce success in reading texts of this level will be severely limited."

Jill chimed in, "It was so exciting to hear them figuring out what that word meant on their own. We were able to walk around and guide them into discovering a definition for *mausoleum* instead of telling them what it means. When I was listening to them discuss, I heard so many students infer the meaning of this complicated word. And the ones who were wrong were so close that they got the idea." Jill's response perfectly captured the spirit of our thinking in those moments when we were conferring with pairs of students.

I then continued, "Our goal is to help them understand how to read and understand a district-mandated challenging text, especially in terms of the big picture, and for that to happen I need to figure out what I want them to take away. Today's lesson was about thinking, not a lesson on vocabulary, and it was amazing to see how well they did with that specific task."

In McKeown's (1985) research on vocabulary development, she found "that instructional strategies needed to focus on the *process* of deriving word meanings, in contrast to the *product* of coming up with the right meaning of an unknown word" (quoted in Beck, McKeown, & Kucan, 2002, p. 105). I observed students doing just this: they were inferring from the context, trying to see what the word reminded them of, using the descriptions from the text to visualize what that word might mean. Although *mausoleum* is not a word that students will likely encounter in grade-level texts, in *Fahrenheit 451* it gives readers critical insight into the emotional state of the character (had the word not been essential, I would not have let students spend so much time on it). Understanding this type of detail allows a student to make meaning in a complicated piece of text. Our students showed that they could use metacognitive strategies to guide them in this complex process.

On another day or with another word, we might have delved into a dictionary to find the formal definition. It is not easy to balance implicit discovery with explicit instruction, as both are critical to robust vocabulary development (Kamil, 2003, p. 12). On this occasion, I felt the benefit of letting them trust their thinking was greater; our students showed themselves that with a little metacognition, they can comprehend and interpret challenging text.

METACOGNITION FOSTERS INDEPENDENCE AND MOTIVATION

The PEBC lab participants seemed satisfied with our answers that day; my own curiosity, however, was piqued. I realized that this issue went beyond vocabulary; it reflected a deeper philosophical belief in what and how children should learn and what it means to be literate.

One of the most important aspects of metacognition is that children become aware of their own thinking. They need to own their use of strategies and should be able to explain how being metacognitive helps them to learn. Research about English language learners by Schmeck (1988) "found that students who perceive themselves as being in control of their own destiny and responsible for their own learning are more motivated to continue learning new skills" (cited in Hernández, 2003, p. 143). Every student who walks into a classroom and feels like she knows how to gauge her own understanding will be willing to take risks and as a result expand her knowledge in that content area.

During another PEBC lab, when visitors were debriefing their observation with our students, one visitor said, "You all seem very independent and in charge of your learning. Does being that independent help you be motivated to learn more and be more successful?"

Ian shouted out, "Yes! It helps me because it makes learning more fun."

Allyson answered, "I feel like I can make more decisions about my learning. I want to know more because I am in charge."

Maria, one of our ELL students, said, "Yes, because in this class I am challenged about my thinking, I am challenged to go deeper. I am used to putting things in simple terms and leaving it like that, but in this class I think more and I'm challenged, so that makes me smarter."

These students' answers speak to the universal value of metacognition and how the process of thinking about one's thinking is crucial for all students in a classroom. Although mine is one particular middle school language arts classroom, the same responses might well be heard from students in high school history or math.

In any content area, engagement increases when students find ways to more actively grapple with text. "Strategy instruction, in which students are taught how to apply specific strategies, may be critical to increasing students' motivation. Guthrie et al. (1996) found that all students who increased their intrinsic motivation across a school year also increased their usage of strategies" (Kamil, 2003, p. 7).

The use of metacognitive strategies can benefit students throughout their education and their lives. "Research shows . . . that students who receive intensive, focused literacy instruction and tutoring will graduate from high school and attend college in significantly greater numbers than those not receiving such attention" (Joftus, 2002, p. 3). If we can teach and encourage children to apply metacognitive strategies to each type of text they read, we will see the long-term benefits of this learned self-advocacy as readers.

We spend our lives as teachers hoping and (in secondary settings) expecting our students will become "adults." We talk to them about how they should act maturely, be responsible for their behavior, and not be influenced by negativity, but rather choose a path toward success. Rarely are students given ample opportunities to practice meeting these expectations. Instead, much time is spent telling students where they fell short.

Citing time restraints and excessive content in the curriculum as our motivating factors, in language arts we may tell them they misunderstood the theme of a book; in chemistry we might be tempted to tell them how to figure out the pH level of a substance rather than wait for them to experiment and draw their own conclusions. What a shame that we as teachers feel we must provide a "correct" answer at the end of every lesson! In Figure 2.1, below, I provide some specific suggestions about how teachers in all content areas can support students in developing their metacognitive awareness.

Even with all the pressures of teaching, we can and should lay the groundwork for our kids to choose their own positive path. A simple way to do this is by helping them learn how to manage and monitor their own thought processes to enable them to understand texts.

SUPPORTING STUDENTS' RIGHT TO OWN THEIR THINKING

I hear many secondary school teachers complain that students are too dependent and will not do anything for themselves. I believe that part of my job is to teach students strategies that will help them become more independent on their road to adulthood. Explicit instruction about metacognitive thinking helps me push kids to take more risks and to work more independently.

Self-reflection and self-assessment should be incorporated into every class. When I grade the writer's notebooks of my students, I ask each student to score his performance using a certain rubric on an entry of his choice. Writing every day is a ritual in our classroom, but it would not be as productive if students were not expected to reflect upon their own growth and monitor their progress from week to week and month to month. In Figure 2.2 I show a specific reflection form I use with my eighth graders that makes this expectation explicit. When I ask students about writing goals for the next quarter, I expect an answer that conveys a sense of seriousness and commitment. For example, Samantha wrote the following: "To

Figure 2.1. Metacognition and Literacy in the Content-Area Classroom

Use the vocabulary of thinking with students.
- "Given that the author of this primary source text uses negative connotations when describing British royalty, I can infer it was written by a colonist."
- "When I read about the subprime-mortgage lending crisis in the newspaper, I had questions about how this connects to our study of percentages and interest rates."

Model how you use strategies to comprehend your course texts.
- Show students how you shift your own thinking according to the sophistication of a task.
- Give examples of ways that different strategies can help you make meaning within or between content areas and their texts.

In one-on-one conferences, ask students to identify strategies most valuable to them.
- "What did you do when you didn't understand that paragraph?"
- "What did you think about as you read this problem?"
- "Which strategy did you use most often as you read this passage? Why?"

Assess students' growth in their use of the strategies.
- Identify sophisticated thinking and how it can help to comprehend the text of your course.
- Keep notes of conferences with students and share their progress in subsequent one-on-one meetings.

Require students to be metacognitive on formal assessments.
- "What steps did you take to interpret this graph?"
- "What inferences did you make as you read this prompt?"
- "What did you visualize as you prepared for your presentation?"
- "How did you decide which equation to use for this problem?"

MODEL

improve my writing next quarter, I know I need to spend time thinking of lots of ideas early on. If I wait to generate ideas until after I have started writing, I tend to get sidetracked and rush to finish an entry. I also would like to expand my vocabulary and learn new words to put in my entry; I'm going to try to use my independent reading book to help me with that."

Class discussions become more powerful when students use metacognition as the foundation for their talk with peers. During our conversation on *mausoleum*, Jill and I saw that our students were invested not just in trying to figure out the right answer, but also in understanding the process that they took to get to that answer. Being literate means not only to read and understand but also evaluate, critique, or interpret what we think of that text.

Figure 2.2. Rubric for Students' Self-Reflection on Their Writing

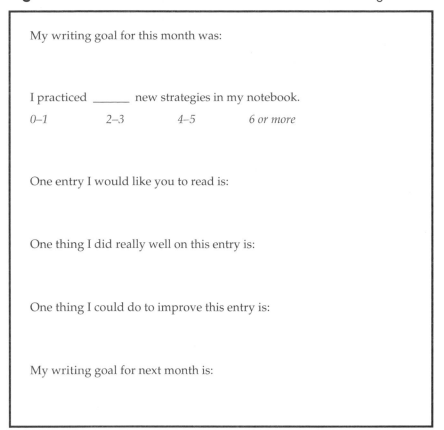

By ensuring young people's rights, we protect their opportunity to achieve at the highest levels possible. We also help to increase their motivation, since they know that we expect excellence and that we will support their hard work to get there. Students must feel free to own their own thinking and aspirations, to dream big and achieve bigger; otherwise they will simply do what is asked and nothing more.

As educators, we strive to hold onto the belief that all kids can learn, but we grapple with providing the authentic opportunities for them to think and to own that thinking. Every day when I walk into my classroom, I am emboldened by the realization that it is within my power to make my middle school students believe in themselves as learners. I take pride in the realization that it is my duty to teach these young men and women to think with confidence and to know themselves as readers, writers, and people.

HOW TO BEGIN

- Start with the strategy that is most comfortable for you to teach to your students and build from there.

- Model how not only to mark your thinking but how to *be* metacognitive.
- Practice each strategy with several texts, from various genres.
- Talk to students about how to identify the strategies most helpful or comfortable for reading your classroom texts.
- Encourage students to make metacognition a part of their peer and group discussions.
- Find ways to *see* student thinking: this is as valuable to you as a teacher as it is to your students. Use the informal data you collect from students' sticky notes or notebooks to inform your instruction minute to minute as well as day to day.

LINGERING QUESTIONS

- How do I balance my belief in process with the need to build students' background knowledge about vocabulary and "right" answers?
- What will ensure that my students will transfer the ability to use strategies to other classes, perhaps with no teacher guidance?
- How can all secondary teachers help students who view themselves as poor readers begin to gain the confidence necessary to recognize their metacognitive thinking beyond the classroom?

LEADERSHIP PERSPECTIVES

From Diane Lauer, former principal of Conrad Ball Middle School:

- *Student thinking.* Students need to know what they are *doing* in order to understand. How can we effectively teach students to analyze their thinking in order to describe the various components of what they do?
- *Instruction in all content areas.* Swinehart has developed a strong process for modeling and for chunking the procedures in clear, understandable ways. Why are these processes and structures important? And how can they be transferred across content areas so they impact student learning?

From Garrett Phelan, principal of César Chávez Charter School (Capitol Hill campus):

- *Explicit literacy instruction.* If you teach literacy in your core content, you will create a critical thinker in that discipline. You not only have to teach literacy, you have to *know* you are teaching literacy, and you have to teach it intentionally. By ignoring the teaching of literacy in every content area, we foster learned helplessness from our students. We must provide our young people with the tools they need to live enriched lives in a democratic society.
- *Professional development.* Teachers need support to do this work well. They are very literate in their content area, but they themselves have not been trained in teaching literacy to young learners. Therefore, it is essential for a school to create a community of literacy. Teachers need to learn with and from each other about what literacy looks and sounds like schoolwide and within each content area.

RELATED READINGS

David Pearson and colleagues' essay "Developing Expertise in Reading Comprehension" (P. D. Pearson et al., 1992) is an articulate piece of research that shares evidence behind each thinking strategy and data that support the notion that being metacognitive helps one become a more literate person.

Harvey Daniels and Steven Zemelman's book *Subjects Matter* (Daniels & Zemelman, 2004) offers a clear overview of the rationale behind content-focused reading instruction and gives practical suggestions for how to teach students to be metacognitive in every classroom.

Regina McKeown and James Gentilucci's article "Think Aloud Strategy"(McKeown & Gentilucci, 2007), focused on English language acquisition students, shares reasons why teaching metacognition is critical to literacy development and gives guidance about introducing specific strategies into the classroom.

CHAPTER 3

Not My Enemy, but My Friend: How Literacy Serves Content-Area Goals

Angela Zehner

IN THIS CHAPTER: Angela Zehner shares how her thinking has evolved regarding the role literacy plays in her work as a content-area teacher. She describes math as a verb, and says that all mathematical operations are manifestations of literacy. She shows how teachers can make deliberate decisions to use time to help students build the literacy skills that are so crucial to mastering content.

KEY POINTS

- Mathematics is thinking.
- Literacy is an essential tool to make mathematical meaning.

I teach math. You may teach a different subject, but we are all teaching thinkers. And thinkers do not learn by content alone. As a content-area teacher, I have learned to use the power of literacy instruction to boost my students' ability and achievement as mathematical thinkers.

I teach at Prairie Middle School, which has one of the most diverse student populations in the state of Colorado. Our nearly 1,600 students speak more than 50 languages and come from more than 70 countries. Approximately 46% of our students qualify for free or reduced-price lunch, 60% are people of color, and 27% are officially designated as English language learners.

In this context, being a math teacher is not just teaching a lesson and assigning problems. It is knowing my students, understanding how they think through problems, and helping them develop in their mathematical thinking. I see this clearly after 18 years in the classroom; it wasn't at all clear when I began.

THAT WAS THEN: HOW I USED TO THINK ABOUT LITERACY AND MATH

As a child, I was great at crunching numbers, but I was not a powerful mathematical thinker; no one asked me to justify, explain, and communicate my thinking. I had teachers who were encouraging and passionate about their content. But none made me talk through, or *think* through, the whys and hows of math.

Not surprisingly, in my early years I taught the way I had been taught: the basics, arithmetic skills, how to "plug and chug" math problems. If students got the correct answer, I never asked them how or why they did it that way. And if an answer was wrong, I would ask students to share their thinking only so I could "fix" it.

I made sure all my students did their classwork and homework, called home on students who did not, and followed my curriculum page after page, rarely straying from the scripts in the teacher's manual. My evaluations were great. I had no pressures on me to perform, nor to have my students perform.

I didn't look at what my students understood. I only knew if they "got" it based on quizzes or the unit test, but this was too little, too late. As a colleague of mine says, "The test is like an autopsy. We should be having little miniphysicals along the way to diagnose the problems before we have to get to the autopsy to say, 'What happened?'"

When I started teaching at Prairie Middle School, Samantha Bennett, a staff developer from the Public Education & Business Coalition worked with my team. She had positive things to say about my teaching, but she also asked me to explain what, where, how, when, and why students were learning the topic I was teaching. She would ask me about specific students' thinking.

I realized that I was not really thinking about my own thinking, or the students'. I was mainly interested in their right answers. I was performing "autopsies," not "miniphysicals."

I would have to change my own thinking and teaching in order to honor the rights of the thinkers in my classroom.

How can you promote metacognition in your content area?

THIS IS NOW: MATHEMATICS IS THINKING

I now believe that regardless of what content we teach, we must teach our students to succeed in a world that will be beyond what we can conceive. Students need to be problem solvers, investigators, social scientists, and explorers. We need them to understand the major concepts of our disciplines not only because of a curriculum guide or district policy, but because we believe that the material presented will make a difference in their lives.

To be a mathematician one has to be able to solve math problems, communicate and justify to others how to solve them and, more important, why it matters. Students need to understand the meaning behind the formulas.

The core thinking processes in my academic discipline are articulated in our *Colorado Model Content Standards for Mathematics* (2005):

> Mathematics is not simply a collection of facts and procedures, and doing mathematics is not simply recalling these facts, nor performing memorized procedures. Mathematics is a coherent and useful discipline that has expanded dramatically in the last 25 years. The mathematics students study in school must reflect these changes, and the ways students study mathematics must capitalize on the growth in our understanding of how students learn.

The standards name six goals for math students:

1. Become mathematical problem solvers . . . know how to find ways to reach a goal when no routine path is apparent.
2. Learn to communicate mathematically . . . learn to clarify, refine, and consolidate their thinking.
3. Learn to reason mathematically . . . gather data, make conjectures, assemble evidence, and build an argument to support or refute these conjectures.
4. Make mathematical connections among mathematical ideas . . . [so math is] meaningful and useful to each Colorado student.
5. Become confident of their mathematical abilities . . . trust their own mathematical thinking by having numerous and varied experiences.
6. Learn the value of mathematics . . . [as] a way of thinking about and understanding the world around us.

Every one of these standards implies and requires strong literacy skills. And a major goal of the standards movement in education has been to ensure equity—to make certain *all* students have access to these tools.

In teaching math, or any discipline, we aim beyond the curriculum and the test scores to the lasting effects we want for students. I want two main things for them:

- To leave my class with the ability to tackle any challenge—in math, other classes, or life—without giving up when it gets hard
- To be powerful mathematicians, social scientists, readers, writers, scientists, and *thinkers*

Here are the key ideas that guide my instruction now:

- Listening: I strive to listen in order to know how students think through their own understanding.
- Literacy: I use reading and writing as tools for students to use as they create meaning.
- Intentionality: I strive to teach, listen, and change what I do tomorrow based on what I heard from students today.

LISTENING TO TEACH: HOW DO YOU KNOW WHAT STUDENTS KNOW?

I decided to do "miniphysicals" in my classroom, rather than just "autopsies." I wanted to know what students knew and how they knew it, in time to intervene and assist. But what does that look like in my actual daily instruction?

Every minute I am with students I have two questions in mind: What do my students know? and What do they need from me to know more?

To gauge what my students know, I must give them time to play with numbers, to explore, and to talk—then listen deeply to understand their process.

One of the hardest parts of my job is listening. It's not the listening itself that is hard; it's restraining myself from rushing in to help the struggling student by giving the answer. Teachers are quick to take the pencil from a student's hand and

[handwritten marginal note: WHAT ARE APPROPRIATE WAYS TO ALLOW STUDENTS TO FIGURE IT OUT?]

say, "Here, let me show you." Meaning well, we interfere with students owning their thinking and learning.

When we listen instead of rushing in, it forces us as teachers to slow down, to choose questions based on a student's actual thought process. Listening to students' thinking is essential; without that, how will I know where to support or challenge them next?

Listening to students is just as important when their answer is right as when it is wrong. Students show us the correct answer; we nod our heads and move on. Wait! Only if we stop and ask them to share their thinking can we truly know if, what, and how they understand.

Consider the conversation I had with students about the following problem:

$$0.2 \overline{)3.2} = 16$$

JASON: I divided and I moved the decimal over to get an answer of 16.
ANGELA: Anyone have any questions for Jason?
MARK: I got 1.6.
ANGELA: Jason, could you explain how you got this answer one more time?
JASON: I moved the decimal over because you want to divide by a whole number and if you move it over one time on the outside you have to move it over one time in the inside.
ANGELA: What does 0.2 mean?
JASON: It is like 20 cents.
ANGELA: What does 3.2 mean?
JASON: It is like $3.20.
ANGELA: So, now explain what it means to divide $3.20 by $0.20.
JASON: If I have $3.20 and I have to break it into groups of $0.20, then I would need 16 groups.
ANGELA: Wow. Thanks for explaining your thought process.

So, what did I learn about Jason from listening closely? I learned that he understands about grouping. He was not simply thinking about moving a decimal (because that is what we do when we divide decimals). Had I just accepted his correct answer and moved on, I would not have known that he sees the division of decimals as money. Having listened, I now can build on that understanding in future lessons, both with him, and with others when they are stuck.

When I began to really listen to my students, I was constantly surprised by their thinking. There are so many ways that our students see the world—what makes us think they see our content the same way we do? And my choice to listen has another benefit. Once students know that I am focused on listening to their thinking, they begin to feel more accountable for that thinking. The learned helplessness syndrome begins to disappear. We all have students who—as soon as you finish going over the directions, ask if there are any questions, and ask groups to begin—immediately raise their hands waiting for you to come and help or rescue them. Teaching students that I am there to listen to their learning and that they are there to facilitate each other's learning, reduces the number of students waiting for me to rescue them.

LITERACY IS A TOOL TO MAKE MEANING

Literacy is crucial to getting students actually thinking about math and doing math with their minds as active as their fingers on a calculator keypad.

A colleague of mine recently asked me, "Angie, how am I supposed to stop in the middle of math class and teach a 20-minute reading lesson? I would much rather spend the time, like today, where my students were questioning whether the table was better than the graph. They were asking questions of me and of each other."

I responded, "You just *did* incorporate literacy into your lesson. That is called 'questioning the text.'"

Put simply, literacy is making meaning from text by reading, writing, and speaking. In math, our text is words, pictures, graphs, equations, and basic problems. Students need specialized vocabulary to make meaning from our text, but the key is still reading, writing, and speaking about math.

I view math as a verb: something one *does*, not knowledge one *has*. And all those "actions" are literacy. Math is about thinking, writing, explaining, discussing, reading, interpreting, analyzing, planning, and problem solving. The same is true in any discipline: Science is more than just facts about chemistry; social studies is more than simply geography.

In Figure 3.1 I show what the types of thinking—the verbs—that I value for students actually look and sound like in my classroom, and the literacy strategies that are embedded in that instruction. These are based on the strategies Woods described in Figure 1.1. In Figure 3.1 I have "translated" some of the strategies into language more familiar to math teachers and have focused on those I find most relevant to my discipline, but they are applicable to any discipline.

If math is a verb (and I believe that *all* content areas are), then students' learning must be active. To help build active minds, I incorporate literacy skills in every lesson. All teachers, regardless of content area, can use literacy strategies to encourage development of powerful thinking. This does not have to be a huge undertaking. It is mostly a conceptual shift; that is, literacy is a tool to make meaning, and if my goal is mathematical thinking, literacy can serve that cause. Furthermore, literacy skills are the single best set of scaffolds to help students get to the mastery of content that we want for them, and to independence as learners. If we enable students to infer, justify, debate, explain, identify, determine, analyze, and synthesize materials (just to name a few literacy strategies), then we are one step closer to empowering our future.

INTENTIONALITY

Students want to succeed. It is their right to have the tools to do so. Our job as educators is to facilitate their drive to learn and equip them with the ability to think. But here comes the hard part: we have to do this with intentionality. We have to call attention to the strategies that we are teaching so that when students use them they know what they are doing and why. We have to know this for ourselves, label it explicitly for students, and teach them specifically how to do it themselves.

Using time up front to model how to think through a performance task produces quicker mastery and independence in the students. One way I do this is with

Figure 3.1. Literacy Strategies in the Math Classroom

LITERACY STRATEGY USED	WHAT IT LOOKS AND SOUNDS LIKE
Determine importance by coding the text: Students identify key components, such as the question they are being asked to answer. They can revisit their coding notes to ask more questions about what they coded.	*During group work:* Brent: I think we need to . . . Aubrey: Wait, you did not code the text. We do not know what is important yet. Brent: OK, what do you think we should code? Aubrey: Look for key words that will help us solve the problem. *Individually:* Students can refer to what they underlined when giving an answer on a unit test or any given prompt.
Predict, then infer: Students preview a unit or section and predict the ideas or concepts that will be covered by "walking through a book." Students look at the cover of the book and flip through the pages to make predictions about what the book will be about. After predicting, students look for evidence to turn their predictions into inferences. As students look through the new unit, they look for evidence as to what it will be about.	Mike: I think this book is going to be about tables and graphs because as I looked through the book I noticed there were a lot of pictures and words that had tables and graphs. Tabitha: As I look through the book, I noticed on page 4, the mathematical highlights. This tells me all about the objectives of the book.
Justify thinking on the basis of evidence: Students show how and why they think the way they do, realizing that an answer is just an answer unless they can prove it. Students need to provide a body of evidence to support their answers.	Angela: What other body of evidence do you know of that will support this answer? Sam: I know that a line is made of 180 degrees and at the half way point it will be 90 degrees. Angela: Tell me more about this. Sam: Well, I know that when I do a 360 degree turn, that means I do a full circle. Half would be 180 degrees, and a fourth would be 90 degrees. Angela: Great. You are justifying your answer.
Summarize the directions for complex word problems: Students use summaries as a way to monitor whether they have comprehended the problem. They work through a prompt, reading through the question to understand exactly what is being asked. Through this process, they recognize the difference between the "real" question and their assumptions (answering a question that was not asked) or incomplete understandings of instructions (answering just part of what was asked).	Today in math class, the prompt asked us to complete a table for two boys mowing lawns. One boy charged $7 per lawn and $3 an hour. The other boy charges $5 per lawn and $4 per hour. When we completed the table, we had to figure out which boy we would hire for a big lawn and which we would hire for a small lawn. (Mi Mi)
Synthesize: Students use the information they collected over the course of the minilesson or group work to come to a conclusion or conjecture about whatever they are working on at the time.	I think the equation for Jake mowing the lawn would be $3x + 7 = m$. I think this because the 3 represents how much he is charging per hour and the 7 represents how much he charges per lawn. However, since he can only mow one lawn at a time, the hours is what would consistently increase, representing the rate of change. (Austin)

Constructed Response, an activity I have my students do every week, all year long. This activity incorporates many of my current thinking beliefs and practices: I listen, I integrate literacy, I am intentional. And I give students plenty of time to actually construct meaning.

EXAMPLES OF CONSTRUCTED RESPONSE

During a Constructed Response, which I outline in Figure 3.2, students work through a challenging mathematical prompt using a process that I call "Plan, Do, Review." Really, students are working on reading and writing strategies intertwined with math.

In a Constructed Response, I almost always begin class with a think-aloud, modeling how I would read through the text. I strive to show students how I think *through* math instead of just mechanically trying to do it.

I begin: "Let's look at today's Constructed Response. I am going to read through it and identify what I am being asked to do. First, let's read the prompt."

Red Cab charges $4 plus $2 per mile or $r = 2m + 4$. Blue Cab charges $6 plus $1 per mile or $b = m + 6$. For what distance does Red Cab charge the same as Blue Cab? When should you take a Red Cab? A Blue Cab?

Note: From *Write About Math*, by M. Thomas, 2004. Copyright School Specialty Publishing, used with permission.

Then I would reread the text, thinking aloud while I coded it: "Hmmm, I better reread but this time I am rereading to pick out essential pieces of information that might help me answer the question, and as I reread, I am going to underline, or code, the text." (In the above problem, I might underline "Red Cab," "$r = 2m + 4$," "Blue Cab," "$b = m + 6$," "distance," "charge the same," "When," "take a Red Cab?" and "A blue Cab?".)

Figure 3.2. Constructed Response Steps: Plan, Do, Review

1. **Read.** Read the mathematical problem to understand the task.

2. **Reread and code the text.** As you read through the problem, code (underline) important facts.

3. **Make a plan of action.** Use a problem-solving strategy (such as a picture, diagram, or chart) to help you arrive at an answer.

4. **Analyze and share thinking.** With the other students share how you each might solve the problem, and share your solutions to the problem.

5. **Edit and evaluate answer.** Evaluate your answer and determine if you need to edit your thinking before writing a final response to the prompt.

Once students have learned the Constructed Response well, I can send them off to work in their groups: "Today we are going to do a constructed response with your tablemates. Your objective is to use inferring skills to construct meaning and then justify your thinking. You will read, reread, code the text, and plan with your tablemates. As you work through the prompt with your group, I will be circulating around the room listening to your discussions. Be sure to hold each other accountable for your thinking. Your job is to complete the task at a proficient and advanced level of thinking."

In Step 1, students read the prompt to construct meaning and identify the task at hand: The who, when, where, why, and how of a problem is essential in determining a process for solving it. This is shown in the example of the red and blue cabs.

In Step 2, students reread and code the text by underlining key words that will help them answer the task. For example, Mi Mi underlines "Red Cab" and "$2m + 4$," the amount the Red Cab charges. She also underlines the very last sentence: "When should you take the Red Cab and when should you choose the Blue Cab?"

In Step 3, after students have coded the text, they plan how to tackle the problem. To get them started, I might model the questions I use in formulating a plan: "Now, that we have identified what is important information to use in solving the problem, we need to make a plan. How should I start? Do I already have background knowledge about this problem that could help me? Should I make a picture or diagram? Maybe I should make a chart?"

Students collaborate on their plan. They use diagrams, charts, pictures, words, and numbers to help display their thinking. Once students come up with a plan together, they share their thinking with the entire class.

For example, students given the problem shown in Figure 3.3 created an elaborate group plan, constructing a table to hold their thinking and using skills from a previous unit to construct equations for each boy (Figure 3.4). They also included a handwritten explanation (not shown in the figure) to communicate their thinking and justify their conclusions.

Step 4, analyzing and sharing thinking, takes the most time, but it is where I have seen my students grow the most as mathematicians, critical thinkers, and strong communicators. Students begin by posting their group's plan on a wall where

Figure 3.3. "Mowing for Dollars" Problem

Jake and John mow lawns in the summer. Jake charges $7 per lawn plus $3 an hour. John charges $5 per lawn plus $4 an hour. Complete the table. Who would you hire to mow a small lawn? Who would you hire to mow a large lawn?

Hours/Lawn	1	2	3	4
Jake	$10			
John	$9			

Note: From *Write About Math*, by M. Thomas, 2004. Copyright © School Specialty Publishing, used with permission.

Figure 3.4. Segment of a Group Plan for the "Mowing for Dollars" Problem

Hours/Lawn	1	2	3	4
Jake	10	13	16	19
John	9	13	17	21

$$\text{Jake} = 3x + 7 = m$$

$$\text{John} = 4x + 5 = m$$

all the other groups can see it. Students then gather on the rug and examine and analyze each other's work.

At this point, students are looking at the other plans to compare and contrast. I often have them write a few sentences here, naming what they notice. For example, students might write: "I noticed that the groups mainly had graphs. I wonder why Group 2 chose to do a table." "I wonder how the graph supports the equation."

Here is an example of what Mi Mi wrote about other posters she viewed: "After I looked and observed the six posters, I notice some groups have different sets of data on their tables. Also, I notice that one group makes a graph and a table. I wonder why some groups started with 0 and some didn't. I wonder why one group didn't put their answer on their papers. I also notice that one group went by 10s and 9s when it is supposed to go by 3s and 4s."

Having students evaluate each other's work allows for them to self-edit, self-question, and self-assess. If I was the only one pointing out what I saw, then the students would not even take the time to look at the plans. They would wait for me to do all the work for them. Students are much harder on each other than I can ever be. They naturally push each other to justify their reasoning if we provide the forum and the structure for them to be successful.

In order to have students respect and trust each other, and be willing to share their thinking, I must create a community of learners. (For more on creating this type of environment, see Chapter 9). This trust is essential. It allows students to share their own thinking and hear the power of their peers' thoughts. I want to encourage students to be mathematical risk takers and articulate their thinking whether or not the answer is right. As I often tell them, "An answer is just an answer unless you can justify and prove it."

Step 5 is editing and evaluating thinking. After students build their understanding about how they are going to tackle the problem together, then they each have the scaffolding they need to write up the problem individually.

Figure 3.5 shows a typed transcript of Mi Mi's response to the problem displayed on page 42. If you look closely at the figure, you will see that in her initial response, she wrote the steps of the Constructed Response process on the top right-hand corner of her paper: "read, reread, code, plan." She was using the scaffold I

Figure 3.5. Transcript of Mi Mi's Constructed Response to the "Taxi Terms" Problem

---

Initial response:

*Read
*Reread
*Code
*Plan

Taxi Terms

Red Cab charges $4 plus $2 per mile or $r = 2m + 4$. Blue Cab charges $6 plus $1 per mile or $b = m + 6$. For what distance does Red Cab charge the same as blue Cab? When should you take a Red Cab? A Blue Cab?

Both of the cabs charges $8 for 2 miles. I should take the Red Cab if I needed to go 0-1 miles, because 0-1 miles for Red Cab costs $4-$6, but for Blue Cab it cost $6-$7. I would use the Blue Cab at 3 or more miles because it would cost $9 +, but for Red Cab, it costs $10 +. I would take either one for 2 miles because it is the same cost.

Later the same day:

Red Car:	Blue Car:
(mile) 1 = $6	(mile) 1 = $7
2 = $8	2 = $8
3 = $10	3 = $9
4 = $12	4 = $10
5 = $14	5 = $11

Taxi Terms

Today in Math Class we did a constructive response on taxis. They told us to compare the two taxis, blue and red Cab. Red Cab charges people $4 plus $2 per mile and Blue Cab charges $6 plus $1 per mile. They asked us what distance the Red Cab charges the same as the Blue. They asked us when we should take the Blue or the Red Cab.

As I look at all of the groups' posters, I noticed that all of the posters got the same answer when the cabs both intersect. I also noticed that all groups said that the Red Cabs by 2's and Blue goes by 1's.

Do you think integrating subjs is a good way for stds to engage in MC? If so, how?

had given the class. Also, notice the coding (underlining) of what she thought was important. Then you will see the steps she took as she prepared to write her final answer. She created a plan, and in her second response, she analyzed other groups' thinking before she finalized her thoughts.

I used literacy strategies to help Mi Mi go slow to go fast. Coding the text allowed her to determine importance. Questioning the text as well as questioning others allowed her to think critically about her thinking. Also, she made inferences based on the body of evidence that was provided. All of these literacy skills helped her communicate her thinking to others.

TIME: GO SLOW TO GO FAST

If we want students to do this type of thinking—to justify their answers and prove their logic is sound—we must give them time to talk, discuss, and even argue about the content. It takes time for students to explicitly develop a repertoire of literacy strategies they need to really think about content. This can be frustrating, since I, like many teachers, feel pressed for time to get through my entire curriculum. But I have come to realize that if I don't provide students the opportunity to explore, think, and justify their approaches and answers then I am shortchanging them as learners. Worse still, I may actually be narrowing their thinking. And I am almost certainly making it harder for them to understand the math I care so much about.

Building a road takes time. But once it is built, drivers from all over use it to go wherever they want to. Teaching kids to be lifelong learners does not happen overnight. We must lay the groundwork for students to explore their thinking and to ask their questions about why, how, and where these skills can be used throughout their lives.

People always ask me, "How do you stay on track with your curriculum?" By giving the time up front, I gain time back in the end. If I want kids to be thinkers, I must prioritize the time to teach them how to do that thinking. I must set up opportunities for students to work on critical thinking, literacy skills, reading strategies, and writing strategies.

Sometimes we teachers find ourselves following the curriculum or book page by page without stopping until the end to determine what kids know. Take time to find out what kids know and you will be able to move quicker than you think. Determine what a student's background knowledge is; find out what you can let go of in order to gain a little time back. Look for ways to streamline the overlaps between your curriculum and your textbook.

The power in a mathematical debate opens up so many opportunities for students to link key concepts and procedures in problem-solving situations and to communicate and defend their mathematical reasoning. Enabling students to ask higher level questions encourages students to give higher level responses. If I don't take time to encourage students to ask questions of others in order to better understand, then I am not preparing them to be mathematical thinkers.

As educators, we are building the pathways for our students to succeed in any endeavors they choose. The instructional approach I describe in this chapter does cost time up front, but pays off with a class full of critical thinkers and stronger communicators. Literacy propels students into the next level of learning in math or any other content area as well as in their lives.

HOW TO BEGIN

- Start integrating literacy by introducing one strategy in one class.
- Listen to your students. Write down anecdotal notes about what you are hearing them say.
- Ask yourself, "How do I know what students know and don't know?"
- Look for patterns of what they know and what they still need to learn.
- Make time for students to talk about, think about, and write about content, as well as to do the work.
- Remember that the student doing the most talking is probably doing the most learning. Encourage students to talk about the content.

LINGERING QUESTIONS

- How can I continue to help students see the connection between the literacy strategies used in math class and their other content-area classes?
- How do I know students understood today's objective?

LEADERSHIP PERSPECTIVES

From Diane Lauer, former principal of Conrad Ball Middle School:

- *Structuring student dialogue.* Zehner has developed a strong process for modeling to students what it means to think like a mathematician. She chunks the procedures in clear, understandable ways, and can describe how she creates structure for student thinking and talking. What is your honest assessment of how much of this you do, and how well? What might be next steps, and who might support you?
- *Naming student thinking.* How can we effectively teach students to analyze their thinking, so they can describe various components of what they do in a way that gives them power over their own learning process?

From Garrett Phelan, principal of César Chávez Charter School (Capitol Hill campus):

- *Teachers as model thinkers and readers.* How might it shift our literacy instruction if teachers viewed themselves as "masters" and saw their students as "apprentices" in literacy and thinking? Given that we read different texts differently, why wouldn't the "experts" (the teachers) in a given discipline teach literacy and deep thinking in that discipline?
- *Assessment.* Might it not be just as important for secondary teachers to teach and assess reading strategies and thinking processes as it is to assess content?

RELATED READINGS

Katherine Schultz's book *Listening: A Framework for Teaching Across Differences* (Schultz, 2003) transformed my teaching. I realized that I was too busy talking to really listen to what my students knew or did not know.

Arthur Hyde's book *Comprehending Math* (Hyde, 2006) offers great strategies for how to build students' conceptual understanding by using the thinking strategies in math.

Joan Kenney's book *Literacy Strategies for Improving Mathematics Instruction* (Kenney, 2005) describes a variety of strategies used in math classes giving examples from the Connected Mathematics Program.

The National Research Council's (2000a) book *How People Learn* is a great resource if you want to understand the way people think through material.

CHAPTER 4

Access and Power Right Now:
From School to World

Marjorie Larner

IN THIS CHAPTER: Marjorie Larner interviewed a group of high school juniors and seniors in a Denver high school about the value literacy plays in their lives. She shares key findings in terms of how students perceive their literacy skills as giving them access and power in their current lives.

KEY POINTS

- Literacy has applicable value right now, not just in students' futures.
- Expanding background knowledge fosters student access to powerful communication and conversations.
- Students increase their power to act in the world through developing the capacity to analyze and consider multiple perspectives.

"If somebody were to tell me," said one of Susan Marion's high school students, "I'm only here so I can get a job later, it would take all the fun out of it—life's all about self-improvement and betterment." The first time I walked into Susan's classroom at the Denver Center for International Studies (DCIS), I was reminded of a college seminar. Students were poring over a script from a public radio interview, identifying the ethos, logos, and pathos employed by the interviewee in building an argument. They posed open-ended probing questions and listened intently to one another's responses. Ana* raised a question about how the interview might have been edited to support the station's point of view or that of the station's funders. There were even moments of silence after some of Susan's questions while they thought before responding.

I am often confronted by teachers bemoaning students' lack of engagement and motivation, and stumped by students asking how they will ever use what is being offered in class. I wanted to hear what the students in Susan's class could

---

*Students' real names are used throughout this chapter, at their request and with their permission.

tell me about how they viewed the experience and learning in which they seemed so engaged.

Susan suggested I join her students at one of their "Thursday coffee houses" where they come to study together after school. Maile (the high school junior quoted above) arrived first and started the coffee. When Warren and Orlinda arrived, they all sat together at one of the seven round tables spread around Susan's classroom. Ana arrived a little later and started talking intently with Susan about a letter she wanted to write in response to an issue she faced as editor-in-chief of the school newspaper.

They welcomed me graciously as I joined them at their table. I told them that I was thinking about how literacy was important for life beyond school and asked them how they saw it would make a difference for them in their lives. They immediately started talking, interjecting examples to support each other's reflections about the contribution to the quality of their lives as they have gained tools to analyze argument, present their own cases, expand their cultural literacy, communicate confidently, and use writing to expand their thoughts.

THINKING HARD ABOUT IMPORTANT THINGS

> *Schools are to provoke young people to grow up intellectually, to think hard and resourcefully and imaginatively about important things.*
> —*Ted Sizer, speech at Coalition of Essential Schools meeting*

For this group of teens, the benefits of analytical and strategic reading, writing, speaking, and thinking has strengthened their sense of their capacity, possibilities, and place in the world right now.

It is perhaps not surprising that their responses to my questions about the value of their literacy development addressed the *present* moment. Their future as adults may feel distant; they have so much to get through before they get there. And given how rapidly our society is shifting, who knows what will be needed in years to come?

Authors of previous chapters posit literacy as a civil right. In this chapter, I show how that right is manifest in many immediate aspects of students' lives. I describe some of the literacy skills and understandings that these students identify as valuable for them. Specifically, I address how access (to knowledge and learning) and power (of analysis, persuasion, and participation) are relevant issues for the students in the here and now.

I will not discuss here the many ways that their highly skilled and dedicated teachers or their focused school have helped students see the value of literacy; Part II of this volume offers excellent examples and concrete strategies about how to get to the benefits these students name. My focus in this chapter is on the students' experiences and perspectives as beacons to highlight possible outcomes of effective literacy instruction.

The students' stories of literacy in their lives point to a vision of possibilities beyond proficiency and readiness for the next level of school to powerful and joyful participation in our world—not only for their future, but for their lives right now.

BUILDING BACKGROUND KNOWLEDGE TO PARTICIPATE IN BIG CONVERSATIONS

You get to be part of the big conversation that's been going on for centuries.
—*Susan Marion, language arts teacher*

The students whom I interviewed are enrolled in AP Language and Composition. On the surface, they do not fit the image you might have of a typical advanced placement class in most schools; their backgrounds reflect Denver's diverse urban population that includes families from Latin America, Asia, Africa, and Eastern Europe, as well as U.S.-born students of African, European, and Hispanic heritage. Approximately 70% of the 420 students in the high school are people of color; about 65% qualify for free or reduced-price lunch.

Ana, Maile, Warren, Orlinda, and their DCIS classmates found and chose a school where, as their teacher Susan says, "there is a sense . . . that this is . . . a good step because of opportunities to think about the rest of the world and you in the rest of the world." What do they find for themselves in this school with rigorous expectations? What motivates them to go even further, enrolling in an AP-level class with significantly more pressure and work?

They describe gaining skills and understanding to impact the world, even while they are still "children" in the eyes of our society. They talk at length about realizations of gaps that can be filled to increase their confidence and capacity to make a difference in the world. As Maile, a junior, said, "I'm ashamed at times. Oh! This is ridiculous. I don't know this. It is easy to feel inferior when you don't have knowledge. The more you know about the world, the more you have to pull from to help people understand what you want to say."

Warren, a senior, described it this way: "You realize you're lacking knowledge in so many areas. When there's something I don't know, I have to target this area and expand my knowledge. It's degrading not to know." For Warren to be able to see the gaps in his knowledge, he needed to feel safe in admitting the lack and to get exposure to knowledge that he could recognize as unfamiliar and of value. With this awareness, Warren could take hold of his own destiny by assessing where he stood, where he wanted to be, and what he needed to add to his repertoire in order to get there.

The students bring to life Paulo Freire's understanding of literacy as a strategy of liberation in which people learn to read not only the "word, but also the world" (Freire & Macedo, 1987), a pathway for people to overcome poverty, injustice, and fear. Freire taught literacy by creating what he called "circles of culture"; he empowered groups of readers and learners by building on their language and background knowledge. He then challenged the groups to discuss national problems in a way that not only opened their perspectives, but also required critical analysis.

Susan's description of her approach to literacy instruction mirrors aspects of Freire's argument:

When students start the year, their most long-term concrete goals are to pass the AP exam, get into a competitive college, get college credit and good grades for that. . . . But rarely is it connected to why college wants those things or why it's good to have those things anyway. Why are those skills valued by college? By people in the world? What does it get you? [At first] they look at me blankly when I say what's exciting about understanding rhetoric (AP curriculum) is that you get to be part of the big conversation that's been going on for centuries, part of the universal discourse—listening to this conversation when you're reading, listening to a speech, the radio—you will have access to this world of ideas.

Though the entry point for these students is an immediate goal of doing well in school, leading to "success" in college and then in life, Susan situates students' learning within a much larger societal context, and helps them realize political, social, and community value in their literacy skill.

Susan realizes that to "read the world," her students need a rich foundation and context to inform their thinking. She therefore focuses on both expanding and deepening cultural literacy, thus filling their gaps as well as learning to draw on the diverse cultural literacy they already carry in themselves. Susan presents the tools and knowledge she offers as "just adding to your repertoire as part of an ongoing learning process."

Warren was particularly articulate in relating a time he became aware of a difference in understanding the meaning of a book when he had some background knowledge of the larger political context in which the author was writing:

> You could think that *Animal Farm* can be a little kids' book that takes place on a farm but when you have some background knowledge and learn that the original intention was to represent Communism and Russia, it means so much more. This is a minuscule example of getting deeper meaning and now when I read I think, "What else is the author trying to convey?"

Warren so clearly points out the necessity for what Jeff Wilhelm (and others) refer to as front loading—giving students oportunities to think and talk about ideas that are part of the cultural context within which a text carries meaning (Wilhelm et al., 2001).

Orlinda adds the power she has found in expanding her vocabulary, an often underappreciated lesson among students. She says, "Now that we're doing vocab, I'm so excited I know these words and I use them over and over." This is not a girl who is learning definitions for a test or to use in a paper for her teacher; she is "owning" new words as a means to expand her capacity for acting in and on her world.

Maile added to Orlinda's comment with a reflection on the impact of both increased background knowledge and vocabulary on her own thinking. "The more successfully you can express yourself, the more complex your thoughts [become]. . . . From reading, I learned new words; I could apply them to myself and could use new words to more effectively interpret my feelings."

Maile says that when she was at a meeting with Palestinian and Israeli girls to talk about their experiences, she drew on her reading and new words to interpret the strong beliefs that were exchanged. Having the words to express, explore, and ultimately name her feelings changed her experience of what can otherwise be an overwhelming and confusing immersion in pure emotional experience. She identifies the generative quality of writing and speaking. She can describe her world with a complexity that matches the depth of her experience. As a result, she is less alone, less at the mercy of events, and more sure of who she in fact is in this world.

THE POWER OF ANALYSIS

Like a key that you look to for help, we learned to look at elements of rhetoric. Not like this shows you where to go, but helps you to see the steps to where you're going.

—Warren, senior

Students in the twenty-first century are faced with the need to organize and evaluate an ever-expanding world of information so as to discern false from accurate, marketing from useful information. Ana speaks with passion about her capacity:

I have become a more analytical reader and a better writer. I have more ability to look at what I read and see: "Are these people really that credible?" . . . I tell my parents to think about who they are listening to. "Are [the speakers] just good masters of English?" [This] is not a bad thing but doesn't mean they are more qualified, but just that they understand how to appeal to us.

In conversation on any topic with Ana, it is evident that she brings a rigorous analytical eye to every claim, argument, statement of fact, or opinion. She cuts through the delivery from the content, the messenger from the message. No huckster stands a chance with Ana. Furthermore, she is sharing this skill with her family and every one of us around her so that we too are alert to the murky areas where evidence or logic are lacking. With this disposition and habit to evaluate others' arguments, adolescents are better able to make wise choices in their lives.

Analysis is about more than discerning truth from falsehood. It is about fullness of thought and developing meaning. As Maile says, "When you can completely understand what you're hearing, see where it's coming from, analyze it, think about why the arguer decided to make it, [that] makes you appreciate what they're saying so much more."

All of these students imply that their ability to analyze others' arguments allows them access and engagement in the world of ideas. Orlinda says that knowing how to recognize rhetorical techniques such as pathos, ethos, and logos "fills an empty spot" for her as a listener and helps her see layers of meaning beneath the surface of what is obvious in a speech.

She remembers bringing this awareness to her ceremony for induction into the National Honor Society. "Listening to one of the speeches, I realized I was critiquing and analyzing, using what I had learned in class—like setting, pace, tone of voice." She has internalized this lens to listening to such an extent that she automatically brings it to every situation. Just as we learn to read like a writer, she was listening like a speaker, fully participating in an interaction with the spoken text.

Warren describes how he has learned to energetically, almost aggressively, listen for meaning: "analyzing style, words they use, background, where it came from, trying to find more about what is being discussed." He talks about finding the "true meaning, understanding the wording of it, the purpose of it to help you identify where you can apply that new wisdom to your life." His self-reported attitude toward school ("The reason I took this class is because my lit skills are not where I want them to be"), his role as a senior guiding younger peers, his view of his future, have shifted as he has opened up to finding meaning in learning, in literature, and in communicating.

I feel hopeful when I hear this 18-year-old boy talking about applying new wisdom to his life. He is thinking deeply and assessing influences, information, and ideas in order to find his own meaning, which allows him to consciously make choices that serve his desired purpose.

THE POWER IN CONSIDERING MULTIPLE POINTS OF VIEW

> *Everything has more than one side to it.*
> *—Warren, senior*

In our conversation, students grow passionate when they talk about learning from different points of view. When they are faced with "pitches" from advertisers, peers, politicians, or even their teachers and parents, students must be able to recognize and respond to multiple perspectives and effectively determine what is right for them. As they learn to develop their own perspectives, teens often are inundated with attempts—from both peers and adults—to capture their minds and hearts with conflicting values and beliefs.

Ana passionately relates a story illustrating the importance to her of honoring multiple perspectives:

> At my other school I was reprimanded for my views and was kept after class so my teacher could explain to me why my comment was wrong. . . . I argued with him for about an hour until I was sent off with my tail between my legs and missed my bus.

Ana intuitively grasped the deep significance of what she experienced. She sensed how this teacher was trying to position her—and her perspectives—within a world that seems to be breaking apart in violent clashes of interests and ideology. She wanted to be able to think about, question, and explore points of view. She wanted nothing to be out of bounds for discussion in the process of discovering what she believes.

Maile suggests listening to language as a means for sorting through and determining meaning and value. "Being able to understand the development of all sides on a literal level helps so much. You look at the kinds of words they use, styles, evidence—these things can make or break writing." Maile brings her understanding of rhetorical elements as a foundation for analysis so that she is neither overwhelmed nor overpowered by multiple viewpoints or sources of information.

Ana explains how the capacity to see multiple viewpoints works in practice for a citizen in a multicultural world. "Being able to understand a person's culture . . . maybe you cannot necessarily relate to them but you can understand . . . and respect it. . . . you realize certain things are valued more in a certain culture. Then you have a way to appeal to them, relating to them, persuading them, getting to their values, helping them to understand you."

I find it hopeful to imagine a generation of youth like Ana, with skills to listen, understand, and communicate across cultures and differences. "Know that everything is in viewpoints, even the stuff you learn isn't completely true. My grandma's opinions sometimes clash with what I hear in school now because she came from Mexico. Like her view of Pancho Villa. The rich hate him. But others love him as a liberator." From her family, Ana sees the immediate relevance of her ability to hold diverse points of view. She understands how cultural background influences how we see and judge both past and current world events.

Ana's open observing or "reading" of another culture relies on her use of analytical skills to identify and organize what she sees, and on the application of her metacognitive skills to inform her communication.

None of these students indicates any tension or threat in considering the validity of potentially contradictory points of view from different cultural perspectives. They talk more like scientific researchers who are open to considering all evidence, or explorers on a long journey who are not going to miss any sights or sounds along the way in the interest of developing further knowledge and understanding.

THE POWER OF PARTICIPATING

Teachers at our school want you to use knowledge to the fullest.
—Ana, junior

DCIS gives students various opportunities to use literacy skills for real purposes. Oliveann Slotta, a veteran math teacher who now works in curriculum development at the school, says that such opportunities are "built into the fabric of the school," with student-led, interview-style parent conferences, a portfolio process, clubs, and school and community service projects, to name but a few.

What makes these experiences significant for literacy development for students at DCIS is that in addition to applying skills to the task, they also use their analytic skills to reflect on the experience and critique their performance.

They critique themselves with the same lens they use in critiquing others. "A lot of us in this school do a lot of speaking, like at the open house for prospective students. We learn how to say what matters, what to say and not to say. Afterward, we think about how it went and why—not enough evidence? not convincing enough?" Through practice, they are developing habits of metacognition, embedding the use of complex literacy skills in the way they live and look at their participation in the world.

Their internalized awareness of process and content provides an entry point to what people with power and privilege have access to, that is, ways of thinking, making meaning, and integrating knowledge to inform strong communication and thoughtful actions (Delpit, 1995). Orlinda says, "There's more to it than you think. Everybody knows about choosing words to get your message across, but now I think about the whole structure of the case and how it is presented. You have an advantage over people when you've had the opportunity to learn these little secrets."

For these students, their awareness of the value of literacy has become inter-twined with who they are and how they interact with the "text" of the world. They no longer assume they are shut out from active participation. In fact, they are tak-ing on leadership roles with peers, in the community, and in the school. Maile says, "If you want to make world change, you also need to establish your credibility or people will be like, 'Who are you to be speaking?'"

Ana often refers to the responsibility she feels as editor-in-chief of the school newspaper to advocate with skill and care:

> Recently there was kind of a little jam with censorship and I was extremely upset. . . . So I talked to my teacher a lot about my options, and she helped me come to the conclusion to write a letter about it. I really wanted to write, "Oh my God! Censorship is horrible and this is about free speech." My teacher helped me think about audience, what are they going to get from this, are they going to think of my school positively if I say my school censors things. I had to think of a lot of good rhetorical strategies and so we had to construct a paper and use an outline. . . . When you get it right and you can say it, [that's] so empowering. . . . When I communicate, I feel strong and good about myself.

As a culminating step in their experiential learning process, these students take a further step in metacognition as they figure out how to pass on their knowledge to younger students. Orlinda relates her current responsibility. "Now I'm doing the training for younger students to talk at open houses for prospective students and their parents—be confident to talk in front of adults. People don't teach you how to speak: posture, convey your message. When you're able to sit and speak with students about this—Wow! I hope they appreciate and use it."

INVESTING AND ENGAGING IN LEARNING

> *Everyone wants a good life.*
> —Orlinda, junior

I have come to believe that at the root of our struggle to engage disengaged stu-dents, there is a disconnect between the tasks of school, what Orlinda describes as "all that is going on in our lives outside of school," and an indeterminate pathway to an unknown future.

Only in the last century have children been lifted out of the real-life function-ing of the community and isolated in buildings where, as they are often told, "your job is to learn." In theory, this is a wonderful privilege: to learn for learning's sake, to live in a world of ideas and possibilities, to perhaps reach beyond the corner of the world in which they were born. In practice, we find a multitude of contradic-tory values and expectations for desired outcomes.

When Maile said, "We are such losers to be thinking this way all the time," they laughed together, perhaps at the irony of acquiring skills that are as much valued in the mainstream adult culture as they are unvalued in their teen culture.

Sitting at the table with this group of teenagers, I could feel their vitality and excitement with this experience of powerful thinking, while recognizing the inner strength required of them to embrace a blossoming identity as analytical thinkers. The students with whom I spoke acknowledged that peer support was often a powerful contributor to their willingness and motivation to engage in rigorous educational experiences.

They feel concern and compassion for those among their classmates who are struggling, and want to help others find access to the learning that is bringing value and empowerment to their lives. Maile joked, "If only we could use our understanding of rhetoric—ethos, pathos, logos—to build a convincing case [to our peers about the value of education, particularly literacy]." There is a seriousness behind the joke—it is possible that these students *will* use their literacy skills to spark their peers' interest and belief in the value of learning.

LITERACY FOR TODAY

> *Knowing and learning take on importance only when we are convinced it matters, it makes a difference.*
> —Deborah Meier, The Power of Their Ideas

Often when confronted with a new group of initially disengaged teenagers, I recall my immigrant grandmother talking wistfully about her lack of education. When asked on her 80th birthday what she would have done if she had been so lucky as to achieve that education, she said, "Oh, so many things. I would have traveled. I would have invented things. I could have talked to people. So much . . . I could have done." In my grandmother's view, education opens doorways to participate more fully in a wider world.

Her words echo in those times when I help students struggling with an assignment, and I am faced with their questions (aloud or implied): "Why should I bother? How will thinking about these questions, reading this text, or writing this essay matter in my life?" Instead of invoking some abstract future defined by future jobs or quality of life, I think of my conversations with Ana, Maile, Warren, and Orlinda. They lead me to teach with a view toward student learning not just for the next school year or for 10 years hence, but for today.

Though planning for the future surely has a place, we cannot guarantee a direct correlation between what students get in school and what they will need in a job 5–10 years from now. And it is unlikely they will create a powerful life for themselves if they do not have a chance to begin practicing, using and experiencing power from their learning for real purposes right now.

Our students have a right to the benefits that literacy brings to their young lives, a right and power they can carry into adulthood as fully participating citizens enjoying both the responsibilities and the rewards. In fact, Susan teaches in the AP Language and Composition class that in this society rhetoric is one of the keys to access and power; if you can analyze and assess rhetoric and use that knowledge in your own speaking and writing, it opens many doors for your future. As Deborah Meier (2002) wrote in *The Power of Their Ideas*, "They've got to see that it matters. Because it does" (p. 173). For this small group of young people, the power of literacy skills and understandings matters, as doors open for them right now.

HOW TO BEGIN

- Ask yourself this question from Theodore Sizer: What are the intellectual habits that your students will carry away from school?
- When planning lessons and projects "with the end in mind," include at least one immediate applicable outcome for students as thinkers.
- Provide regular consistent opportunities for students to use the skills and understandings in conversations with each other and with other people about topics and issues that matter to them.
- Encourage students to be metacognitive about how they are applying their literacy abilities.

LINGERING QUESTIONS

- How do we quickly find relevancy and points of entry for students who are initially deeply resistant to learning in school?
- What are the implications for school reform if we were to create more opportunities for students to practice literacy skills in authentic situations?
- What is the role of simulated experiences (such as Model UN, debate clubs) in providing authenticity of opportunity for practicing literacy skills and understandings?
- How do we continue to identify current relevance and opportunity for application in real time for teenagers?

LEADERSHIP PERSPECTIVES

From Diane Lauer, former principal of Conrad Ball Middle School:

- *Authentic learning.* Middle school students are just blossoming. Their brains are opening. They are so passionate about justice, fairness. We can inspire their hearts and activate their minds by thinking beyond the detailed skills. We can envelop skill development in an authentic, engaging, inquiry-based learning opportunity. They are ready to be hooked *right now.*

From Garrett Phelan, principal of César Chávez Charter School (Capitol Hill campus):

- *Relevance.* We should teach the moment. Teaching powerfully what's in this moment, for this moment, takes care of the future. If we teach only for the future, we lose the student. Students know that we, like them, have no real idea what the future might be. We have to give them tools to make meaning of the world now, as well as the world they will face when we are not there.

RELATED READINGS

The Rethinking Schools and Essential Schools websites (rethinkingschools.org and www .essentialschools.org, respectively) offer invaluable support and ideas for approaching education in a way that is directly relevant to students' current lives.

Duke Helfand and Howard Blume's article "Left Out, Students Want a Voice in Reform" (Helfand & Blume, 2008) provides an example of students expressing and demonstrating for a voice in what affects their lives.

James Beane's book *A Reason to Teach* (Beane, 2005) provides specific examples of class-rooms where students are engaged in important issues and actions.

John Dewey's book *Experience and Education* (Dewey, 1938) is essential reading for every teacher to understand the roots of best practice instruction that matters for students.

James Moffett's book *Teaching the Universe of Discourse* (Moffett, 1966) offers teachers a foundation in teaching rhetoric and discourse.

Reflecting on Part I

- Given the content and students you teach, what resonated with you about these authors' vision of thinking and literacy? What aspects challenged you?
- How do the authors' comments apply in particular to students with special needs or who are English language learners?
- In respect to your group (faculty, department, team), what might be important for you to reaffirm or reassess in terms of what, how, and why you teach?
- Zehner asserts that literacy is a powerful way for content-area teachers to achieve their goals. Do you agree? In your content area, what relationships do you see between thinking, the subject-specific literacy skills needed to excel in your class, and the role of metacognition?
- Woods argues that thinking is the "only enduring freedom." Based on student data, how well is your school doing in ensuring that all students have this freedom? What might be key issues and possible next steps?
- Swinehart claims that students must learn to be metacognitive if they are to succeed within school and beyond. How do you respond?
- Larner argues that students can use literacy skills to gain access and power "right now." How might you and your colleagues capitalize on this as you plan and teach?
- Do you agree that "literacy is a civil right"? If so, how so? If not, why not?

LEADERSHIP PERSPECTIVES

From Diane Lauer, former principal of Conrad Ball Middle School:

- *Culture*. For a school leader, the jumping-off point is shifting a school culture to see this as vital work. If we as a group of teachers really care about thinking and not just knowledge, then how can we *not* teach in the ways these four authors described?
- *Reflection*. I wonder, can we teach students to be metacognitive thinkers without being consciously metacognitive thinkers ourselves? In our work with each other as adults, can we model this practice of being reflective?
- *Synergy*. As a principal, I am always thinking about how to create synergy in the building, a way to formulate a shared dream and vision of what we want to accomplish. Literacy truly does run through all our content areas. This provides a sense of interconnectedness, the thing that ties us all together, even though at the secondary level we are typically going off in all directions. What is literacy, and what does it mean in the twenty-first century to have these students be complete, capable, empowered people? We have to have a dream beyond basic skills.

From Garrett Phelan, principal of César Chávez Charter School (Capitol Hill campus):

- *Rituals.* As colleagues, consider this: What values, rituals, and traditions will make for a culture of literacy in your school and in your classroom?
- *Student motivation.* If we want to rid the classroom of student comments like "This is boring," or "I don't know," or "Whatever," we must give students the tools and opportunities to make meaning from all texts and artifacts as they read the world. Motivation starts with literacy. Motivated students trust their thinking. They have confidence, and they can make meaning from what they are doing. They have some control in grappling with their world.
- *Advocacy.* I always want students to advocate for themselves. If we are not teaching young people to read well, analyze deeply, listen keenly, write powerfully, and speak precisely, then they will be powerless to advocate for themselves or for anyone or anything else.

Beliefs into Practice: Literacy as Means to Content Teachers' Ends

The cliché of "reading and writing across the curriculum" does not show you as a secondary content teacher how literacy truly serves *your* particular goals for students: to understand this particular content deeply and to develop independence in how to think, learn, read, and write about this particular content.

Part II includes portraits of four classrooms—math, science, social studies, and language arts—in which the teachers help students acquire and use content knowledge through literacy. In each chapter, readers see how literacy links to the central cognitive tasks of that particular academic discipline, illustrating how the concept that "students have a right to literacy and a right to think" works differently in each content area.

- What, concretely, does this work look like?
- How does each teacher use literacy (reading, writing, vocabulary, and oral language/discussion) to help students understand key concepts, make meaning of difficult texts, and develop independence as future learners in this academic discipline?
- What beliefs does each teacher hold that enable and challenge him or her to teach in these ways?
- How does each teacher in effect "apprentice" students in his or her discipline? (see Schoenbach, Braunger, Greenleaf, & Litman, 2003).
- What does this type of teaching make possible for students in terms of engagement, understanding, achievement, and power?

As with Part I, you might read this section in various ways. If a full faculty is reading the book together, ideally each teacher might first read the one chapter in Part II that is most relevant to him or her and discuss it with colleagues who teach the same content area. Then the full faculty could meet to discuss similarities and differences across the four chapters. Alternatively, an individual reader, team, or department could select a few of the chapters that seem most relevant either to the content or grade levels you teach.

Each author describes instructional practices that you can implement in your own classroom, but these practices are not formulas, programs, or tips and tricks. Rather, the way these teachers interact daily with students is a manifestation of the vision outlined in Part I.

Individually, these chapters aim to help you see what it looks like—concretely, specifically—to teach in this way, and how students benefit. Collectively, these chapters drive home the point that adolescent literacy is a shared effort; every secondary teacher plays a key role in respecting and promoting the students' right to think.

CHAPTER 5

Mathematics Teaching for Understanding: Reasoning, Reading, and Formative Assessment

Paula Miller and Dagmar Koesling

IN THIS CHAPTER: Paula Miller and Dagmar Koesling describe the role that literacy plays in three central elements of Koesling's mathematics instruction: teaching for understanding by solving complex word problems, reading mathematical text, and assessing student understanding. Readers see how literacy helps all students, including English language learners, "marry" skills and understanding.

KEY POINTS

- Students, even those with weak math skills, can develop problem-solving and reasoning skills that make advanced mathematics courses accessible.
- Teachers can "marry" the mathematical reasoning process with a reading process that helps students understand the real-world context and mathematical concepts of a problem.
- Rich word problems provide the teacher with in-depth assessment of a student's skills, which in turn helps teachers determine what additional instruction students need.

Delia Jones, a student at Boston's Fenway High School, represents many students who make it through middle school still lacking basic math skills. Unlike most of those peers, however, Delia is now a senior precalculus student—and doing well. Asked about her school experiences in mathematics, Delia recalls:

> When I came into the ninth grade, I didn't even know how to do long division. My teachers in elementary and middle school would . . . show us how they'd work a problem. It felt . . . like watching a magician pull a rabbit out of a hat. "See how easy this is? Now you do it, too." But the problem was, I never figured out why the rabbit got into the hat, much less what steps the magician used to make it reappear. Then the teachers would give

us . . . [similar] problems to do in class and finish as homework. I'd try, but then I'd give up. The teacher made it look so easy, but I felt stupid when I couldn't do it, so I just started hiding.

Delia admits, "It was easy to hide in middle school. You know, you just keep quiet, keep your head down . . . don't cause trouble. The teachers didn't know how lost I was until I'd already failed the test. Then it was too late and they were already moving onto the next thing," Delia says. "But here at Fenway, teachers figure out what I don't know even before *I* know I don't know it!"

ACCESS FOR ALL: THINK IT THROUGH VERSUS DRILL IT IN

Fenway High School is a small high school (within the Boston Public School system) with approximately 300 students, 65% of whom qualify for free or reduced-price lunch, and 85% of whom are people of color (although few formally qualify as English language learners).

Teachers at Fenway believe that problem-solving and reasoning skills, as well as content skills, can be taught best in the context of a literacy-based math curriculum. Such an approach goes beyond drills and memorized procedures. It not only equips students with the skills to pull mathematical rabbits out of hats, but also challenges students to understand how those rabbits got into the hats in the first place.

Dagmar Koesling teaches math at Fenway and works as a math consultant with the Public Education & Business Coalition, where Paula Miller is a staff developer. In this chapter, we describe three central components of Dagmar's mathematics instruction that help her make advanced mathematics courses accessible to all students:

1. Using complex word problems to teach higher level math skills by giving students a concrete real-world situation and applying progressively more abstract algebra tools
2. Modeling the mathematical reading and reasoning process, coaching students as they learn difficult concepts
3. Assessing and naming students' thinking as they work, and reshaping teachers' next steps accordingly

MATH LITERACY AS A CIVIL RIGHT

Advanced math courses are a gatekeeper. In order to receive a high school diploma, Dagmar's students must pass the high-stakes tests of the Massachusetts Comprehensive Assessment System (MCAS), which require mastery of algebra, geometry, and process skills. And beyond these basic graduation requirements, students need to master higher level courses such as calculus, or the door to careers in science, economics, and technology will be closed to them.

Many students enter high school either having never mastered mathematics or not retaining that mastery:

• Students may have experienced math as isolated skills and formulas leading to solutions that make little sense.

- Students who "live in poverty, students who are not native speakers of English, students with disabilities, females, and many non-white students . . . [often are the] victims of low expectations" (National Council of Teachers of Mathematics, 2000, p. 13).

Dagmar believes that "to level the playing field for my students, I must facilitate the learning of higher level math like algebra and process skills like problem-solving and reasoning to kids who have been judged by others as not having the aptitude to achieve at that level. Learning algebra and process skills is a civil right."

TEACHING ALGEBRA SKILLS THROUGH COMPLEX WORD PROBLEMS

Dagmar and her colleagues use the Interactive Mathematics Program, a math curriculum that challenges students to learn math concepts through complex, language-based problems. This approach is supported by leading math educators; Arthur Hyde (2007) asserts: "To raise mathematics achievement in the United States to higher levels it is essential that we infuse language and thought into mathematics. We can do a far better job of teaching students to understand and love mathematics if we enrich our teaching with practices from reading and language arts adapted by cognitive science" (p. 48).

"Leading students toward building their own understanding of a math concept takes time," says Dagmar. "I could give students the answer to the problem much earlier in the game . . . but students would have lost a lot of learning." Instead, as we show in this chapter, Dagmar may spend the better part of a class period helping students deconstruct and solve one word problem.

The results are impressive: Though 65% of Fenway High School students qualify for free or reduced-price lunch, the school boasts a 99% graduation rate, and 84% of graduates enroll in colleges. And even though half of the entering ninth graders were deficient in math and reading skills, 91% of sophomores met or exceeded state mathematics proficiency standards as measured by the state MCAS test on the first try, and 100% met or exceeded proficiency on the English MCAS.

These successes, as measured by statistics, result in part from the teachers' use of a three-pronged process: using complex word problems, coaching students on how to read math problems, and assessing students' thinking in order to revise instruction.

REASONING AND READING LIKE A MATHEMATICIAN

Like most secondary math teachers, Dagmar received no coursework in reading during her formal teacher training. Yet she has made it her business to include reading in her pedagogical toolkit. In this chapter, you will see her challenge students to develop algebra skills through word problems by teaching them a mathematical reading process (see Figure 5.1).

"I have students read the problem at least twice before they actually try to solve it," Dagmar says. "This gently guides students through their thinking about the text. I ask open-ended questions to further understanding and uncover conceptual

Figure 5.1. Mathematical Reading and Reasoning Process

First Read: Read for Understanding

- What vocabulary do I not know?
- What's the real-world context of the problem?
- What's the situational setting of the problem (not the mathematical skills)?
- What questions are being asked?

Second Read: Identify a Problem-Solving Process

- What is the pertinent information in this problem?
- What problem-solving strategies could I use?
- Which of those problem-solving strategies is best suited for this problem?
- How will I represent the problem in the symbolic language of mathematics?
- What mathematical details will I select as I reason and solve this problem?

Third Read: Solve the Problem and Check for Reasonableness

- Now that I understand the problem's content, how can I best use my math skills to solve the problem?
- How can looping back to the original setting help me interpret the solution?

---

misunderstandings. It's not 'here's how you do it.' It comes from breaking the problem-solving process into small pieces that the student is able to successfully negotiate."

Students watch her model as they read the problem together three times, in specific ways that support mathematical reasoning:

> *First read*. Reading for understanding: What is the real-world setting of the problem?
> *Second read*. Identifying a problem-solving process.
> *Third read*. Solving the problem and checking for reasonableness.

Dagmar also uses these multiple reads to assess students' conceptual understanding, reasoning, and communication (Cai, Lane, & Jakabcsin, 1996). Below, we show Dagmar taking students through these three reads and describe some of her assessment strategies. For the second read—perhaps the most complex— we also describe how Dagmar provides additional support to English language learners. At the end of the chapter, we explain Dagmar's assessment strategies in more detail.

THE FIRST READ: READING FOR UNDERSTANDING

Dagmar asks a student to read the problem aloud to the whole class:

A chemical company spends $2 million to buy machinery before it starts producing chemicals. Then it spends $0.5 million on raw materials for each million liters of chemical produced.

1. The number of liters produced ranges from 0 to 5 million. Make a table showing the relationship between the number of million liters produced, L, and the total cost, C, in millions of dollars to produce that number of million liters.
2. Find a formula that expresses C as a function of L.

Note: From *Functions Modeling Change: A Preparation for Calculus* (p. 10), by E. Connally, Deborah Hughes-Hallett, and A. M. Gleason, 2000, New York: Wiley. Copyright 2000 by John Wiley & Sons, Inc. Reprinted with permission.

Clarifying Vocabulary

Dagmar knows that students must understand the key words before they can understand the full problem. So she asks, "What is a liter?" Her question meets blank stares. She considers two choices: She could tell students, "There are roughly 3.5 liters in a gallon," or she could show students a visual image of a liter to help them make connections to their background knowledge. She quickly pulls a liter Coke bottle from the recycle bin, holds it up, and says, "This is what a liter looks like. Pass it around so you can make the kinesthetic connection between a bottle and a liter."

Comprehending the Context

Dagmar wants students to take ownership of the problem and rephrase it so it makes sense to them. "Who can tell me in their own words what the problem is about?" Dagmar asks the class. Xiomara responds by saying, "A company makes chemicals and it costs money." This is a good summary of the big picture.

When a student shares such a summary, all students benefit: the repetition reinforces comprehension, and students have a chance to ask clarifying questions.

Stating the Problem's Questions or Tasks

In the first reading Dagmar makes sure students can state the questions or tasks of the problem. If students can't, then Dagmar doubles back to give more direct instruction around vocabulary or the problem's setting. This immediate remediation reduces potential student confusion.

In this lesson the class struggles to correctly state the questions. Xiomara got the big picture, but she did not state that the problem asked her to make a table and set up a function. This shows Dagmar that Xiomara needs more instruction on how to read to identify the questions or tasks.

Dagmar then gives that instruction to the class. "When you read an essay, you have a topic sentence and supporting ideas. The most important idea is generally at the beginning. But in a math problem, you read the information first, and the most important part, the question or task, is at the very end. That's why you must read a math problem several times. It's important to ask yourself not only 'What is this problem about?' but also 'What are we supposed to do?' Look at the problem again and try that out. Look at the very end to see if you can find the question or task to be solved."

ASSESSING THE FIRST READ: STUDENTS' UNDERSTANDING OF THE REAL-WORLD CONTEXT

It is important to assess whether students have mastered the goals of the first read. If they do not understand the setting, vocabulary, or meaning of the questions or tasks to be solved, they will not be able to continue the problem.

To assess, Dagmar sometimes asks students to write down the problem questions they have identified, or she may ask students to state the questions verbally to the class. Today she pulls a "dipping stick"—a wooden tongue depressor inscribed with a student's name—from a cup, and asks, "Chris, now that you've reread the problem and focused on the last part, what does this chemical company want to know?"

"This chemical company wants to figure out the actual cost of making stuff," Chris says.

"That's it!" Dagmar responds. "And what helped you determine that this is the question that needs to be answered?"

Another student raises her hand. "That thing you said about the important part being at the end of the problem—that helped us out a lot. Before we were analyzing every sentence looking for the question."

Students have accomplished two parts of the problem-solving process: They understand the setting of the problem, and they have identified the questions to be answered. During this first read and the related assessment, Dagmar gave her students two literacy gifts: a process to follow, and an opportunity to reflect on how that process helped them accomplish the task.

THE SECOND READ: CHOOSING A PROBLEM-SOLVING STRATEGY

Without rereading the problem, the math problem-solving process would grind to a halt. The second read is more complex than the first and actually incorporates multiple, increasingly precise rereads. Although a skilled reader might be able to perform all these tasks during and after one second read, Dagmar addresses each part separately in order to build students' problem-solving skills.

Looking for Pertinent Information

"If Chris is on target, that the question this problem asks is what's the actual cost of making products for the chemical company, then what do we have to do with this problem? Reread the problem and underline phrases and sentences that you think may have important information for us. Find data that could help the company determine how much it will actually cost to make their new product. We may not know exactly how to use that information yet, but we have a hunch it will be useful. Talk it over with your neighbor."

Dagmar lets students read the problem again and gives them a minute to chat with each other.

She wants to make the process of identifying pertinent information explicit to all students. Circulating as students work, she sees that Maurice has underlined several pieces of information, and asks him to share with the class. "So, Maurice, what pieces of information did you find that will help us determine the cost to produce?" Dagmar asks.

"This company has spent two million bucks on equipment before they've even made a dime," Maurice says.

"So what questions were you asking yourself, Maurice?"

"Right here it says the company spent $2 million to buy machinery before producing chemicals. So I wondered if that should be included when the company adds up all the costs. Won't they need to add that $2 million to the list?" Maurice says. He is modeling for his peers how to think through what is most important.

Determining Problem-Solving Strategies

Students next need to consider possible strategies. Dagmar helps students do this by first labeling Maurice's thinking for the class. "Maurice took a piece of information from the text itself, that the company paid $2 million up front for equipment. He asked himself a question, 'Shouldn't that be included in the total costs for the new product?' And that question is worth considering as he thinks about the problem-solving strategy he'll use."

She asks Maurice, "So what math operation would you use to make sure the chemical company includes that $2 million in their final costs?"

"You need to add up all of the company's expenses first thing. And the cost of equipment is one of those expenses," he responds.

Dagmar affirms his response, then questions the class, "So what other information do you think is important here? What are some of the other costs we'll need to include?"

Another student responds, "They spend $0.5 million for each million liters produced."

The class now has correctly identified all the pertinent information in the problem and one math operation to use in solving it.

Representing the Problem in Mathematical Symbolic Language

The next part of the second read is perhaps the hardest: Students need to move from the concrete, real-world situation to representing it in abstract mathematical symbols.

In this case, students need to make a table for 0 to 5 million liters of chemical produced. From experience, Dagmar knows that not all students will be able to do this immediately.

Again, she makes the reasoning and reading explicit. She asks them what the problem asks them to do next. Noticing that few students have their eyes on the text, Dagmar redirects the class. "Look at the problem again."

She knows that students tend to read only the main part of the problem, not the questions or tasks at the end. "When you fail to read the question and tasks at the end of the problem," Dagmar explains to the students "it's like telling a joke without the punch line."

Students read the question quietly to themselves. Some hands go up. Dagmar waits until all students look up, an indicator that they are finished reading.

ASSESSING THE SECOND READ: STUDENTS' ABILITY TO ABSTRACT

As with the first read, Dagmar begins to assess how well students are mastering the goals of the second read.

She draws a dipping stick with Maria's name. "What do you think, Maria?"

Maria answers, "Make a table."

"Right," Dagmar responds. "Question 1 does give us the problem-solving strategy of 'make a table.' And it also provides specifics about the table. What might those be?"

Students now need to represent the problem in mathematical symbolic language. They must transition from the concrete problem situation (i.e., the cost of producing chemicals) to the abstract algebra concepts of dependent and independent quantities. They also have to grapple with the abstract concept of variable, correctly identifying the variables L and C and their precise meaning in terms of the problem. And since the text is not explicit about the format of the table, students must draw on their algebra skills and a correct interpretation of the facts of the problem to set up the table.

While students read the text they must ask themselves the key algebra question for the entire problem: Which quantity depends on which? Adults may easily see that cost depends on volume of chemicals produced. But that is not obvious to many of Dagmar's students.

Visual Representations: Drawing a Table

To help students make sense of the abstract concepts in the problem they just read, she draws a blank table on the board.

Through open-ended questions, she gets students to label the table correctly. She asks, "What are the variables mentioned in the text?"

Students respond, "L and C."

"What does L stand for?" Dagmar asks the class.

Students call out, "Liters."

Dagmar continues to push for more information. "Is that all I should put in the table? How can we make this more specific?"

"Number of millions of liters of chemical produced," Jasmine says, and Dagmar adds that clarification to the table.

"And what's the other variable?" she asks.

"It's C," several respond.

"So what does *C* represent with units?" she asks.

"Cost in million of dollars," they reply.

Dagmar pulls from the students the information they are finding in the text, and writes their words on the board.

She has now modeled how to find the variables and correctly identify each one in terms of the problem setting. Next, she quickly thinks aloud about how she processes pieces of this word problem.

"Here's what I ask myself when setting up a table, 'What depends on what? Does the amount of chemical depend on the final cost or does the final cost depend on the chemical produced? Which quantity goes on the left side of the table and which on the right side?"

Shifting the thinking responsibility back to students, she asks: "What do you think?"

"*L* belongs on the left and *C* on the right," James responds. Dagmar enters the variables in the top row.

Checking for Misconceptions

She quickly assesses the class by asking the class who agreed with James. Most students raise their hands, but not everyone. This indicates that some did not make the conceptual leap to the dependent and independent variable.

Instead of delving into an abstract conversation about independent and dependent variables Dagmar decides to go back to the text and keep the conversation at the concrete level.

"Look at the question one more time," she tells the class. "Where are the numbers we care about right now?" She waits ten seconds.

Assessing Students' Understanding of Technical Vocabulary

"Now we have this table that's begging to be filled in with numbers. What do we call these numbers? They have a special name," Dagmar tells the class as she points to the Word Wall (see Figure 5.2) loaded with math terms students have learned.

Figure 5.2. Mathematical Word Wall

Independent Variable	Dependent Variable
X	Y
Input	Output
Domain	Range
Horizontal axis	Vertical axis
Input value	Function value

"Oh! You mean independent variable," cries out Monica.

"Right!" Dagmar said. As she points to the first empty spot in the table, she asks, "What goes here?"

Monica responds, "Zero."

"Why do you think that?" Dagmar quizzes.

Monica looks at the text again, then responds, "The left column holds the independent variable *L* because these are the input numbers. Whatever happens in the right column *depends on* the number in the left column. That would make the right column the dependent variable. The second question reads, 'Find a formula that expresses *C* as a function of *L*.' I think this means that *C* is the dependent variable."

Dagmar knows that Monica understands the most important concepts of the abstract algebra component of the problem: dependent and independent variables and where to put them in the table. She checks that this assessment is correct by asking, "So what do I write here on the left side of the table, Monica?"

Monica quickly rattles off, "0, 1, 2, 3, 4, 5 because that's what it tells us in the first line of the problem."

Monica has achieved the main goal of the second read: She has translated the real-world context of the problem into a mathematical representation (i.e., a table).

THE SECOND READ: ADDITIONAL SUPPORT FOR ENGLISH LANGUAGE LEARNERS

During the second read, Dagmar often provides additional support to her English language learners and others who may need more scaffolding. "For an ELL, the targets are (a) to stretch the student towards conceptual learning of the content at the next level and (b) to bring her or his language development forward at the same time" (Bay-Williams & Herrera, 2007, p. 49).

Dagmar knows that Charlie, an ELL student, often needs extra time and support to fully understand a problem. She does not want to lose track of Charlie or let him off the hook; he too can master reading and math.

To assess his current understanding, Dagmar points to the empty spot on the table across from where $L = 0$, and asks Charlie, "What goes here?"

Charlie responds, "$C = 0.5$."

This is incorrect, yet Dagmar does not correct him. She wants to give him the challenge of thinking this through.

Additional Processing Time for ELL Students

Charlie may have chosen the wrong number because he did not fully comprehend the problem. He may simply need more processing time.

"Read the beginning of the problem again, Charlie. What does it say?" In effect, Charlie gets a chance to repeat the second read.

As an English language learner, Charlie may need this extra time in order to "translate" the math into his native language. As ELA expert Sally Nathenson-Mejia has noted, math is a language with a specific syntax; typically, whatever language students *first* used when learning to calculate math is the language they will revert to whenever they calculate math (personal communication, December 15, 2007).

Chunking Text for ELL Students

Charlie reads the first sentence aloud. Dagmar asks him to stop there. She doesn't want him to read the information in the following sentence because that isn't pertinent to understanding what needs to go into the table. Thus Dagmar breaks the reading down into small chunks for Charlie. As an unskilled math reader, Charlie might jumble up additional information and get confused.

Clarifying Vocabulary and Wait Time for ELL Students

Dagmar knows that English language learners often struggle with technical math vocabulary. She asks Charlie directly if he needs clarification on any vocabulary. He says he is fine.

She waits as he continues to look at the first sentence for an answer. After a few seconds, she can tell by his body language—a smile on his face and his body physically relaxing—that he is able to do this. She confirms this when Charlie looks up and says, "Oh. It's 2."

"That's exactly right. And what in the text helped you figure that out?" she inquires.

Charlie looks at the ordered pair $L = 0$ and $C = 2$ and says, "Because in the beginning of the word problem, it says before they make anything, it cost two million dollars."

Dagmar's assessment helped her adjust her instruction so Charlie arrives at the right answer on his own, giving him the opportunity to learn and gain confidence.

Naming Success for ELL Students

Dagmar points to the next empty spot on the table and asks, "So try that out, Charlie. Look at the next number in the L column of our table and tell me what goes on the right side."

"2.5!" Charlie exclaims.

"And the next spot?"

"3!" he says.

With a big smile on his face, Charlie continues to fill in the rest of the missing numbers (see Figure 5.3).

"So Charlie, why is that? What's happening here?"

"Well, there's a pattern. It goes up each time by 0.5 million dollars," he says.

Students have read the problem twice, identified the setting and the questions, translated the problem into mathematical representation, and made a table. They now are now ready to set up the function that models the problem.

THE THIRD READ: INTERPRETATION OF THE SOLUTION

The most abstract part of solving complex word problems is translating the concrete word problem into an algebraic equation, or function, in this example, $C(L) = 0.5\,L + 2$.

Figure 5.3. In-Out Table for Cost of Chemicals Produced Depending on the Number of Liters Produced

L Liters of chemicals produced (in millions)	C Cost (in millions of dollars)
0	2.0
1	2.5
2	3.0
3	3.5
4	4.0
5	4.5

By laboring through the table, students have had to think about the pattern involved, which makes it easier to set up the equation. They are able to identify the 2 as the initial cost of $2 million and the 0.5 as the variable cost of $0.5 million per million liters produced. Both contribute to the total cost C.

After all this work many students don't remember anymore what they were supposed to do and what it all means. So it is important to have students verbally summarize and interpret their work. Students need this final processing opportunity to help them solidify the skills learned and put it all in its proper context.

In this problem, students were to make a table and set up a function to model the cost of producing 0 to 5 million liters of chemicals. After Dagmar writes the cost equation on the board she asks the class about the meaning of the equation. As she points to the equation, she asks, "Who can tell me what each part of the equation represents?"

Students look at the problem one more time as they struggle to make sense of the equation. The answers come one by one and Dagmar asks that students label the equation as she writes on the board (see Figure 5.4). She wants students to interpret the equation on both a concrete and an abstract level.

Only now can Dagmar be confident that students have mastered all aspects of the problem: text, table, equation, and understanding.

These three reads named students' mathematical reasoning processes so everyone could begin to see how to get the rabbit out of the hat.

ASSESSMENT LEADS TO STUDENT EMPOWERMENT

Dagmar used informal assessments throughout all three reads in order to understand student progress. These informal assessments let her look at students' mathematical reasoning and reading and determine whether they are on target or not.

Figure 5.4. Interpreting All Parts of the Equation

C		(L)	=	0.5		L	+	2

C	L	0.5	L	+ 2
Total cost	Mill. liters of chemicals produced	Expense of $0.5 mill. for each mill. liters produced	Mill. liters of chemicals produced	$2 mill. for equipment before production starts
(Dependent variable)	(Independent variable)	(Variable cost or rate of change)	(Independent variable)	(Fixed cost or initial condition)

Note: Typically, this equation is written as follows: $C(L) = 0.5L + 2$. When Dagmar teaches this, students frequently do not understand what all the symbols in the equation mean. Therefore, she spaces out the equation and explain the real-world meaning and the mathematical meaning of each symbol.

She then can adjust her next instructional moves accordingly to prevent the cycle of learning shut-down that plagues many students.

As shown in Figure 5.5, informal assessments take many forms. Dagmar used many of these informal assessments as students worked through the chemical company word problem. She consistently questioned students about their thinking to assess when their conceptions were accurate or off-target.

Using the dipping sticks helped insure that she talked with many students versus only those who raised their hands. Having students write gave accountability to each student and also helped them process their thinking to share with partners.

The thumbs check allowed her to quickly determine how many students needed more teaching and how many were ready to move ahead. For those needing more teaching, she conferred with them individually or in small groups. For those ready to move ahead, she challenged them to fill in the table on their own before sharing with the class.

SKILLS AND UNDERSTANDING GO HAND IN HAND

The guiding focus for Dagmar's math instruction is her belief that students must do the thinking and explain why they select specific math processes to work toward solutions. When students construct knowledge, it becomes more enduring knowledge. Literacy becomes the tool that lets them access and assess math concepts, bringing together formerly disparate skills and approaches to solving problems into a coherent whole. Literacy provides students a key—especially important for those who might otherwise be locked out—to mathematical understanding and skill, which in turn empowers them to open many doors.

Figure 5.5. Informal Assessment Methods in Literacy-Rich Math Instruction

INFORMAL ASSESSMENT METHOD	HOW OR WHEN TO USE IT
Questioning	Use throughout each of the three math reads to help students clarify their thinking and identify misconceptions
Conferring	Meet with each student or small groups to query their thinking as they work on a math task: • Where are you stuck? • What have you tried to get unstuck? • What are you considering as your next move? • What is the question asking of you?
Dipping sticks	Randomize whom you call on by using wooden tongue depressors with a student's name on each stick and pulling them from a container, grab bag style, to involve everyone in class conversations
Thumbs check	Students give the following signals to help the teacher assess their understanding during class: • Thumbs up: "I understand the concept." • Thumbs sideways: "I sort of get it." • Thumbs down: "I need you to teach a bit more."
Exit slips	Students take the last 5 minutes of class to write three or four sentences that: • Explain the main point of the lesson (e.g., what a function is) • Name one strategy used in class that helped the student solve a problem
Journal writing	Writing daily to short prompts, such as: • Explain this answer • Explain how you solved this problem

HOW TO BEGIN

• Experiment with the 3-part math reading process.
• Let students wrestle with word problems. Don't rescue.
• Coach students to articulate their thinking, and to ask themselves these questions:

Do I really understand this problem?
What process should I use to solve this problem? ·
What skills do I need to use?
What does the answer mean?
How can I communicate this to others?

LINGERING QUESTIONS

- What must mathematics teachers give up to find time to teach this mathematical reading process? What will students gain?
- How can content area teachers in different disciplines collaborate to understand the differences students face as readers in various content areas?
- How might such conversations help teachers to help students access text across all disciplines?

LEADERSHIP PERSPECTIVES

From Diane Lauer, former principal of Conrad Ball Middle School:

- *Importance of scaffolding.* We tend to think that older students don't need us to break things down for them. But Koesling shows the benefits of scaffolding the type of reading and reasoning she values most for her high school math students. She models, coaches, gives them time to practice, and asks them to reflect on the tools they are learning. She explicitly teaches students how to think mathematically. Consider to what extent you do, could, or should do this for your students in your content.
- *Leaders must walk the talk.* School leaders must ask themselves, "Am I, as a principal, doing the things Koesling does to help students learn when I help my teachers learn? What do I model? What scaffolds or supports do I provide? When and how do I give teachers time and space to practice new skills? When and how do I bring my staff together to reflect on new learning?"

From Garrett Phelan, principal of César Chávez Charter School (Capitol Hill campus):

- *Value of rereading.* I encourage my teachers to have students read the same text multiple times. Rereading with literacy strategies does more than help a student understand the given text; it creates a lifelong habit in students of probing, asking more of themselves and of the texts they encounter. Thus it shifts the responsibility for learning back onto the student.
- *Informal assessment.* Miller and Koesling say, "When students construct knowledge, it becomes more enduring knowledge." Informal assessments—conferring, seminars, reflection slips, writing prompts, and so on—help individual students construct knowledge. They have to do the thinking and explaining of the process they are using to solve math problems or problems in any discipline.
- *Access for all.* We can make advanced classes accessible for all students if we create the conditions for success, honor student thinking, and give students literacy

skills. Consider how shifting instructional practices in math might mean giving more access to more students at your school.

RELATED READINGS

Arthur Hyde's book *Comprehending Math* (Hyde, 2006) explains step-by-step how students can use reading and thinking strategies to approach word problems.

Lainie Schuster and Nancy Anderson's book *Good Questions for Math Teaching* (Schuster & Anderson, 2005) gives models of how to ask purposeful questions that build student understanding.

Douglas Fisher and Nancy Frey's book *Checking for Understanding* (Fisher & Frey, 2007) provides various engaging activities to help build and assess student understanding.

Jan de Lange's essay "Mathematics for Literacy" (de Lange, 2003) discusses different forms and definitions of math literacy.

Joan Kenney's book *Literacy Strategies for Improving Mathematics Instruction* (Kenney, 2005) is full of concrete examples and advice on how to teach math literacy skills.

CHAPTER 6

The Scientist in the Classroom: The Place of Literacy Within Scientific Inquiry

Moker Klaus-Quinlan and Jeff Cazier

IN THIS CHAPTER: Moker Klaus-Quinlan and Jeff Cazier describe how to create the "fire" of powerful content-area instruction, specifically when using an inquiry-based approach to teaching and learning science. They show how teachers can combine subject-specific knowledge and best-practice literacy instruction to create powerful results for students.

KEY POINTS

- Scientists observe, use their background knowledge, ask questions, interpret evidence, and read, write, and discuss to explore new understandings.
- Inquiry-based teaching engages students and fuels their conceptual understanding.
- Best-practice literacy instruction is crucial to help students engage in authentic scientific pursuit.

A guiding question emblazons the front wall of Jeff Cazier's seventh-grade classroom: "What will the earth look like in 100 million years?" Students are not pursuing a question already answered long ago, nor are they working to memorize and regurgitate a fixed set of facts. In Jeff's class, student curiosity—their innate desire to ask questions and seek answers—drives the pursuit of scientific understanding.

How does Jeff set students up to successfully answer this question using evidence from the scientific record? In short, through inquiry, scaffolded with specific thinking and literacy skills. Jeff creates a series of experiences that put students in the role of scientists, examining evidence and "uncovering" scientific information while constantly revising their own theories and understandings based on each new piece of evidence.

As a staff developer with the Public Education & Business Coalition, I have had the honor to observe and learn with Jeff (a PEBC National Lab host). I regularly bring groups of educators for facilitated visits to his classroom at Prairie Middle

School in Aurora, Colorado, which serves 1,600 students, approximately 46% of whom qualify for free or reduced-price lunch, 60% of whom are people of color, and 27% of whom are English language learners.

This chapter describes instruction in Jeff's classroom to give you a picture of the kind of content-area learning that we'd all like for ourselves, our students, our children. Students in Jeff's class engage in authentic academic pursuits, spending time "being scientists" rather than "learning science" (Schoenbach et al., 2003). The chapter address three components of Jeff's practice:

1. Belief in students' ability and right to engage in authentic scientific pursuit
2. Use of inquiry-based teaching methods to engage students and help them understand scientific concepts
3. Use of literacy strategies to support the inquiry process

Teachers often feel so pressured to cover required content that they get caught up in trying to cram sets of facts into students' brains, hoping those facts will be correctly replayed on tests. What if we taught based on an expectation that the ability to engage in inquiry—and the right to pursue a scientific career—is essential to twenty-first-century citizenship? We can't expect students to memorize in school, then somehow transform into critically thinking citizens and scientists when they enter the "real world."

All children can and must learn to use reading and writing to analyze, evaluate, critique, and question the world around them. How can we ensure that students have the opportunity in our classrooms to master this kind of thinking?

INSIDE JEFF'S CLASSROOM

Groups of students sit together, examining artists' renderings from *Ancient Denvers* (Johnson & Raynolds, 2006), a book depicting Denver at specific points over the last 100 million years. Examining the drawings, they work to generate as many observations and questions as possible. Their goal is to develop a theory of what is going on in their picture and to guess what time period it represents.

The students record their thinking in two-column charts: the left column labeled "What I see," and the right column "What it means."

"Was this an explosion that made things extinct?" one student asks. Jeff listens in, then interjects, "Write down what you just said. Are you right or wrong? Who knows? You'll find that out later." Jeff encourages students to ask as many questions as possible, knowing that doing so engages their natural curiosity.

With another group, Jeff prompts, "Have you found the animals in your picture? What do you see this time that you didn't notice before?" He moves on. The students get out a geologic time line and start trying to identify the plants and animals in their picture to determine the time period.

Jeff lets groups work, then shares with the whole class some questions he has heard.

He says, "Questions are what it's all about. In science you come up with a guess. Then you look for evidence, which will either support your guess or not. Next I'll show you how to confirm or refute some of your guesses by reading about your picture."

On the overhead projector, he displays a short text about the time period in one of the *Ancient Denver* drawings. He shows how he "dissects" the text—reflecting on it and making meaning from it. He models underlining passages, making margin notes, circling unknown words to look up, and finding answers to some of his questions.

The guiding question "What will the earth look like in 100 million years?" anchors the work Jeff's students do each year, creating coherence among topics such as biology, geology, and ecology. Before distributing texts to each group, he reminds his students, "Remember, for our big project we need to know about the life, climate, geology, and environment of each time period. Your purpose as you read is to see how well you did interpreting the picture." Having already generated observations and questions, the students now know why they are reading: to gain information to help them interpret what's happening in the image they looked at.

INSPIRING YOUNG THINKERS: LIGHTING THE "FIRE" OF LEARNING

The work of Jeff's students, described above, mirrors the work of real-world scientists, who do the following:

- Observe the world
- Try to make sense of it by considering what they already know (their background knowledge)
- Ask questions
- Seek to interpret evidence
- Discuss their ideas and hypotheses with peers
- Write to explore new understandings
- Read to compare their ideas with those of other scientists

This should be typical of a secondary science class, but it isn't.

Scientific literacy—just like mathematical or historical literacy—is more than knowing a body of information. It includes the "abilities and habits-of-mind required to construct understandings of science, to apply these big ideas to realistic problems and issues involving science, technology, society and the environment, and to inform and persuade other people to take action based on these science ideas" (Yore, Bisanz, & Hand, 2003, p. 690).

Under the right conditions, instruction results in high student engagement and interest. Students see the value and relevance of the content to their lives. They think deeply about and remember the concepts with which they have engaged. How do we teach so that our classrooms mirror authentic scientific pursuit?

To light a fire, you need three interdependent ingredients: oxygen, fuel, and heat. Similarly, to get our students "on fire" as science learners, teachers can combine the following:

- *Oxygen.* A belief in students' ability and right to engage in authentic scientific pursuit
- *Fuel.* Content-specific pedagogy—in this case, inquiry-based teaching methods—that engages students and leads to deep understanding of content

• *Spark.* Use of best-practice literacy teaching strategies to support the inquiry process

Fire's warmth, light, and magic can only be sustained when all three elements are present. Below, we elaborate how each element manifests itself in Jeff's instruction, and the impact on his students.

In this "fire" of content-area learning, the oxygen is Jeff's belief that students walk through his door as scientists, equipped with ample curiosity and background knowledge upon which to build. He also believes that they will successfully learn—and love—science.

He begins helping them develop the habits of mind required of scientists in a very simple way. Each day as students enter, he displays a *Far Side* cartoon on the overhead. Today the cartoon depicts a chicken walking away from a house carrying a human baby under its arm, passing a woman returning to the house with a basket of eggs (Larson, 2003). Students open their notebooks and work to record three things:

• What do I see (observe)?
• What background knowledge do I have?
• Why is it funny (can I combine what I know with what I see to interpret the cartoon)?

In the process, students ask questions of themselves, each other, and Jeff. Listen in on one table of students:

MARIA: I don't get it.
JEFF: So what do you do? Where do you start?
MARIA: Observation. Is that a chicken holding a baby? Oh . . .
ASHLEY: I see a lady holding a basket of eggs and a chicken holding a baby. My background knowledge tells me that the chicken laid the eggs and the baby was the lady's, so I conclude that the chicken snuck in the house and got the baby for revenge.
KAYLA: I think they traded.
JAMES: I think the chicken was trying to teach the lady a lesson because she's always taking her eggs.
MARIA: How can a chicken carry a baby?

Students then write their responses in their notebooks. Figure 6.1 shows a typical student response.

These students clearly are at different levels of conceptual understanding. But this daily practice of interpreting *Far Side* cartoons engages them in a microcosm of the habits of mind of scientific thinking: using their background knowledge, making observations, asking questions, and attempting to come to conclusions about what they see.

Jeff builds this habit daily and uses inquiry-based instruction to sustain it.

INQUIRY: FUELING CONCEPTUAL UNDERSTANDING

The fuel for effective content-area instruction is pedagogical content knowledge: the knowledge and instructional strategies teachers need in order to teach their

Figure 6.1. Student Writing About the "Chicken and Egg" Cartoon

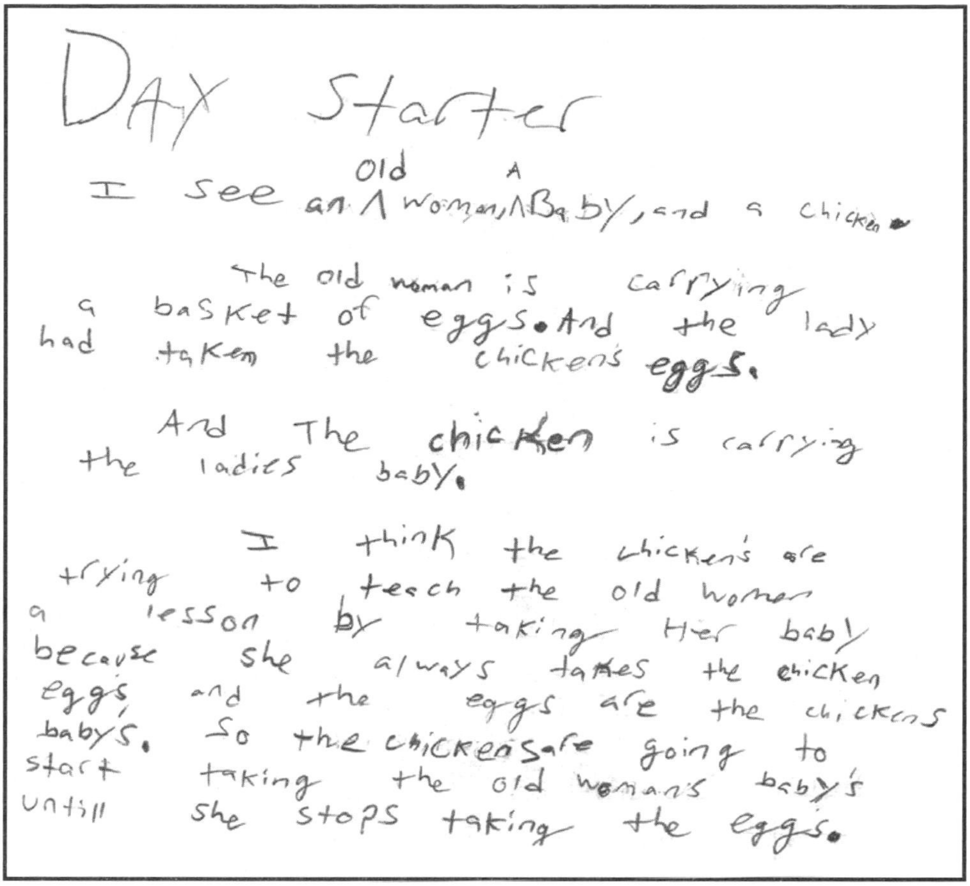

DAY Starter

I see an old woman, A Baby, and a chicken.

The old woman is carrying a basket of eggs. And the lady had taken the chicken's eggs.

And The chicken is carrying the ladies baby.

I think the chicken's are trying to teach the old woman a lesson by taking Her baby because she always takes the chicken eggs and the eggs are the chickens babys. So the chickens are going to start taking the old woman's baby's untill she stops taking the eggs.

content well (Shulman, 1986). In science, this includes an understanding of the inquiry process, and of what, when, why, and how scientists read and write as part of that inquiry process. "Inquiry refers both to the abilities and understandings students should develop . . . and it refers to the teaching and learning strategies that enable scientific concepts to be mastered through investigations. . . . Teaching science through inquiry allows students to conceptualize a question and then seek possible explanations that respond to that question" (National Research Council [NRC], 2000b, pp. xii–xv).

The inquiry process, shown in Figure 6.2, harnesses students' innate curiosity and builds on it, teaching students how to gather evidence, do research, propose explanations, and share their findings (NRC, 2000b). Inquiry is not the same as the rote run-through of "The Scientific Method" (question, hypothesis, procedure, results, and conclusion) as is often taught in science classes. Inquiry requires students to think, not just follow procedures (NRC, 2000b, p. 18). The pursuit of truth can start with simple experiments, but it has to go farther, to the point where students are developing and using the habits of mind of scientists in undertaking complex investigations. As Jeff states,

Figure 6.2. Essential Features of Classroom Inquiry

- Learners are engaged by scientifically oriented questions.
- Learners give priority to evidence, which allows them to develop and evaluate explanations that address scientifically oriented questions.
- Learners formulate explanations from evidence to address scientifically oriented questions.
- Learners evaluate their explanations in light of alternative explanations, particularly those reflecting scientific understanding.
- Learners communicate and justify their proposed explanations.

Source: National Research Council, 2000.

Simple experiments can help to create background knowledge, but it is the application of that new knowledge toward answering students' own questions that differentiates true inquiry from the standard practice in most classrooms.

Jeff, rather than having everyone do the same lab—with experiences predetermined by the teacher and one lab write-up identical to another—immerses students in the sometimes messy, authentic world of *being* a scientist.

Using Background Knowledge to Propel Student Questions

Jeff uses inquiry as the foundation to plan his year, units, and daily lessons. Daily guiding questions address pieces of the larger yearlong question. He writes today's question on the board: "How has our earth changed?"

Jeff begins by helping students activate their background knowledge: "We're *not* talking about human history, like the Revolutionary War. Earth history is much longer. Make a two-column chart in your notebook. Remember to draw a line down the middle of the page. Title the left column, 'I know.' Then title the right column, 'I want to know.' Once you have constructed your chart, take 2 minutes to write down everything you already know about how the earth has changed."

After thinking and writing, students share at their tables: "The land has changed"; "Animals went extinct"; "There used to be dinosaurs"; "Volcanoes made new islands." Jeff listens in on students' conversations. Then writing on the board again, he says, "Here are four questions that will help you think about geologic time: How old is the earth? What has changed on earth since the beginning? How is geologic time organized? How do we *know* things have changed on earth?"

Students go back to their notebooks, think some more, then share again: "Earth was created by a big bang"; "Continents were together and then drifted apart"; "Volcanoes erupt under water"; "Life changes over time." One student concludes, "It's like Earth has its own life cycle."

Another student asks, "Can we go to the 'want to know' column?" Here we see how the inquiry process fuels students' scientific thinking; their background knowledge drives them to ask questions, which in turn will drive them to want to learn new concepts and deepen their understanding.

"Yes," Jeff says, "let's work to ask questions that aren't yes or no. Try to ask how and why questions. Here's an example: 'How did scientists know what weather was like in the past?' Take 3 minutes to ask questions."

Students think, write, share at their tables, and then share with the class as a whole:

"What makes volcanoes erupt?"
"Do hurricanes come from wind or earthquakes or eruptions?"
"Will water come over Africa and America and cover those lands?"
"When will the world end?"
"Will we ever be able to go to other planets?"
"When will global warming happen?"
"How did the earth start making land?"
"How did life start?"
"How old is the earth?"

Creating the Need to Know: Starting with an Engaging Experience

After students finish sharing, Jeff continues: "As we go through class today, keep asking questions. Now, stand up. How old do you think the earth is?"

"More than a thousand million years," ventures José.

"That's a billion. If you agree with José, go over to the front of the room. If you disagree, go to the back of the room." Students move; many go to the front.

"Now, move to the front if you think it's more than 2 billion." A few more students move forward.

"Older than 3 billion years?" Most move, but a few stay put.

This quick inquiry-based experience has both activated background knowledge and created a purpose and a desire: Students want to know the answer and see who was right. This all comes *before* students read.

Jeff introduces another prereading inquiry activity that will generate more questions and challenge students to consider what they already know. "Today I'm going to give you a group of cards. You'll organize them in order from earliest to most recent, and you'll have to tell why."

Jeff gives each pair of students an envelope with cards; each card has a drawing or photograph, some with captions. The images range from single cells, to trees, to dinosaurs, to prehistoric creatures, to cavemen. "Look at these cards. What order do they go in? For example, you might put the dinosaur card before the ape card. But why?"

A student ventures, "Because there's a photograph of an ape, but only a drawing of a dinosaur?"

"Exactly. Take out your cards. These are all real things. Just so you know, I don't know if *I* could do this 100% right. It's about *why* you're putting one before another."

Carlos and Victor pair up, and Carlos jumps right in: "Insects were the first. Cavemen were like the last." Victor asks, "Where's the aliens?" Kayla and Jasmine work at another table.

KAYLA: Bugs were before dinosaurs. This one looks like a mouse.
JASMINE: It's a primate.
KAYLA: Were shells before fish?

The girls group all the cells together. Jeff comes over and asks, "Which of these was first?"

> KAYLA: One cell.
> JEFF: Why?
> KAYLA: Because one might have created another?
> JEFF: So which comes first, simple cells or complex cells?
> KAYLA: Simple.
> JEFF: We're making an inference that simple came before complex and that single came before multicellular.
> JASMINE: We think that plants came before dinosaurs because dinosaur drawings always have plants in them. Otherwise what would dinosaurs eat?

Using Text to Revise Thinking

Jeff introduces text now, when students have sorted out all their cards and are excited about whether their order makes sense. Like scientists, Jeff's students will bring their theories to the text and then use the information they encounter to revise their ideas and increase their background knowledge. "Take out your books and open to page 30, the geologic time line of the earth's history. Go through and try to rearrange your cards. The only way you'll be able to do this is by reading."

Carlos and Victor scramble to locate page 30. Carlos asks, "So, what was the first thing?"

> VICTOR (*orienting himself to the time line*): "Let's see. That's the future (*pointing to an image of a city*). See back here are bacteria, algae, then jellyfish. The plants happen more in the middle." (*The boys take their cards and move the jellyfish to the left.*)
> CARLOS: Where are the cells?
> VICTOR (*reading aloud*): "Earth's history begins; seas form; mountains begin to grow; oxygen builds up in atmosphere; first life forms in sea"(Maton et al., 1994, p. 30). (*They move a few cards, then move to the question of which order the grasses belong in.*)
> CARLOS: I know grass had to be here (*pointing to the Permian era*) because I see grass at the bottom of this tree.
> VICTOR: "Guess what? Grass is a flowering plant, so it moves over here." (*He points to the Cretaceous era where the textbook says "first flowering plants appear," and he moves a card.*)

Eventually, Jeff asks the class, "How many of you have rearranged things? Guess what? Scientists change their ideas when they learn new things. You went to the chart today and learned something new. That's just what scientists do."

Class is almost over, so Jeff asks students to grab an index card on which to write an exit ticket with their three best questions about the earth's history, as well as two *inferences*, "things you put together from combining your background knowledge with what you saw."

Science classrooms should be places where students engage in the authentic work of scientists. Through incorporating inquiry, and by having students do the kinds of reading, writing, and talking that scientists do, we can move toward that goal. However, as content-area teachers, the "how" of the reading and writing can be elusive. Next we consider specific strategies that Jeff uses.

SITUATING TEXT WITHIN THE INQUIRY PROCESS: SPARKING SCIENTIFIC UNDERSTANDING

Reading, writing, speaking, and listening are as much a part of the authentic work of science as designing experiments or gathering data. Scientists read before, during, and after conducting experiments, to update their knowledge and to review others' research. Scientists read "with pencil in hand, jotting down interesting ideas, checking calculations, and often writing margin notes" (Yore et al., 2003, p. 695). Scientists also write and talk to each other, presenting and debating ideas.

Without certain literacy skills students cannot successfully learn content. And without effective strategies for literacy instruction, content-area teachers can find that their best efforts fail to ignite students' curiosity and understanding. The needed "spark" is best-practice literacy strategies. As Jeff states,

> The inquiry and framing of a task fuels student curiosity. The literacy strategies then allow students to think through a problem, argue based on evidence, and synthesize their own discoveries with what the standards require them to learn.

It is not until we interact with information that we start to assimilate it into our understanding of the world. The greatest books are useless if we don't have the reading skills to make sense of texts for ourselves. Research by Guthrie et al. (2004) indicates that students' reading comprehension increases when they read about compelling content and concepts.

Revisiting the Need to Know: When and How to Use Text

A typical science class might consist of students reading about a topic in a text-book, and then discussing the text afterward. By contrast, Jeff creates a need or purpose, so students understand and retain what they read. For example, within the larger framework of understanding the earth's past to predict what it will look like in the future, a subunit focuses on the question: How are volcanoes and plate tectonics related?

Jeff asks students to write the day's guiding question in their notebooks as he passes out two maps. One map relates to plate tectonics, the other to locations of earthquakes and volcanoes. He instructs students to look at the maps and try to figure out what they show. Students begin recording observations in their notebooks, and Jeff circulates to confer with small groups.

After a while he displays an image of the plate tectonic map on a white screen, and students pose questions: "Are the arrows wind, or is that the way the plates are moving?" "Why are some arrows short and others long?"

Next Jeff shows the earthquakes and volcanoes map on the screen, and again students supply observations and questions: "There aren't a lot of deep earthquakes near us, but there are a lot in Asia."

Jeff notes this on the board, demonstrating how to record information. He says, "So an observation would be: 'deepest earthquakes near New Zealand and Japan.'" He goes on, "Hopefully your observations will help you answer today's question. I want a list of clear, detailed observations for each map."

Students work for 10 minutes, while Jeff continues questioning and listening to students talk in small groups. Then he instructs them to read over their observations and star a few they would like to share that will help answer the question of how volcanoes and plate tectonics are related.

Students share these observations with the class:

"Volcanoes happen near edges of plates."
"The North American and Pacific plates are transforming."
"The Ring of Fire is the volcanoes ringing the Pacific plate."

Already, student observations are more precise than 10 minutes ago. Only now does Jeff introduce text.

Text Selection

Jeff has chosen a text that is not a whole chapter, not even from a textbook, but a short article entitled "Where Do Volcanoes Occur?" It fits his question of the day perfectly, since he compiled it from various online sources and modified it to match his students' reading level. He uses the readability tool in his word processing program to gauge difficulty and adjusts vocabulary if necessary.

Jeff is constantly seeking short texts that his students can read after having experiences that have generated questions they want answered. Sometimes the textbook is a great resource, but he also uses trade books, picture books (including children's books), and the Internet. These offer quick reads to deepen student understanding.

Modeling: Showing How to Read Like a Scientist

Jeff never hands his students a text without first modeling how readers of science approach a text and record their thinking. As he passes out the volcano article, he asks, "When I say 'read,' what do I mean?"

Students chime in: "Code the text." "Underline." "Write what you think it means."

"Exactly. Pick out things that help you answer today's question. When you have questions, write them down. Also be looking for answers."

He displays the article on the overhead projector screen and models how he would read the first paragraph, taking time to underline key words, put question marks next to confusing sections, and make connections between the text and the maps. The margins of his text (see Figure 6.3) are filled with thinking in response to the text.

As students read, Jeff circulates to confer. The text informs the thinking that students generated about the maps. By talking to them about what they are thinking as they read, Jeff can help them make connections, use their background knowledge, pose smart questions, and interpret the textual information.

Figure 6.3. Jeff's Coded Text

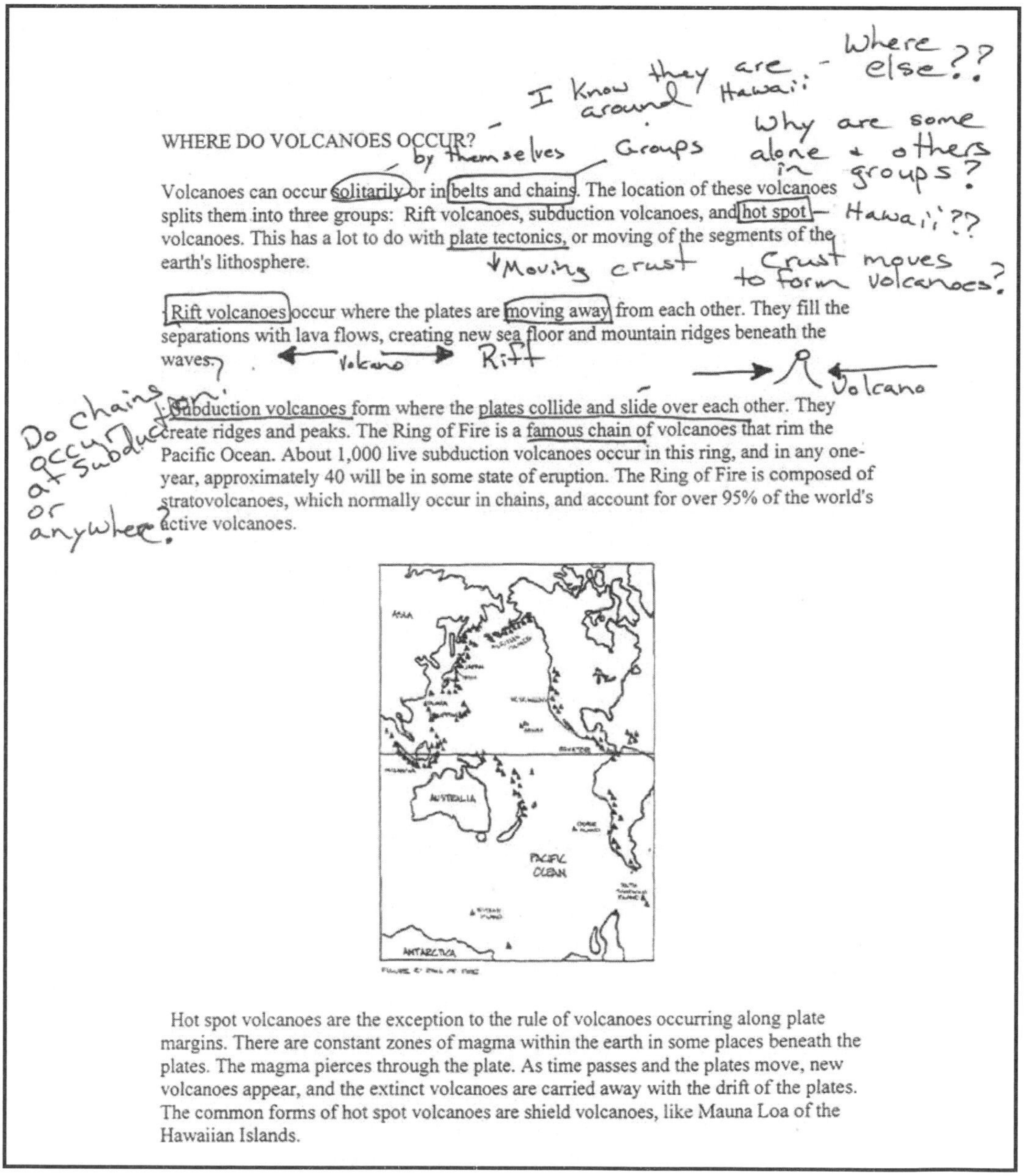
WHERE DO VOLCANOES OCCUR?

Volcanoes can occur solitarily or in belts and chains. The location of these volcanoes splits them into three groups: Rift volcanoes, subduction volcanoes, and hot spot volcanoes. This has a lot to do with plate tectonics, or moving of the segments of the earth's lithosphere.

Rift volcanoes occur where the plates are moving away from each other. They fill the separations with lava flows, creating new sea floor and mountain ridges beneath the waves.

Subduction volcanoes form where the plates collide and slide over each other. They create ridges and peaks. The Ring of Fire is a famous chain of volcanoes that rim the Pacific Ocean. About 1,000 live subduction volcanoes occur in this ring, and in any one-year, approximately 40 will be in some state of eruption. The Ring of Fire is composed of stratovolcanoes, which normally occur in chains, and account for over 95% of the world's active volcanoes.

Hot spot volcanoes are the exception to the rule of volcanoes occurring along plate margins. There are constant zones of magma within the earth in some places beneath the plates. The magma pierces through the plate. As time passes and the plates move, new volcanoes appear, and the extinct volcanoes are carried away with the drift of the plates. The common forms of hot spot volcanoes are shield volcanoes, like Mauna Loa of the Hawaiian Islands.

Synthesizing New Understandings: Talking and Writing

Just as it is critical to have a question in mind while reading, students also need to continue to grapple with new information and concepts after reading. Like scientists, Jeff's students spend time talking about what they have read after finishing a text. Jeff instructs, "Share what you learned with your tablemates. I'll come around and listen." When arguments arise, Jeff asks students for evidence from the text to support claims.

At the end of class, Jeff brings the inquiry full circle, referring to the guiding question and reminding students where they have been. "Today you looked at maps, read, and talked to each other. So, what do we know now about volcanoes and plate tectonics?" On the board, he models making a concept map, as students volunteer information. Students then create their own concept maps in their notebooks.

Finally, Jeff assigns a scenario for homework. "You are a geologist predicting the locations of *new* volcanoes. Explain where and why three new volcanoes will occur in the next 100 million years. Use information from the maps and reading as evidence to support your predictions. Start by figuring out where and why, then do the writing." This assignment will allow students to "own" their new knowledge by applying it to a real-world scenario.

CLASSROOM INSTRUCTION THAT MIRRORS AUTHENTIC SCIENTIFIC PURSUIT: TEACHING TO MAKE A DIFFERENCE

We move toward creating classrooms full of student scientists by engaging learners in scientific inquiry and equipping them with the literacy skills that the National Research Council indicates are essential to the inquiry process (see Figure 6.4): asking questions, reading and experimenting to explore hypotheses, and speaking and writing to communicate findings and to transfer understandings to new scenarios (NRC, 2000b, pp. 161–171). When we help students develop the literacy skills needed to grapple with information and construct their own understandings, it is like holding a lit match to dry tinder.

Teachers can use the template in Figure 6.4 as a guide to sequence authentic learning experiences that combine best-practice literacy instruction and scientific inquiry. This template has all the "ingredients" necessary to build the fire of effective content-area learning.

Recently, I met with a teacher to help her create an upcoming unit on weather. We designed a series of experiences in which students would become meteorologists; she got excited thinking about the ways her students could take the information they were learning and apply it to real-world situations.

When I checked back in with her later to ask how it was going, she told me she was not implementing any of those plans. She said that instead she just needed to cover a set of discrete bits of information to prepare her students for a district-mandated exam on the topic.

I asked how students were doing at learning the information. Not very well, she admitted. No wonder. Wouldn't any of us prefer to be a meteorologist than

Figure 6.4. Inquiry Supported by Best-Practice Literacy

STEPS IN THE LEARNING PROCESS	WHAT IT LOOKED LIKE IN JEFF'S CLASS
1. Exploration of preinstruction understanding through individual or group concept mapping	Recording what students know and want to learn about the earth's history in two-column note format
2. Prelaboratory activities, including informal writing, making observations, brainstorming, and posing questions	Analyzing *Ancient Denver* drawings, recording observations, and trying to anticipate what things mean Examining plate tectonics maps, writing down observations, and generating questions
3. Participation in laboratory activity	Sorting cards to try to create a geologic time line Analysis of rock samples from *Ancient Denver* time periods
4. Written reflection to articulate own understanding of laboratory activity	Recording observations in scientist's notebook, such as the reasoning behind the order of the cards in the geologic time line Creating a concept map to explore the relationship between plate tectonics and volcanoes
5. Sharing and comparing data interpretations in small groups	Collaborative learning groups Discussion, debate, dialogue Partner work
6. Reading textbooks and other printed resources to build on and revise one's growing scientific understanding	Reading about the *Ancient Denver* time period in order to confirm or refute conclusions arrived at by looking at drawings and using background knowledge Reading an article about volcanoes to better understand their relationship to plate tectonics
7. Individual reflecting and writing	Daily reflection at the end of class Notes written in scientist's notebook Scenario in which student takes on the role of geologist predicting earthquakes
8. Exploration of postinstruction understanding through concept mapping	Putting together a project that explains the student's theory of what the earth will look like in 100 million years and why

Source: Hand, Wallace, & Yang, 2004.

someone reading a textbook to prepare for a test? Teaching that uses the "quiz show" approach leaves students without a sense of how the knowledge will be useful to them, which results in a lack of motivation (NRC, 2000b).

To ignite all students' learning, we must create an atmosphere in which they experience being scientists (or mathematicians or historians). We can fuel learners' curiosity with content-specific pedagogy and spark their understanding with literacy skills to do the reading and writing of the discipline. By teaching in this way, we inspire the kind of learning that illuminates our common future.

HOW TO BEGIN

- Consider what scientists (or practitioners in your field) do.
- Create opportunities for your students to *be* scientists (or practitioners of whatever discipline you teach).
- Search out and use provocative, accessible texts that your students will want to read.
- Provide prereading activities that activate background knowledge and create a purpose for reading.
- Show your students how you make sense of texts in your field and have them practice using the strategies proficient readers use to make sense of text.
- Scaffold students' reading, giving them structured ways to interact with and respond to text so they can make meaning for themselves.
- After reading, engage students in activities that extend and solidify understanding.
- Make sure your students have opportunities not just to read about topics, but also to engage in experiences, write, and talk their way to understanding.

LINGERING QUESTIONS

- "Real" science is messy and time-consuming; how can we create a classroom where students act as scientists, within established constraints (schedule, standards, and so on)?
- What is the best way to incorporate vocabulary instruction into the inquiry process?
- What happens when teams of teachers with the same students incorporate common literacy practices across disciplines?
- What can we let go of to make the time required to plan effective inquiry instruction?

LEADERSHIP PERSPECTIVES

From Diane Lauer, former principal of Conrad Ball Middle School:

- *Inquiry-based instruction.* As a staff, are we creating opportunities for kids to learn like scientists? Or do we just use traditional instruction to fill their brain with scientific knowledge? Can inquiry-based instruction be transferred to other content areas beyond science? Should it be? What might be the benefits in terms of student engagement, motivation, and achievement?
- *Action research for teachers.* Teachers tend to be most driven when they learn in authentic situations—answering questions that matter deeply to them. How can a staff learn like scientists? How might we use action research as a professional

development method so teachers research their own questions about student learning?

From Garrett Phelan, principal of César Chávez Charter School (Capitol Hill campus):

- *Facts vs. learning.* What we know as fact today may not be fact when our students are adults. This chapter reminds me of the importance of preparing students for an uncertain future, and of the crucial role that literacy plays in helping students make meaning and seek change.
- *We choose how we teach.* I always remind teachers that, although we may not have tremendous choice over *what* we teach, we get to choose *how.* Jeff Cazier chooses to teach in a way that "mirrors authentic scientific pursuit." Do you choose to teach in such a way that students actually experience what it is like to be a writer, scientist, mathematician, historian, or linguist?

RELATED READINGS

The National Research Council's book *Inquiry and the National Science Education Standards* (NRC, 2000b) offers science teachers a clear and thorough overview of how to implement inquiry-based instruction.

Grant Wiggins and Jay McTighe's book *Understanding by Design* (Wiggins & McTighe, 2005) thoroughly explains how to create essential questions and authentic assessments as part of backward curricular design.

Steven Zemelman and colleagues' book *Best Practice* (Zemelman, Daniels, & Hyde, 1998) has a great chapter on best-practice science instruction, including classroom examples and practices to increase (such as having students hypothesize to explain data) and decrease (such as instruction based on lectures or overemphasis on memorization).

Harvey Daniels and Steven Zemelman's book *Subjects Matter* (Daniels & Zemelman, 2004) is a helpful resource for thinking about text selection and tools for students to use while reading.

John Guthrie and colleagues' article "Increasing Reading Comprehension and Engagement Through Concept-Oriented Reading Instruction" (Guthrie et al., 2004) describes a research study that indicates that engaging students in reading about rich scientific concepts increases students' reading comprehension, reading motivation, and reading strategy use.

CHAPTER 7

Argument and Advocacy: Rigorous Talk About Culturally Relevant Text in Social Studies

Joanna Leeds

IN THIS CHAPTER: Joanna Leeds describes how Gerardo Muñoz, a high school social studies teacher, teaches his academically at-risk students to value literacy, in particular the importance of analytical argument. Leeds describes how Gerardo establishes relationships, designs curriculum that is compelling, and uses specific discussion strategies to foster students' engagement, critical thinking, and use of evidence to support their reasoning. Leeds shows how teachers like Gerardo balance connection and challenge to reach all students.

KEY POINTS

- Teachers' beliefs about students impact everything: what, how, and why they teach.
- Teachers must design culturally relevant curriculum that engages their students.
- Social studies teachers must teach students to value their voices and effectively argue their views.
- Rigorous oral discussions help students develop their thinking and writing skills.

Gerardo Muñoz's 10th-, 11th-, and 12th-grade students are in the midst of what he calls a "Scored Discussion" about an article that discusses Arnold Schwarzenegger's veto of a bill banning the use of Native American–related terms as mascots for football teams in California. Gerardo begins with a question, "Why did the governor veto the bill?" He then sits back and lets his students discuss the question.

> JENNIFER: This is just like that other article we read 2 weeks ago about football teams.
> MICHAEL: I don't understand this part. What are the rules around the governor's veto? (*Jennifer explains the veto rules and Michael nods.*)

Luis: I sure wouldn't want some racial slur about Mexican Americans being used as a mascot. I'd protest too.*

Students are making connections, disagreeing, debating, and respecting each others' opinions. Gerardo keeps "score," documenting whether each student takes a position, makes a relevant comment, uses evidence to support a position, makes an analogy or connection, or demonstrates other skills that indicate overall understanding of the text and ability to think critically about it.

Gerardo teaches at the Contemporary Learning Academy (CLA), an alternative high school in the Denver public school system that serves students who have either failed at or been kicked out of their "home" (neighborhood) schools. Of the approximate 225 students, 73% qualify for free or reduced-price lunch, 92% are people of color, and about 9% are designated as English language learners. But these demographics may vary over the course of one school year, since students come to CLA for a single quarter, or up to a year, but don't graduate from CLA; they just come to get back on track so that they can return to their regular schools.

Gerardo motivates students who have had a history of failure—to debate, learn, and see the impact their learning will have on their futures. I first met him when I came to CLA as a staff developer for the Public Education & Business Coalition. He was one of six teachers who received one-on-one coaching and participated in a study group to improve their teaching practice. We planned, I observed his class, and we debriefed the observations. The more time I spent with Gerardo, the more I saw and heard something different from what I was seeing in other classrooms. I kept coming back to this question: Why are these students—who sit silently in the back of other classrooms, have failed countless classes, and have largely given up on school—engaged and learning in Gerardo's classroom?

In this chapter, I examine Gerardo's practice to identify the components of his success with students:

1. How Gerardo's beliefs inform his teaching and impact his students
2. How Gerardo designs curriculum and uses "culturally responsive teaching" to help students connect learning to their lives
3. How Gerardo uses critical literacy and helps students learn to craft effective arguments
4. How Gerardo uses his "Scored Discussion" assessment to foster rigorous student "talk" that promotes student learning
5. How helping students craft effective oral arguments is essential to students' success not only in class, but as active citizens and change agents

TEACHERS' BELIEFS MATTER

Sonia Nieto (2001) states: "Through their work, teachers articulate their greatest hopes and dreams for the future. . . . What they do and say with and about their students reflect what they believe their students are capable of and deserve"

---

*Students' real names are used in this chapter, at their request and with their permission.

(p. 13). The three beliefs I describe below are crucial to Gerardo's success in motivating students to impact their world.

Relationship: The Foundation from Which Learning Grows

Gerardo believes that what motivates students is "the relationship teachers have with their kids." Mutual respect underlies his ability to reach them. Gerardo is Latino, grew up in Denver, and has a past similar to many of his students. Yet while some research has found that minority teachers are better able to reach students in their own ethnic group because of shared culture (Salinas, 2000), Gerardo does not emphasize his background. "I don't want to say, 'I came from where you came from.' I'd rather they figure it out as I go along." To him, developing relationships is based on taking the time to know and listen to students without judging. "If you even hint that you value what they're saying, they will tell you everything. There are just so few places where they're heard."

Three of Gerardo's former students—Patrick, Yolanda, and Carrie—spoke with me about their teacher. "He made a difference in the outlook I had about learning," Carrie explained. She felt comfortable expressing her opinions in his class, which changed the way she thought about school. "The way he taught, I was interested."

High Expectations Build Students' Self-Confidence

Gerardo believes that all students can perform at the highest levels. He says, "I've never had a student who showed up and didn't want to succeed. The difference is whether they do what it takes and whether I show them how." Once students believe they are being taken seriously, they gain confidence in the power of their voices and minds.

"It has to be about academic rigor," says Gerardo. "They want to know that their minds are being respected. They think they want easy work, but ultimately they want to be challenged. When students get an A or B, it wasn't easily earned and they feel good." His students step up to the challenge. Says Yolanda, "[That class] made us learn more and push ourselves."

He believes challenging work is especially important for students who have struggled in school. "So many of our students have had so much failure. They've never really felt like students, [but] felt passed by. When they learn the discipline of being a student, they start to think like one: 'Maybe today I'll start carrying a backpack. Maybe today I'll bring a pencil to class.'"

A Teacher's Mission: To Prepare Students to Be Active Citizens

Gerardo believes that students have the right to be empowered as citizens. "To teach a student to be a citizen—that's the mission of a social studies teacher—to educate citizens for participation in a democracy," he explains. "It's about civil rights—that you are a member of society, you have a voice, and you need to use it."

Social studies, to Gerardo, is much more than imparting facts. He teaches students to insist on their right to literacy, and helps them internalize how being literate helps them stand up for their beliefs beyond the shelter of the classroom. He shows them how and why they should fight for literacy, as self-advocates and community members.

"My kids see society as being disinterested, dismissing them. It's my job to teach them how to challenge that. How can you demand justice if you don't know what you're speaking about? It's about giving them knowledge as a mode of empowerment."

Gerardo's beliefs affect his students. "I have always been a feminist," Carrie explains, "but I never said anything. He gave me practice to speak out."

CULTURALLY RESPONSIVE TEACHING: CURRICULUM THAT MAKES THE CONNECTION

Gerardo's beliefs drive his curricular decisions. He strives teach so students see how content relates to their lives.

Geneva Gay (2002) defines *culturally responsive teaching* (CRT) as "using the cultural characteristics, experience, and perspective of ethnically diverse students as conduits" for more effective instruction. This practice assumes that "when academic knowledge and skills are situated within the lived experience and frames of reference of students, they are more personally meaningful, have higher interest and appeal, and are learned more easily and thoroughly" (p. 106).

Gerardo teaches several electives, such as Chicano History and Native American History, in which the course content already may be relevant to many of his students' lives. But CRT is most important in classes where content is less clearly linked to students. And since diverse content is important regardless of students' racial or cultural background, CRT is effective with all students.

Padrón, Waxman, and Rivera (2002) outline the four key benefits of CRT:

1. Improved acquisition and retention of new knowledge by working from students' existing knowledge base
2. Improved self-confidence and self-esteem by emphasizing existing knowledge
3. Increased transfer of school-taught knowledge to real-life situations
4. Exposure to knowledge about other individuals or cultural groups (p. 6)

These four benefits accrue daily in Gerardo's classroom. While he aims to make the content accessible, his goal is not to make it easy. The confidence gained from talking about something familiar pushes students to learn new and challenging skills. Gerardo leverages this engagement to help them see this learning as something worth fighting for.

CRITICAL LITERACY AND EFFECTIVE ARGUMENT: TAKING A STAND ON ISSUES THAT MATTER

If students are to be truly "literate," able to read the world (Freire & Macedo, 1987) and take action to change it, they must learn not only the curriculum but also how to critique it and argue for what they believe. "You have to show them they have a voice and then show them how to use it," Gerardo says. "Sometimes, we teach them about their voice but then don't let them do anything with it. We teach about democracy, but we practice dictatorship."

Gerardo encourages students to question everything they read and learn. He believes that if they have the power to question, they will ultimately retain and comprehend content more deeply.

Gerardo teaches the sort of critical literacy defined by McLaughlin and DeVoogd (2004) as "read(ing) from a critical stance—a need to question rather than passively accept the information we encounter"(p. 53). He designs the sort of curriculum described by McLaughlin and Devoogd as a curriculum that "by representing alternative perspectives" encourages readers to take action, and "to become text critics in everyday life" (p. 53).

Gerardo encourages students to, as Len Holt (1965) put it in another context, "challenge the myths of our society, . . . to find alternatives and, ultimately, new directions for action" (Holt, quoted in Elsasser & John-Steiner, 1987, pp. 55–56).

Teachers who promote a critical stance, as defined by McLaughlin & DeVoogd (2004), incorporate several essential components:

- Examining multiple perspectives
- Juxtaposing alternative texts, photos, videos, and lyrics
- Posing problems
- Pushing students to question these materials

Engaging Questions, Requiring Evidence

As an example, how does Gerardo bring the topic of Christopher Columbus back to life to develop students' critical literacy?

First, he abandons the textbook, adding two alternative texts: (1) actual journal entries written by Columbus and (2) a picture book *Encounter* (Yolen, 1992) told from the perspective of a Native Taino boy who witnesses Columbus's landing at San Salvador.

Then he pushes students to examine these texts and form an opinion, connecting the topic to their own lives. "The great thing about teenagers," says Gerardo, "is that they'll say what they think. Then I can start questioning them and asking them to back up that opinion."

"Most kids have some background knowledge about Columbus," explains Gerardo, "enough to be surprised when we start examining the facts."

Students read Columbus' journal entries, written to communicate his progress to the King and Queen. This helps students learn the facts, and see Columbus as a human being.

A discussion illustrates the students' emerging understanding. Gerardo offers a guiding question for their Scored Discussion: "How should Columbus be taught in schools today?"

"Columbus was a murderer," says one student. "He was a bad guy."

Gerardo pushes him, "What evidence do you have that proves that statement?"

"He writes that the Taino are so generous, and then he goes and kills them. He was the ring leader who prepared his men."

Another student disagrees. "But Columbus was just one man. You can't pin it all on him."

"Why not?" asks Gerardo. "What makes you feel that way?"

The student responds. "The first big massacre didn't even happen until 1494 when he was back in Madrid asking the Queen for more money. . . . Then there was the mass murders of the Taino leaders, but that happened after Columbus was in prison." Gerardo strives to form questions that will draw students to the knowledge that they learned in class, yet not lead them to a predetermined single specific answer. Gerardo explains, "The current that runs through my teaching is that you have to take a position. By choosing to argue that point and back it up with evidence, you are learning."

Structuring Arguments

Gerardo's students are learning to craft arguments based on Toulmin's (1958) model, which describes an effective argument as having six components, the first three of which apply here:

- *The claim.* The statement you are trying to get someone to accept
- *Grounds.* The basis of real persuasion; made up of data and facts
- *The warrant.* The link from the data to the claim, showing the data presented is relevant to the claim

Researcher and educator George Hillocks (1986) calls argument a habit of mind integral to good thinking in any content area. He asserts that students learn best to craft strong arguments through inquiry, by exploring compelling content, not by regurgitating the formulaic structure of a five-paragraph essay or having a teacher name the various parts of an argument.

So rather than teach students Toulmin's formula, Gerardo engages students in actual thinking about issues that interest them, insisting they back their thinking up with evidence or data. "You raise the standard a little bit: 'You've stated your opinions. That's a good first step. Now you need to support it with evidence. OK, now you need to use *textual* evidence.'"

Some students argue that everyone should be exposed to the documents they saw today to form their own opinions. "Kids learn he's a hero," one student remarks. "I thought that too until I read his journal!"

"At the very core of my philosophy, beyond argument, is the feeling that democracy is broken because the electorate is full of people who don't ask questions. I hope to instill the skill of argument so they can participate in society and make a difference."

DISCUSSION MAKES A DIFFERENCE

To help students find their "voice," take a critical stance, and craft effective arguments, Gerardo strives to create "a forum where they can talk and where what they say is valued." His weekly Scored Discussions provide this: Clear expectations provide the basis for structured feedback and a grade.

Scored Discussion: How Does Talk Promote Literacy?

For several years, Gerardo has been using Scored Discussions, a technique he learned from John Zola (2003) at the University of Colorado at Boulder. Scored Discussions work as follows: Students read a piece of text, such as a newspaper article, or watch a piece of film, usually relating to an issue they have been studying that week, and are asked to discuss it. Gerardo scores participants using the rubric in Figure 7.1, which assesses students' contributions, their critical thinking skills, and their interaction with other participants.

Figure 7.1. Discussion Score Sheet

Name _____

Topic _____

Positive	Negative
1. States an opinion (2) _____	1. Does not pay attention/ distracts others (–2) _____
2. Makes a relevant comment (1) _____	2. Interrupts (–2) _____
3. Supports a position with facts (2) _____	3. Makes irrelevant comment (–1) _____
4. Draws another person into the discussion (1) _____	4. Monopolizes the discussion (–3) _____
5. Recognizes contradictions in another person's statements (2) _____	5. Engages in personal attacks (–3) _____
6. Recognizes irrelevant comments (2) _____	6. Uses inappropriate language (–2) _____
7. Makes a connection/ analogy (2) _____	
8. Asks a question that moves the discussion along (1) _____	
9. Evaluates or refers to another person's opinion (1) _____	
10. Builds on previous point (1) _____	
11. Uses vocabulary regarding specific content or concepts taught in this class (1) _____	

Note: Numbers in parentheses indicate the score awarded for each item.

The score sheet helps students focus on crafting an argument by naming the specific skills required, awarding points for stating an opinion ("the claim") and supporting that claim with evidence ("grounds"). This, says Gerardo, "creates a safe space for student opinion. The rubric and agenda provide structure that they can understand."

Gerardo tracks students' contributions on a master sheet; each student also has his or her own sheet to refer to during the discussion. And since Scored Discussions happen weekly, students can work to improve their score as the quarter progresses.

These discussions let Gerardo push and assess both students' ability to think critically, craft arguments, and participate in thoughtful conversation, and also students' understanding of the content they are learning. "He wants to know what you know, what you understand," says Carrie.

Gerardo uses a "fishbowl" structure for the discussions. Half the students sit in an inner circle and actually discuss the topic; the others sit in an outer circle, observing. Each observer scores is assigned to score one participant, using the rubric. Students keep score on a simplified version of Gerardo's rubric. They use tally marks to indicate whether their classmates demonstrate each specific skill listed. When the discussion is over, the observers give oral feedback to their peers. Gerardo also makes photocopies of the outer circle's feedback sheets, and then gives those sheets to the students in the inner circle, who then reflect on their participation. In effect, says Gerardo, "it's an assessment of the outer circle too: Do they know what a good discussion is?"

Keeping Score: Hooking the Reluctant Learner

Scoring is key, according to Gerardo. "I keep stats on their scores, and averages, and make it clear to them that the scores are a reflection of their progress. They get a little competitive. I have seen students congratulate each other on high scores and have heard that they even ask each other about their scores in other classes." He keeps a Discussion Wall of Fame, which came out of his self-proclaimed obsession with sports statistics. "The kids like the Wall, especially when they see their names up there. It actually gets them engaging each other, something I rarely saw before." Yolanda agrees, "It made us learn more and push ourselves on our own."

Some might argue that the use of points is inconsistent with the idea that students are intrinsically motivated to learn and demonstrate mastery of the skills. But the points give reluctant students with years of experience of failure the initial push they need to realize that the skills and content are valuable.

"At the beginning, I just didn't want to be there [at school]," explains Carrie. "Since I've taken his class, I have a whole different point of view on school. He inspired me. He made me push myself." Patrick explains, "We got minus points if we put someone down. It made us realize that we had to listen to what other people say."

Gerardo sees additional benefits. "Scored Discussion has elevated their level of participation in other classes. And in my class, they participate more and more without even thinking about it."

Gerardo says that discussion-based assessment is not easy. "One of the hardest things is to sit through a discussion when no one was prepared. They realized it's not as easy as they thought." Students learn from being put on the spot in this way. "It's a kind of accountability that's hard to get from other kinds of assessment."

The Type of Talk: The Quality of Discussion Affects Learning

Padrón, Waxman, and Rivera (2002) note that "instructional conversations" are key to reaching unmotivated students. Research bears this out: In a study of 44 classrooms in 25 schools, students were found to be more successful in classrooms where teachers helped students engage in thoughtful dialogue (Close, 2005, p. 2).

Nystrand, Gamoran, Kachur, and Predergrast (1997) go further in arguing that the quality of student learning is closely linked to the quality of classroom talk. They found that in most classrooms, teachers asked questions to assess how much students know or to check for task completion. Students were expected to respond mostly in what they call "recitation," which focuses on remembering and guessing and puts no value on thinking. According to Nystrand et al., students learn more through discussion, when they are asked to explain their thinking instead of just reciting someone else's, they feel as if they are a primary source of information. That lets them interpret the content within their own frame of reference.

It is not just the presence of "talk" in a classroom that makes a difference, but the *quality* of that talk. Nystrand et al. (1997) compared two different groups of eighth and ninth graders to see whether differences in the quality of discourse between low- and high-track classes result in inequalities. When they controlled for other variables, they found that "time devoted to discussion, authentic questions, [and] uptake . . . had a strong positive effect on achievement" (p. 62). "The bottom line is that learning to think requires effective interaction" (p. 72).

AN EXAMPLE: COMBINING CULTURALLY RELEVANT TEACHING AND THE TEACHING OF ARGUMENTATION

I observed an example of such interaction in Gerardo's class during a Scored Discussion on ancient pre-Columbian societies.

He asked students to compare contemporary society with ancient societies and then to compare them with the societies of the Europeans who arrived and conquered them. "We look at primary and secondary sources and then discuss how to evaluate these sources," says Gerardo. "We break apart and determine perspective and bias. We're learning how to use tools, how to form opinions."

Gerardo asks, "If you had been with the Spaniards, what would have been your first reaction to seeing the Aztec cities?"

"It would have been amazing. I don't think I would have expected it," says one student.

"Why not?" asks Gerardo. "What makes you think that?"

"Well, what we saw in that documentary [from the History Channel], the cities were clean and organized. And if you look at the printouts of the Aztec codices, you can see how advanced the cities really were."

Another student recalls, "They had these calendars that were really advanced. They used it to predict that a God would come from the East. Then when the Spaniards came, they thought it was their prediction coming true."

This leads another student to speculate. "If the Spaniards hadn't come from the East, I wonder how it would have been—or if they had never come, or if they had come at a different time. How would things have turned out differently? I think that if they hadn't come, the Aztecs would still be standing."

Gerardo prods, "What do others think of that?"

A third student offers her thoughts. "They were organized, they built things—with the knowledge they already had, and the land, their power would have just kept extending. They could have really made something!"

These students are doing more than just recalling facts. They are engaged in inquiry, which Hillocks (1986) argues is so important. And they are using what they have learned to formulate hypotheses and discuss them, practicing Toulmin's model of effective arguments. They are backing up their opinions with evidence from texts they have read.

The discussions help students use oral arguments and internalize the content. "Every time we would do it, we would do it on a topic we studied before," explains Yolanda. "Mr. Muñoz wouldn't interrupt. He'd just sit and listen. In the beginning I didn't like it. Once I figured out that you got to say your opinion . . . it opened my mind to want to try."

"The discussions forced them to recall factual information, that hard history stuff, because without that evidence, they can't make the comparisons," Gerardo explains.

Through these discussions, students retain the content and connect it to their own lives. As Yolando says, "He wants to know what you think about everything that's going on. He'll teach you something and you'll remember it due to the Scored Discussions. You talk about it amongst your peers. You get to know how they feel. You link that to how you feel."

Scored Discussions also give students authentic practice being active, well-spoken citizens. "They learn about how to speak to and with other people," says Gerardo. "They look on the rubric and see 'Oh, I'm interrupting a lot,' or 'I'm monopolizing the conversation.' Well, a good citizen doesn't monopolize. A good citizen allows other voices to be heard too. The skills they get in discussion are skills they can use wherever they go."

Gerardo explained, "I adopted the Scored Discussion structure because I knew my students had beliefs, values, experiences, but I didn't know how to tap into it. I didn't imagine that it would prove transformative in [terms of] how our society goes. [Now] it's central to my core philosophy that these skills can be used anywhere."

Students take these skills beyond his classroom. "It started to transform teacher/student interactions," says Gerardo. Patrick confirms this: "What I've learned in his class, I've taken out of that class to other classes."

Gerardo recalls: "One teacher came to me and said 'Manuel loves to do these discussions. His participation has gone up.' When students feel involved, they are more motivated to actually go to class. [That means their] chances of finishing high school and being successful go way up."

LINKING ORAL AND WRITTEN LANGUAGE: NEXT STEPS FOR GERARDO

In this chapter, I focus on Gerardo's use of oral argument. Of course, this is not enough; students must transfer these skills into their writing. So often, teachers skip over oral argument in their rush to get students writing; for all students, and particularly English language learners, oral language can serve as a preparation and support for writing.

When I began working with Gerardo, he acknowledged that he was not having students write enough. I pushed him to build on his students' enthusiasm for the content and incorporate more writing into his curriculum. He knows that he, like his students, must grow.

"Maybe the most important take-away is this," he explains. "A strategy is only a strategy if you build on it; otherwise it's only a tip or trick that keeps the kids from revolting. You have to say, 'OK, that was good, now where do we go from here?' or 'This is working, but how can I improve in areas where they're not so confident, like writing.' This cannot be an end. It's just the beginning."

So Gerardo has made changes. Now during Scored Discussions he asks those who are observing to write while their peers talk. "I still have 7–9 students in a given discussion," explains Gerardo. "Now those outside the circle are paired up and they do written conversations. I'd like to start having students build off of what they've written in these conversations."

The foundation Gerardo has established—by asking students to craft their oral arguments in Toulmin's model around compelling content—serves as a great springboard for writing.

SCHOOL IS DIFFERENT NOW

Gerardo has found an effective way to guide students toward literacy, with the belief that their awareness of its value and their assertion of their right to it is as important as the literacy itself. This propels students to take a more active role in their own lives and their communities.

"I was a quick-tempered person; I was always quick to jump on something someone said," says Patrick. "He made me stop and think about what was going on. [Now] in every other class I try to listen and understand. So I'm going to work to reach out to others and see what's up."

"School is different for me now," says Carrie, "It has a lot more meaning. Now I'm the type of person where education's not a problem. I can go to college where, before, I was bored with school. I'm going to finish high school and do my best to make my brain like a tool for my life."

Gerardo's students are not only building literacy skills, they are grasping the value literacy brings. He has developed relationships that foster trust, created curriculum that students relate to, and structured his class around authentic discussion that empowers students to gain and use knowledge, speak up, and defend their views. Other teachers can pull specific strategies from his practice to improve their own ability to ensure that the civil rights of their students—all students—are not denied.

HOW TO BEGIN

- Get to know your students and let them know you.
- Listen without judgment. Build students' confidence that what they have to say has value.

- Explicitly teach students citizenship skills. What will it take for them to engage actively?
- Look for curricular connections that are relevant to students' lives. Build on their background knowledge.
- Provide structured discussion as a form of assessment. Model and give students opportunities to practice.
- Let students talk. Oral language is a rehearsal and scaffold for polished written products.
- Let students argue about things that matter; then teach them the components of effective argument.
- Encourage students to question what they learn. Provide different perspectives on the same issue or event.
- Ask questions you truly don't know the answer to. Answer student questions with more questions.
- Explicitly teach students the value of their education.

LINGERING QUESTIONS

- How much do teachers' relationships with students depend on some common background?
- What are the benefits and drawbacks of using extrinsic rewards to motivate students?
- How can we make sure the oral skills students gain from discussion also help them better express themselves through writing?

LEADERSHIP PERSPECTIVES

From Diane Lauer, former principal of Conrad Ball Middle School:

- *Critical stance.* How might teachers in all content areas incorporate the strategies listed in Figure 7.1 to help students develop a critical stance? And what in terms of control over the texts and talk in our classrooms—might we have to be willing to give up in order to do this?
- *Student voice.* How are we encouraging student voice not only in our classrooms, but in the broader school community? Where, when, and how do we give students the opportunities and support to take a stand and defend their reasoning?

From Garrett Phelan, principal of César Chávez Charter School (Capitol Hill campus):

- *Relationships, affirmation, and engagement.* What makes a student want to come to class? To bring her texts, her materials, her work? Imagine if a student were engaged in authentic work in every class, and if teachers affirmed and valued what that student thinks, says, and does. Giving students literacy strategies and allowing time for thinking allows for such affirmation.
- *Discussion.* Authentic high-quality discussion—around open-ended questions and legitimate topics of inquiry—promotes learning. Historians, mathematicians, scientists, writers, and artists all talk to each other to expand their views and

perceptions. I encourage teachers to share with each other various ways to structure discussion to promote student thinking: seminars, fishbowls, workshops, debates, panels, and so on.

RELATED READINGS

Geneva Gay's article "Preparing for Culturally Responsive Teaching" (Gay, 2002) offers clear descriptions of how to design curriculum to connect with and engage a diverse student population.

Maureen McLaughlin and Glen DeVoogd's article "Critical Literacy as Comprehensive: Expanding Reader Response" (McLaughlin & DeVoogd, 2004) is a brief and teacher-friendly introduction to critical literacy.

Stephen Toulmin's book *The Use of Argument* (Toulmin, 1958) is somewhat dense, but Chapter 3 helps teachers understand the structure of argument.

CHAPTER 8

Self-Assessment of Standardized Test Data: Empowering Students to Plan and Own Their Learning in Language Arts

Lesli Cochran

IN THIS CHAPTER: Cochran describes why and how she has taught her eighth graders to analyze their high-stakes test data and design their own plans to master all the literacy standards. She shows how, in the current test-driven environment, teachers can harness student achievement data in the service of multiple goals: students' mastery of standards; "data literacy"; and engagement, independence, and self-awareness as learners.

KEY POINTS

- Students have the right to access their own achievement data.
- Students should be taught how to analyze data about themselves.
- Teachers must develop relevant, engaging materials that allow for personalization as students work to achieve their own learning goals.

One late spring day, my eighth-grade students confirmed and clarified for me the power of providing them with their specific testing data. They were restless and I was tired, but I launched into a lesson about "packing." We looked at two texts: one about taking everything and the kitchen sink on a trip and another about bringing only what you could carry in a backpack. Our discussion focused on "packing" for what life would throw at you. What would my students need to take with them from middle school to ensure their success?

"In history this year I learned about my rights. I think I'll need to know about that." There were chuckles.

"I can finally solve for *x*!"

"I like the essay format we learned this year—it will work in every class."

And then a student asked, "Will the high school teachers have our new data?"

"They should," I responded.

"Yeah, we need that so we can see if we reached the goals we set, and so we can set new ones."

Even though these were students whom many people might not expect to have their noses in spreadsheets, they animatedly discussed how having their data helped them decide what to work on this past year.

MOTIVATION AND MASTERY

The rewards for all my instruction about students' data were right in front of me: students who know what they know and are able to do and who are motivated to improve in areas they previously struggled with. We had created a situation in which we shared instructional decisions, set goals based on sound information, and increased student motivation. Students no longer asked, "Why do I have to do this?" or "When will this ever matter?"

I teach at Conrad Ball Middle School in Loveland, Colorado. Of our approximately 780 students, about half qualify for free or reduced-price lunch; 32% are people of color, and 28% are English language learners. Our district, like every district in this country, has come to terms with the fact that high-stakes tests are not going away. And we language arts teachers are also facing the fact that we bear much of the burden of preparing students for these tests. How can we make these tests relevant to students and use them to raise student achievement?

The answer for me has been to use students' data to drive many of my instructional decisions. I am now teaching two types of literacy: the literacy defined by our state language arts standards, and "data literacy"—the ability to understand, analyze, and display information.

This focus represents a shift in how I view my role. When I began my career as a language arts instructor, I wanted nothing more than to share my love of literature. And I still do that. But I now believe that to fully prepare students for their future, I must focus more on skills, "what you use," than on information, "what you know" (Glasser, 1992).

TWO LITERACIES: LANGUAGE ARTS STANDARDS AND DATA ANALYSIS

The Colorado Student Assessment Program (CSAP) is based on a set of skills or standards the state has decided our students need to know and be able to do. Initially, I resisted these tests. I resented the implication that my students weren't learning enough.

Now, however, I believe that the CSAP provides valuable information about a student's progress and can be used to provide specific direction in planning instruction for particular students. Such focused instruction not only raises students' scores on the state assessment; more important, it helps build their confidence and prepare them to tackle the challenges of college and work.

Many middle school students are resigned: If reading has always been hard, it probably always will be. Specific data helps me show them how they can improve, which in turn helps them change their thinking about themselves and their futures. They have a right to know that it's not too late.

Until 2 years ago, I was the only person in my classroom who got that awful feeling in the pit of my stomach when the CSAP scores came out; my kids didn't care much. Some teachers in my building had begun to discuss student responsibility; but few of us were giving students the tools that responsibility requires. We began to realize that in order for students to be self-directed, they needed information with which to make decisions.

I decided to give my students their data: trends in class assignments and quizzes, class averages on tests, and the most frequent comments I make on writing assignments. Armed with this information, they can make instructional decisions with me: They can ask questions, get help, and target areas of improvement.

When I asked a student if having these data made a difference, he stated simply, "Now I have an idea of where to start. Before it all seemed so big. I'm not stupid; I just have a few things that are holding me back."

When I get data about an individual student's weakness, it's as if that student is asking me for help. Students have the right to expect that we will do our best to meet their individual needs, especially when we know what those needs are.

Over the past few years, I have restructured my teaching to meet the individual needs of every student. Central to this has been demystifying high-stakes testing data so students can use it to analyze next steps.

ANALYZING DATA: HOW WE BEGIN

I begin teaching students about data at the start of the school year. I want students to understand the following:

- How to read a spreadsheet and extract information from it
- How to use data as evidence of their thinking
- How to use data to make their assertions stronger

We start by reading sports data. We analyze which sport is the "toughest." Usually it comes down to a statistical battle between football and ice hockey. We look up players' average minutes of playing time, the average number of injuries per year per team, the number of games played, and other obscure facts like how long a career usually lasts and the amount of insurance carried by some players.

Then we break into teams and debate which is the toughest sport. Every argument must have statistical backing. Students begin to see how data can be manipulated to support a variety of positions. I love hearing students explain that the 16 football games are tougher than the 82 ice hockey games because no one can predict how long a football player will have to play. This spirited debate serves three purposes:

1. *Students apply their understanding of statistical information.* If they understand how to use data accurately and convincingly, they are less likely to try to dismiss data or make excuses if their data isn't "good news."
2. *Students learn how to effectively discuss and disagree.* Sometimes students try to dodge a classmate's insightful rebuttal with a quick, "Whatever . . ." I use these moments as an opportunity to discuss what constructive discussion looks and feels like.

3. *Students see a personal side of me.* I am a huge hockey fan, and I passionately strive to prove that hockey players are more accomplished than football players. My involvement in the debate makes me real.

We next search newspapers and magazines for articles with graphs and charts representing statistical data, such as weather or election-season polls. We discuss authors' purposes and bias. This lets me transition to discussing why I would want to share individual test data with students.

"What would happen if I told you that I already knew exactly what each of you needs to work on?"

"Like we wouldn't have to do the stuff we're already good at?"

"Well, no. You can't just check out because you got it right once on a test. But what would change about this class if you knew I was teaching a lesson about something you didn't get, and I spent less time on the stuff you did get?"

Most students agree that school is easier if they know exactly what they need to do and why. When I focus on both types of literacy, students can use the data literacy to set priorities for mastering the language arts standards.

ANALYZING STUDENTS' CLASSWIDE LITERACY ACHIEVEMENT DATA

After the first few weeks, students are fairly skilled at reading data. I then bring in data from each class to analyze. I have groups of students visually represent the class proficiency in each state standard (see Figure 8.1). Groups tend to create bar graphs or pie charts. I divide the charts by reading and writing. Figure 8.2 shows an example of two classes' reading data (Standards 1, 4, 5, and 6).

The next day, I post the data displays around the room. I pose a big question, referring back to our sports discussions: "If you were the coach of this team, what would you do to make sure you got a playoff spot?"

Figure 8.1. Colorado State Standards for Reading and Writing

1. Students read and understand a variety of materials.

2. Students write and speak for a variety of purposes and audiences.

3. Students write and speak using conventional grammar, usage, sentence structure, punctuation, capitalization, and spelling.

4. Students apply thinking skills to their reading, writing, speaking, listening, and viewing.

5. Students read to locate, select, and make use of relevant information from a variety of media, reference, and technological sources.

6. Students read and recognize literature as a record of human experience.

Note: From Colorado Model Content Standards for Language Arts, 2005.

Figure 8.2. Student Group Graphing of Class Proficiencies in Colorado Language Arts Reading Standards

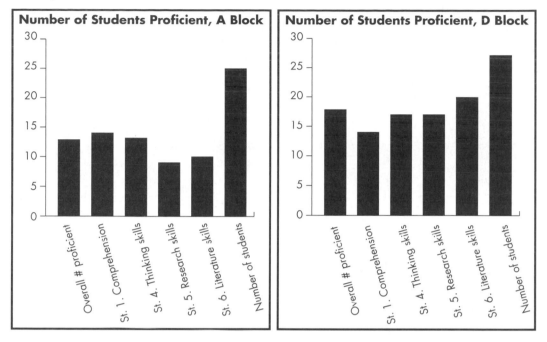

I then send students on a "Gallery Walk" to look at each data display and take notes on their ideas. I strive to stay quiet; they need to own this, since personal investment will increase their motivation to change.

This past year, when Chandler returned to the whole group, he said, "Man, Ms. Cochran, I feel sorry for you. You have a lot of work to do. We're not good at anything." I reassure my students that I'll help them take this on, one step at a time.

Prioritizing and Unpacking the Standards

Next, we prioritize based on the standards and the benchmarks that make up each standard (see Figure 8.3). Sometimes we spend 30 to 40 minutes before we reach consensus about which standards to work on most during class time in the coming months. This analysis gives students a clear picture of their needs, and helps build their buy-in, which in turn increases their motivation. Listed below are some questions I use to facilitate this discussion.

GUIDING QUESTIONS FOR CLASS DATA

- What do you notice about strengths of the students in our class?
- How can we use these strengths to help us work on our weaknesses?
- What does the framework indicate the state thinks is most important?
- What do you think is most important?

Figure 8.3. Colorado State Standards, Benchmarks for Standard 1

1. Students read and understand a variety of materials.

1.a. Compare and contrast texts with similar characters, plots, and/or themes.

1.b. Summarize text read (for example, newspaper and magazine articles, technical writing, stories, and poetry).

1.c. Determine the main idea or essential message in a text.

1.d. Make reasonable inferences from information that is implied but not directly stated.

1.e. Infer by making connections between separated sections of a text.

1.f. Find support in the text for main ideas.

1.g. Use word recognitions skills (for example, roots, prefixes, and suffixes) to comprehend text.

1.h. Find the sequence of steps in a technical publication.

1.i. Use context clues to determine the meaning of unfamiliar words.

Note: From Colorado Model Content Standards for Language Arts, 2005.

- Are there skills that you and the state think are important that we need to work on?
- What are some factors that might suggest that the test data is not 100% accurate?

This is what I hear in the discussion:

"How are we supposed to practice comprehension?"
"What if the story is stupid or boring? Then I have a hard time paying attention. I can read interesting stuff."
"I get good grades in school, but I hate taking the tests. I don't see how that shows what I know."

These responses tell me what the students think influences their success or failure. And analyzing their data serves two important instructional purposes:

1. Students develop data literacy: they know how to read a spreadsheet to make sense of all these numbers and rankings. I am preparing them for the future as professionals and informed citizens.
2. Students can look at the test more objectively. We have demystified an exam they usually feel nervous about. They become motivated to show what they know.

Adding Real-World Input

The data analysis is important, but it is imperative that my students see beyond the test. I want them to really get that the standards are a set of skills that will lead to a successful future. So I invite people from our community to come in and talk about what these standards look like in the real world. One guest speaker who develops digital cameras talked about how important it was for him to be able to make accurate predictions based on text about what people will want. He described how his department reads pages and pages of customer comments before they develop their next camera. Another guest talked about how important precise writing is when you are sending e-mail to another country and you are not sure how much English the recipient will know. By tying aspects of these jobs directly to the standards, I show students how they will use the skills we call standards.

PLANNING FOR WHOLE-GROUP INSTRUCTION

An Integrated, Team Approach

To address my district curriculum and my students' needs, I must allocate every minute of class time for maximum efficiency. I am fortunate to have 98 minutes each day with my students. They have two other teachers: one for math (every day, 98 minutes); the other for science and social studies (alternating days, 98 minutes).

To make it possible for me to have this much instructional time with my students, we integrate the science and history curricula into language arts. I build students' background knowledge through a variety of science and social studies texts, so my colleagues can move forward at a faster pace. I have learned that students master standards best when they read a wide variety of text structures and topics. And students seem more invested when we teach similar concepts in multiple classes.

The Workshop Model

My team's approach to shared instruction helps me determine how to best use my class time. I use the workshop model (which Samantha Bennett describes in Chapter 12). I save the last 30 minutes three times a week for individual work. During that time, students are responsible for working on activities that help them achieve their goals while I circulate to confer with them. Later in this chapter I elaborate on how we use the independent goal and reflection time.

Over the past few years, I have had 55, 73, 80, 90, and now 98 minutes with students. You might set aside a certain number of minutes per day or one day per week for this work. The fewer minutes you have, the more important it is to share the responsibility of student achievement with them. There is one benefit to this: When students pursue some of their goals independently, you have less pressure to cover everything with a whole group.

For our first few months, I do independent goal time every day. As students start to reach their goals, I cut back the independent goal time to 2–3 days per week and include more crafting time, during which I introduce new material and model how to deal with it. Having had time to fill their learning gaps, students are more confident and can master new material more quickly. Ultimately, this saves instructional time.

Choosing the Focus for Whole-Group Instruction

I make sure my use of the workshop time is quite noticeably tied to the priorities each class identified. Students must see that my purpose is to meet their goals. It can be overwhelming to balance what I know about kids and their data, what we decided as a class to focus on, and what the district expects me to cover. But if I want students to accept responsibility for their learning, I cannot let go of our class goals; that would give students permission to slack when their work becomes difficult. And I know it will become difficult because I am asking them to focus on the skills they find most challenging.

Designing Whole-Group Lessons

When I first tried to design lessons based on students' class data, I thought I had to create entirely different lesson plans for each class. The planning and preparation made me crazy. Ultimately, I decided to use the same piece of text for every class but alter the focus of my crafting lesson based on each class's needs. (For more on the crafting lesson, see Bennett, 2007, Chap. 12.)

For example, I may select a piece of nonfiction text about climbing Mt. Everest. In my A Block class, the data indicates that we need to work on Standard 5: "Students read to locate, select, and make use of relevant information." So we spend a significant amount of time looking at headings, bolded vocabulary, the captions for the pictures, and the footnotes. This conversation will help them better tackle this kind of text and determine what information is important based on the purpose for reading.

With my D Block class, however, their data indicates they need to focus on Standard 1: comprehension. Therefore, I alter the crafting lesson to include a discussion about how the text features help us to understand what will be presented in each section. We stop at each section and underline five key words from the section. Then I ask students to use those key words to write one sentence that summarizes the section. Both classes would receive instruction on the text features, but I would tailor the crafting lesson to their needs.

Analyzing Students' Individual Literacy Achievement Data

Once students see how analyzing their class data is helping the entire class, it is time for them to analyze their personal data. This is a hard day; some students get quite disappointed. Consider Caryn. She works hard, is a good student, and loves school. But for as long as she can remember, she has been a struggling reader.

On the first day of school, I asked Caryn what her goals were for the year. She simply said, "I have to learn to read better and faster." From reading her file, I knew she had been determined for the past several years and that her parents also were very invested. They had Caryn tested for special education and dyslexia. Caryn received 3 years of vision therapy and had been held back in the third grade. So now she's here: still frustrated at her lack of proficiency, yet still determined.

After I handed out students' individual data, I noticed Caryn slouching down in her chair trying to avoid the inevitable, "What did you get?" I knew that Caryn was partially proficient. But she had held out hope until today that all the work she put in last year had paid off.

In order to be deemed "proficient" in Colorado, Caryn needed an overall proficiency score above 620. Caryn's score was 608. Colorado also gives a score for each standard. Caryn had scored 543 in Standard 1, 606 in Standard 4, 624 in Standard 5, and 631 in Standard 6. Thus she was proficient in Standards 5 and 6, but not in Standard 1 (Comprehension) or Standard 4 (Thinking Skills). I did a little investigating into the state assessment frameworks to see how those standards were tested. I found that the primary text type for both comprehension and thinking skills was nonfiction. This information helped me focus Caryn's attention on how to improve her ability to read nonfiction texts.

I began my conference with Caryn by asking, "What are you noticing?" She answered, "It didn't work. I have to be able to read better." She was only focused on the fact that she was partially proficient. To help her identify her strengths, I had her look at the individual elements that made up her score:

LESLI: What does this data show that you are good at?
CARYN: The one about recognizing different cultures, six I think.
LESLI: Why do you think six is somewhere you excel?
CARYN: Because like I travel a lot so I know about other people.
LESLI: You know that's a valuable skill in the real world, especially since technology continues to shrink the planet.

I then asked her why she thought her Standard 1 score was so much lower than the others. She wasn't sure, so we started down the list of benchmarks (see Figure 8.3). Caryn said she knew she wasn't good at some of the items tested. When I asked her what it meant to *infer* in the Benchmark 1.e, she had no idea. So I asked her about her work to improve her reading:

LESLI: What did you focus on last year?
CARYN: Reading.
LESLI: Yes, but what about reading?
CARYN: All of it. I have to get better at reading and I have to get faster, so I can finish all the reading in the CSAP.

I asked her if she could see why focusing on just being better and faster wasn't working. She needed to focus on specific skills, not just speed and endurance.

I explained that together we were going to focus all of her independent class time on improving Standard 1: integrating reading strategies to improve her comprehension. She would still receive instruction in all the other standards during the crafting lessons and whole-group instruction.

Based on how quickly Caryn focused on the negative aspects of her data, I designed whole-group instruction for the next day as an "Expert Review." We identified people who were experts in a particular standard or benchmark. Thus students celebrated the area where they were successful and also identified class-mates who could help them work on areas of weakness.

PLANNING FOR INDEPENDENT STUDENT LEARNING

Once the students have identified their goals, I must create a culture where students take risks, give them predictable time to pursue their goals, provide relevant and challenging materials, and give timely and honest feedback.

Classroom culture is essential. For students to take on the two literacy goals of improving their skills on the language arts standards and improving their ability to analyze data, I must create an environment in which they will take risks, admit there are things they are not good at, consult one another without the fear that they will be judged, challenge one another respectfully, and take on challenges independently. (For more on creating such a classroom culture, see Chapter 9.)

I also must protect time for individual work and support. As I said earlier, this actually saves time for presenting new material to the whole class because students who begin to see success in their problem areas gain confidence, build background knowledge, and need less time to learn new material.

Materials: Practicing with Engaging, Relevant Texts

Perhaps the most difficult aspect of asking students to set and work toward their own goals is finding sufficient appropriate materials. The first year, I ran around trying to find texts and relevant materials that weren't just packets of worksheets. My goal is to have students working toward mastering the standards, not completing a packet. I was teaching three classes a day, each with 31 students; each student created an individualized plan. I felt like I was preparing 93 lessons every day! At one point I even created a message center where kids could write a specific need on a post-it note and I would spend my afternoons on the Internet or flipping through books to find something that would meet their needs.

Now, I have created a library by standard and benchmark. It is housed in three filing cabinets. Two cabinets are full of texts from every genre imaginable. The texts are not leveled, but rather are arranged by topic, so students can select text that they find appealing. I can't imagine asking students to attack a skill they find difficult by reading text they find boring.

The third cabinet has a series of lessons and activities for each standard that progress from a Level 1 (meaning the student scored "unsatisfactory" on CSAP) to a Level 4 (for students who scored advanced, but want to keep improving). Figure 8.4 shows an example of four lessons for Standard 2: Students write for a variety of purposes and audiences.

Conferring: Providing Timely, Honest, and Meaningful Feedback

Meaningful feedback is crucial. My conferences focus on the goals the students set, a discussion of their progress, and instruction for their needs. (See Chapter 9 for a

Figure 8.4. Examples of Differentiated Lessons for Standard 2

LEVEL OF ACTIVITY	ACTIVITY
Level 1: For students who scored "unsatisfactory"	Students create packing lists for two different destinations. Then they sign up for a conference so we can discuss the idea of writing for a specific purpose: Why aren't the lists the same?
Level 2: For students who were "partially proficient"	Students write two notes about a time they were in trouble—one note to a friend and one to their parents. The conference at the end of this lesson will include a discussion about determining importance. What details were left out of the letter to their parents?
Level 3: For students who were "proficient"	Students choose from series of RAFT writing prompts based on Role, Audience, Format, and Topic. Once they complete the writing, a reflection exercise asks them to identify the key elements they considered and how those elements affected their writing.
Level 4: For students who scored "advanced" but want to deepen their understanding	Students analyze a text passage, and then revise it in three different ways. Can the student make each version deliver the same information but meet the needs of a very different audience?

detailed description of conferring.) Here is one example, from a conversation with my student James:

> LESLI: What are you working on?
> JAMES: Drawing Conclusions, but I don't get it.
> LESLI: What don't you get?
> JAMES: Well, it seems so simple with this activity, but my scores are really low.
> LESLI: What level story did you choose?
> JAMES: Two. Nonfiction.
> LESLI: So what do you think would happen if you tried this activity with a piece of fiction text? And try using the same skills you thought made this easy with the nonfiction text.
> JAMES: Oh—I've been practicing with the wrong text?
> LESLI: That's what I think. Give it a try and see what you think.

These conferences let me guide students in developing self-monitoring strategies. They need to learn what it feels like when they don't get it and what to do about that feeling. They need to develop that "self-knowledge to know what works for them" (Costa & Kallick, 2004, p. 51).

REDEFINING MY ROLE AS A LANGUAGE ARTS TEACHER: THE PAYOFF FOR STUDENTS

Since beginning to work with data, I have come to believe that my primary responsibility is to teach students the skills they will need to access information about the world around them. If they love to read poetry and fiction, that's a bonus.

My approach has paid off. On average, students who analyzed their data and then had choices about how to target their learning scored 8% higher on the CSAP than their peers in our school. And Caryn, my determined "partially proficient" student, improved her scores 146 points in that one school year, compared to just 27 points average growth that year for students in our school. More important, Caryn is now succeeding in high school and making plans for college.

Students have the right to access all the information we have available about them. They have a right to master both data literacy and the standards-based literacy of language arts. We have the obligation to give them this opportunity to choose to be successful.

HOW TO BEGIN

- Analyze class data with your students. Have them create graphs and set class priorities.
- Show students the reasons behind your instructional decisions.
- Begin with whole-class data in order to motivate students by sharing your thinking.
- Gradually add standards to your list of priorities as you and your students are ready.

LINGERING QUESTIONS

- How can we be explicit about testing vs. teaching? How do we show students that the test aims to measure skills relevant to their futures?
- What is the primary role of language arts teachers? Which of our students' rights are we responsible for protecting?

LEADERSHIP PERSPECTIVES

From Diane Lauer, former principal of Conrad Ball Middle School:

- *Data-driven dialogue.* Cochran shows how teachers can help students use data to self-assess and plan what they need to learn. In what ways do we, as teachers, use data to drive our reflection and professional development?

- *Data literacy for adults.* Teachers in all content areas can and should share students' data with students. Yet before doing this, teachers need to be able to access their students data and understand that data themselves. How can we help demystify data and help teachers analyze and own it?

From Garrett Phelan, principal of César Chávez Charter School (Capitol Hill campus):

- *Time.* Cochran has made very intentional decisions about how to spend class time. I urge all teachers to ask, "Why am I using class time the way I am? What is my ultimate goal?" To be literate is to have tools to face a future where the truths of today no longer hold. Are we using our time in a way that prepares students for that?
- *Students' right to know.* Students should be empowered to know where they are in the learning curve of each class. They then know how they are being evaluated and can take responsibility for their learning. Students in our math classes discussed and analyzed citywide math scores to see where they were, hypothesize about why, and recommend how they might improve. A literate look at their own data was motivating for them. As a result, our math department now has a Saturday academy, Monday extended hours, and after-school tutorials, all with student input and buy-in. This would have been impossible without sharing the data with students.

RELATED READINGS

Mike Schmoker's book *Results Now* (Schmoker, 2006) gives a matter-of-fact look at instruction and what the data tells us about how we utilize our instructional time.

Lori Conrad and colleagues' book *Put Thinking to the Test* (Conrad, Matthews, Zimmerman, & Allen, 2008) gives great insight into how to approach testing without giving up the integrity of your instruction.

Reflecting on Part II

- How was your thinking about your own instruction pushed by seeing these portraits of literacy-rich classrooms?
- As a content-area teacher, what do you think your academic discipline is "mostly about"—in terms of the kind of thinking you really want students to do? To what extent might you argue that students have a right to think in these ways as a part of their secondary schooling?
- In what ways do you see literacy as a means to your ends? Or as an obstacle or distraction?
- Compare your academic discipline to other content areas. How is the thinking and literacy in your content unique? How might you demonstrate and explain that to your students?
- Part II presents many specific literacy practices (ways for students to read, write, speak, or learn). How might you apply or adapt one of those practices? What might that "get" your students, both now and later?
- In order to apply that practice in a way that feels authentic (for you) and effective (for students), what else do you need to know?
- Each author in Part II uses particular scaffolds (support or assistance) to help students make meaning of difficult texts. In what ways might these scaffolds be particularly useful to your students who are English language learners?

LEADERSHIP PERSPECTIVES

From Diane Lauer, former principal of Conrad Ball Middle School:

- *Self-assessment.* Use the chapters in Part II as a launching pad for collegial conversation about concrete instructional practices in everyone's classrooms. Integrated teams might discuss what is familiar, emerging, or a challenge. Which practices described in these chapters remind you of strategies you are already using consistently and with fluency in your teaching? Which practices are emerging in your own teaching, and how might you build on those? And which are totally new to you: "Aha!" "Wow, I'd never considered doing that!" If everyone is using a bunch of different strategies, and there is no consciousness that "I am using this, and you are using it, and this is how it looks to you," then we can't have conversations to help us in our own professional inquiry.
- *Beliefs into practice.* In order to help our faculty understand the *why* behind the *what* of the instructional strategies, our PEBC staff developer had us complete a three-column chart. In Column 1, we listed the tools and strategies that PEBC teachers used: for example, think-alouds, or coding text. In Column 2, we named

the purpose for those tools: for example, coding text helps students make their thinking visible so they can go back and build on that thinking later. In Column 3, we inferred the core belief that sits underneath. For example, Gerardo Muñoz believes that students must be change agents. So he regularly asks them to take a stand. Consider: do the tools you are using in your classroom truly match your core beliefs? If not, what are the implications? And if you as a full faculty can come together around your core beliefs, what are the implications for the tools you use with students schoolwide?

From Garrett Phelan, principal of César Chávez Charter School (Capitol Hill campus):

Subject-specific literacy expertise. If you are an expert in your discipline, then you are a literacy expert in your discipline. You read, write, speak, listen, and think like an expert in that discipline. So shouldn't you be modeling and teaching such literacy to your students to enable them to be authentic members of that community? If we see our students as apprentices under the tutelage of masters, then we need to model for them. We must give them the tools and instruments to follow our lead and then set them off on their own in authentic work of our discipline.

Our purpose. Can we tell students, based on data, why we are studying what we are studying in the ways we are studying? Our data indicated that literacy is key. A few years ago, Chávez teachers came together to determine why our students were not achieving. We have an incredibly talented faculty, a rigorous and exciting curriculum, small classes, and time. Based on the data, we concluded that our students' literacy was the key obstacle. But we felt insecure—could all teachers teach literacy? After a year of struggling, we invited PEBC to help us. Our reading scores have increased markedly every year since. Through various professional development structures—coaching, labs, PEBC consultation—we now all see ourselves as literacy teachers for our disciplines.

Essential Frameworks: How to Help All Adolescents Engage, Think, Understand, and Develop Independence

Many secondary teachers work in isolation. Some who are more fortunate may collaborate with a small group of colleagues. Rarely is an entire faculty on the same map, heading in the same direction, using the same strategies.

In Part III, each contributor describes a key concept or theoretical framework that a full faculty can embrace, in service of five central goals—for students to do the following:

- Authentically *engage* in learning, rather than merely completing a task or pursuing a grade
- Actively *think*, rather than passively receiving information
- Actually *understand* content, rather than simply memorizing information
- Gradually *develop independence* in making meaning from difficult texts, rather than relying solely on teachers to tell them what matters or how to make meaning
- Build skills that give them *access* to and *power* in their communities

Combined, these chapters give a faculty, department, team, or individual teacher a clear starting point—a common language, common principles, and a set of practices that work in all content areas—so you can implement the type of instruction described in Part II. The authors write about how teachers can create the classroom environment and conditions that protect students' right to literacy and let students engage in authentic experiences in every academic discipline.

Thus, if Part I laid out the vision and Part II showed that vision in practice, then Part III now answers two questions:

- How do I get there?
- How can we get there together?

If your entire faculty is reading this book, we encourage all teachers to read all four chapters in Part III, so you can develop a common understanding, language, and set of frameworks that will help you move forward as you "design for thinking." Of course, individual teachers, teams, or departments could do the same. Alternatively, your staff may "jigsaw" the four chapters: a subset of staff reads each chapter, discusses with those who read the same chapter, and then shares out with colleagues who read other chapters.

The authors hope the chapters in Part III serve two purposes. The first is to either solidify or provoke a crucial shift in secondary teachers' thinking. Rather than focusing on what or how we teach ("I taught it; why didn't they get it?!"), we can begin to focus on what and how students learn ("As I plan and teach, what do I need to consider to be sure that students both master the content and grow as thinkers and learners?"). The second purpose is to leave you as readers—whether a full faculty, a department, a team, or a lone teacher impassioned to make a difference—with a clear road map for how to begin.

CHAPTER 9

Engaging Classroom Communities: Belonging, Rigor, and Support as Three Pillars of a Thinking Classroom

Michelle Morris Jones

IN THIS CHAPTER: Michelle Morris Jones articulates how teachers can create a classroom environment that promotes a culture of thinking. She revisits the work of Jennifer Swinehart and Jill Dreier (see Chapter 2) with eighth-grade students at Bruce Randolph Middle School. Jones argues that in order to help students become thinkers and to promote their literacy, teachers must create classroom environments with three pillars: a sense of belonging, a dedication to academic rigor, and an unwavering net of support.

KEY POINTS

- A sense of belonging provides a foundation on which teachers can facilitate inquiry, collaboration, and deep thinking for students.
- A dedication to rigor propels students beyond a skills-based experience to one that is transactional and critical in nature.
- A strong net of unwavering support allows teachers to provide differentiated challenges to promote student success.

Imagine a young man, an eighth grader: Mario is a little quieter, softer, and larger than the others. Long hair hangs over his soft brown eyes, a shy grin appears occasionally. One day after independent writing time, he volunteers to share, stands, and begins to sing a song he has written. Thirty-five pairs of eyes turn, gum stops popping, and a hush falls over the room. At the end of the song his peers clap and begin to ask him questions.

His teachers, Jennifer Swinehart and Jill Dreier, facilitate the discussion. "What did Mario do well in his writing today?" "What can we add to our chart 'What We Do Well in Independent Writing'?" As other students share their writing publicly, Jennifer and Jill name and record the brilliant thinking, risks, and writers' craft their students are exhibiting during their daily independent writing. The students demonstrate a sense of confidence, camaraderie, and genuine interest.

Mario, a Latino student with learning disabilities, finds both writing and reading challenging. He tries to fly below the radar. But this year in his language arts class, he has found his writing voice, a sense of purpose, and an understanding of text that he has never experienced before.

Jennifer and Jill are ensuring that Mario and all their other students have access to quality instruction that leads to content-area understanding and improved literacy skills. They view literacy not as an innate skill, a fortunate accident, or an enrichment opportunity, but rather as a student's civil right. They believe that the freedom of intelligence is the only enduring freedom (Dewey, 1938). The classroom environment they create both manifests this belief and makes possible its realization.

ENVIRONMENTS THAT SUPPORT STUDENTS' RIGHT TO THINK

About 3 years ago, I came to Bruce Randolph Middle School (BRMS) as a staff developer with the Public Education & Business Coalition. Of the approximately 650 students, 94% qualified for free or reduced-price lunch, and 54% were designated as English language learners.

Jennifer welcomed me into her classroom, and Jill joined our work the following year. My role as instructional coach has taken many forms: cheerleader, flame-keeper, and teammate. Mostly I have been a witness—of great growth and extraordinary teaching that has led students (whom many might view as on or over the edge due to socioeconomic and cultural differences) to engage in and take responsibility for their learning.

In my work with the PEBC, I have observed and coached secondary teachers in all content areas. Teachers who believe that all students can learn to read difficult material and make meaning, write with voice and purpose, and communicate their thinking and understanding effectively also believe in the importance of belonging, rigor, and support:*

1. *A sense of belonging.* Jennifer and Jill believe that learning is social and that an inclusive classroom will allow students to build trusting interpersonal and scholarly relationships. Students understand each other as people, writers, readers, and thinkers. Leonardo, an English language learner, states, "They help my learning 'cause I am comfortable and don't have to worry about anything else but learning."
2. *A dedication to rigor.* Jennifer and Jill never shy away from challenging texts, extensive writing projects, and metacognitive tasks. High expectations permeate. Students read, write, speak, listen, and *think* every day. "They have challenged me to go deeper into my thinking," explained Christina, another English language learner. "They don't give me the answer; they just give

---

*My framework has been heavily influenced by my colleagues at the PEBC, including our founding staff developer, Ellin Keene, who expands on the concepts of intimacy, rigor, and inquiry in her new book *To Understand* (Keene, 2008).

me a little tip to get me going so I can figure it out myself because they know I can do it."

3. *A strong net of unwavering support.* By using formative assessments and conferring, Jennifer and Jill set the bar high and support a range of learners. As Richard notes, "I feel comfortable being here and sharing my thoughts because I know students and teachers won't make bad comments. They help me instead on what I have to improve."

In this chapter I describe this three-part framework, with illustrations from Jennifer and Jill's classroom, and share how teachers can create classroom environments that help increase student engagement and encourage students to take intellectual risks. All teachers, regardless of content area, can do this crucial work, which serves as the foundation for helping students develop strong literacy skills and deep content-area understanding.

A SENSE OF BELONGING

"Who wants to share?" asks Jill. Donald eagerly raises his hand and practically jumps out of his seat.

"Great, go ahead," says Jill.

Donald eagerly reads a piece he just wrote about his changing body. Jennifer and Jill facilitate as students ask serious questions about mustaches, maturity, and Donald's growth over the past months. Donald confidently fields questions about his writing and his development.

"Anyone else interested in sharing?" asks Jennifer. "T" smoothly raises his hand and offers to share his own piece. He reads the title: "My Manhood."

"Oh my, I guess we have development on the brain," teases Jennifer. Jennifer understands that by allowing students to make choices about their independent writing, topics may occasionally be dicey or even titillating.

"I guess so!" chimes in Jill. "Let's hear it!" Encouraged, "T" continues:

"My Manhood." How I know is because I'm getting taller and muscular a.k.a. stronger. And now I know that is because I've seen my BODY and I'm quite impressed. I'm also getting the facial hairs and to me I think that's a BIG ACCOMPLISHMENT and I think it attracts more females and women and I love that attention. I also know that my voice is getter deeper by the time period and I think that females think that males sound way cuter with deeper voices but that's they way I'm. I'm also getter bigger in clothes, wise and etc. So that's how I know I'm getting my MANHOOD SKILLS!!

After a brief discussion of the changes many students are experiencing, Jennifer and Jill add "writing about personal topics" and "being honest" to their chart entitled "Things We Are Trying in Independent Writing." They are not worried that the occasionally edgy content of their students' writing may derail their instruction; rather, students glean important lessons about topic choice and writers' voice.

Jennifer and Jill affirm students' academic and cultural differences. They know the importance of a multicultural stance and how it can be crucial in helping students get into a state in which they are ready to learn (Gay, 1994). By honoring students' work, voice, and culture, Jennifer and Jill make it more likely that students will rise to meet the academic challenges they present.

Connecting to Students' Interests and Academic Strengths

Building rapport and trust enables teachers to stay connected to their students. Being aware of current trends and popular culture, talking with students about their interests, watching their television programs, listening to their music (liking it is not required), and observing them in action allow teachers to connect with students. By knowing more about students' lives outside of the classroom, teachers can honor each student's individuality, which encourages students to engage and think.

Of course, staying connected doesn't mean just knowing students personally. In this era of high-stakes testing and stifling accountability, we must be conscious of our students' academic and personal distinctiveness. Later in this chapter I discuss ways teachers might collect data on students' skills and understandings.

Donald Graves, author of *The Energy to Teach* (2001), concurs that teachers must understand their students in order to make sound instructional decisions. He created an exercise to gauge how well teachers know their students, which my colleague Annie Patterson and I have adapted (see Figure 9.1).

Cindy (pseudonym), a veteran eighth-grade science teacher, completed this exercise with me. She noted that when she was a 1st- or 2nd-year teacher, she could have listed all of her students' passions and interests; yet now, after 15 years of

Figure 9.1. Know Your Students as Learners

List all your students in a particular class. Note whom you listed and in what order, and whom you omitted. Then complete the remaining columns. When you have filled in as much as you can, analyze your chart. What do you notice? What were you unable to complete? What were you able to complete with little effort? Why?

Student Name	Interests and/or Passion Areas	Strengths as a Learner	Needs as a Learner	Instructional Moves to Consider

Note: Adapted from Graves, 2001.

teaching, she realized she knows her students well as scientists and thinkers, but not very well as people. Her expertise in her content has steadily increased; so it made sense to her that she would be able to identify her students' strengths and needs in terms of their scientific knowledge and thinking strategies. Yet she worried because she couldn't note a passion for each student and vowed to make personal contacts with those she felt she knew little about. We have found it useful for teachers to complete the exercise and reflect on their findings.

Noodling

Michael Smith and Jeff Wilhelm (2002) have noted the importance of "noodling" (fishing around) to teachers: "We can teach our aspiring teachers how to make lessons and units and how to implement the plans they develop. . . . But we can't teach them how to 'noodle' [citing Lopate, 1975, as cited in Gere et al., 1992] around with the kids during the passing periods or notice and remember the musical artists adorning their T-shirts. We can't teach them to care" (p. 187).

In Jennifer and Jill's classroom this "noodling" happens through independent writing and sharing. They get to know their students' interests, worries, passions, and needs by reading over their shoulders during writing time, hearing their pieces, and reading their self-selected entries. Through these interactions, Jennifer, Jill, and their students create and sustain a palpable sense of belonging.

Secondary teachers must build in structures to "noodle" and learn about students as learners and people. Two strategies include reflection journals, in which students write about their learning, and "conversation calendars" (Tovani, 2004). A conversation calendar is an actual calendar on which students and teachers jot notes to each other, which they pass back and forth on a regular basis. The exchange between teachers and students can be about personal topics ("How are you doing?") or academic issues ("I don't understand this chapter").

Individuality sustains the democratic nature of the classroom and helps students feel more engaged in and responsible for their learning. Karla affirms this belief: "I feel really comfortable and successful in this class because my classmates and teachers help me out when I need help. And that makes me want to learn more."

Students in urban settings should not have to worry about cultural differences or about being ridiculed for their successes or shortcomings. Teachers must nudge and nurture individuals to think broadly and take risks, so they can begin to take hold of their education, gaining access to all of the skills (reading, writing, speaking, and critical thinking) that will allow them to practice intellectual freedom and fully participate in a democratic society.

A DEDICATION TO RIGOR

"What do you think?" asks Karina, as she and her partner Raquel (both English language learners) pause from independently reading a selection from *Fahrenheit 451* in which Bradbury (1953) compares a character's smile to a melting candle.

"Well I don't know," begins Raquel. "It is kind of confusing. Let's reread it."

The girls continue to read and discuss the text, pencils jotting and heads nodding.

"It kind of makes you . . . it makes you think hard. Not a question either," Karina says. "I am visualizing that candle."

The girls jot down "visualizing" on sticky notes and put the notes in their books. Later they will go back to the quote, copy it in their writers' notebooks, and write a short response about its meaning and importance. They also will share with the class why they chose this quote and how visualizing helped them construct meaning.

Fahrenheit 451 is a tremendously challenging text for these eighth graders. Jennifer and Jill confer with small groups and partners. They ask questions like "Think about your thinking—which of our thinking strategies are you using?" They probe: "Go back into the text. Think about our strategies that good readers use. Which of these can you use to help you make sense of these new words?" After spending 25 minutes reading and discussing two or three pages, the students are worn out.

They gather to debrief. There is a quiet rumble as 30 eighth graders huddle around the overhead projector on the floor, books open and hands raised. They all have found a meaningful quote and written a brief response—some questions, some connections to their lives, and some visual images—that the text evoked. Some share their work. Jennifer records one student's quote and inference on the overhead.

What is rigor? *Rigor* is intellectual independence. Ron Ritchhart (2002) argues that rigor is fostered when teachers are oriented to learning within classrooms. The learning orientation is contrasted with a working orientation, in which the focus is on getting work done, and a work-avoidance orientation in which all parties do as little as possible.

A learning orientation sets the stage for rigor, which has three dimensions: engagement, authenticity, and transferability (see Figure 9.2).

Engagement

Engagement is commitment, not compliance. Students engage more deeply with content when teachers implement the Workshop Model (see Chapter 12) and balance process and product. Within a workshop, students have an opportunity to practice and engage with their content in meaningful ways and to serve as apprentices to their teachers or real-world models (Schoenbach et al., 1999).

For this apprenticeship to succeed, teachers must emphasize both process and product. If we overemphasize process, students do not have opportunities to create products that are accurate and polished. Yet if we overemphasize product, students do not reflect on, grapple with, or refine their work.

Authenticity

Adolescents are savvy consumers; they disengage from bogus materials and activities. *Authenticity* refers to the validity, realism, and genuineness of our course materials and performance tasks.

Often students in high-needs schools are denied access to authentic texts and tasks, and are inundated with worksheets, controlled readings, and skills-based assessments. A colleague once asked me to consider the "Barnes and Noble test": Why would we ask students to write something that might not be published and sold at a store like Barnes and Noble?

Figure 9.2. Dimensions of Rigorous Instruction

ENGAGEMENT	AUTHENTICITY	TRANSFERABILITY
Workshop model: • Students engage in focus lesson or crafting session while teachers model the activity. • Students practice and refine new skills while teachers confer and gather data. • The class reflects and shares new learning. *Process vs. product:* • The learning process is valuable and meaningful work. • The students' work products are engaging and thought provoking for adolescents.	*Age and cultural appropriateness:* Texts and tasks connect to issues in students' lives, and to their native languages and cultures. *Social discourse:* Teachers provide many opportunities to discuss ideas. *Inquiry:* An inquiry stance is employed. *Relevance:* Learning is meaningful; student work is significant.	*Thinking strategies:* • Thinking strategies are metacognitive. • Thinking strategies serve as mental models across content areas. • Students internalize these strategies and apply them in a variety of settings. *Global perspective:* • There is a sense that student work is connected to a larger entity. • Students are asked to read, write, and reflect with a critical lens.

In terms of text selection, we must consider the following:

• Students' interests, native language, gender, and reading levels
• Age appropriateness
• Ways to pair required texts that are often less considerate (Keene & Zimmerman, 2007) of our students' needs with accessible texts that are gripping and comprehensible
• Cultural relevance
• Whether the texts we use with students were written for a real-world audience

Students also need opportunities to talk, discuss and digest information verbally with their peers. Engaging in genuine inquiry is an underpinning of authenticity (see Chapter 6), as students ask real questions that compel them to want to read materials deeply, talk, and seek meaning.

Transferability

Rich learning transcends content areas. Students can apply their understandings in new contexts and can use these understandings to think critically about their lives and the world. Particularly in high-needs schools, the learning that takes place in our classrooms must be able to benefit our students in their other courses as well as their everyday lives.

Some may ask, How does reading a text such as *Fahrenheit 451* transfer to the real world? Jennifer and Jill designed their unit based on essential questions (Wiggins & McTighe, 2005) including this: What do good readers do when they encounter challenging text? By framing the reading with this question, the teachers helped students see how the skills and strategies within this unit would serve them in many situations for years to come.

In Jennifer and Jill's class, we see how the dimensions of rigor (engagement, authenticity, and transferability) interconnect. The Workshop Model helps students engage in challenging texts with a myriad of supports. Jennifer and Jill use the thinking strategies (Pearson, Roehler, Dole, & Duffy, 1992) as a vehicle to explore the various aspects of their language arts curriculum and to continually build the cognitive challenges presented to their students. As students work through the text, they are focusing on understanding and on their process for making meaning. The task itself is authentic: Students are asking real questions to make meaning of a difficult text and are dialoguing with peers along the way.

Rigor is also promoted by a unique teacher mind-set or disposition. Teachers with this mind-set could be called "warm demanders"(Gay, 1994; Kleinfeld, 1975). They strive to do the following:

- Maintain strong systems of management
- Build relationships with students that are mindful of individual students' needs
- Hold high standards and expectations for individuals and the collective
- Design instruction with students' culture and learning styles in mind

A STRONG NET OF UNWAVERING SUPPORT

"As you and your partners move to each poster, read the quotation and record your questions, inferences, schema, and other thoughts you have. Be sure to discuss the quote with each other," instructs Jennifer as she models the activity on a chart.

The eighth graders set out, traveling in small groups from poster to poster, reading, discussing, and jotting down ideas as a cooperative group (for this Carousel activity, see Critical Friends Group, 2002). They are examining quotations from immigrants and recording their thinking in order to write survey and interview questions to use in their study of immigration. In this unit of study the students are reading excerpts from an anthology of memoirs related to the immigrant experience, interviewing immigrants, and creating surveys for immigrants, all in hopes of crafting an essay that depicts the historical and personal story of an actual recent immigrant to the United States.

During this activity, Jennifer and Jill confer with groups and individuals. Then, after a first round of recording their responses, Jennifer asks each group to synthesize their comments on a poster, note one "burning question" for that immigrant, and share their findings with the class. After this discussion, many students decide to ask their interview subject if he or she regretted the decision to immigrate and what made the experience difficult.

Effective teachers shape their classroom environment to support a variety of learners. Dewey asserts that teachers must "recognize in the concrete what surroundings are conducive to having experiences that lead to growth" (1938, p. 40). In the activity above, Jennifer and Jill have conversations with each of their students about their thinking and their work, and get crucial formative data from which to plan their next instructional steps.

Support takes many forms. Here I focus on two: formative assessment generally, and conferring specifically. Both link directly to the work of Brian Cambourne (1995), who claims that learners need response and feedback from "more knowledgeable others." Such supports let all students become critical thinkers and exercise their right to literacy.

Formative Assessment

"So, would you like to take a look at some of your assessments?" I asked Jennifer as we were reflecting on an upcoming unit of study.

Jennifer rolled her eyes. We both laughed, and Jennifer admitted, "I don't want to waste our time on assessment, especially the state tests. I have had it with all of that!"

As we talked, however, it became apparent that assessment is crucial to her decision making. For example, as students were engaged with the Carousel activity, Jennifer and Jill were able to assess students' reading comprehension, concept understanding, use of metacognitive strategies, cognitive language learning, and group collaboration in real time and make individual suggestions to enhance understanding.

It is hard to support student learning without a clear picture of students' skills, strengths, and needs; by collecting data from a variety of sources we strengthen our net of support. Teachers can evaluate how well their students are progressing and then tailor their instruction to capitalize on strengths and to meet individual needs. Rick Wormeli writes, "Good assessment advances learning, not just documents it: it's accepted as integral to instruction, not outside of instruction. We cannot have good instruction that does not assess, just as we cannot have good assessment that does not inform" (Wormeli, 2006).

Formative assessments allow teachers to make complex instructional decisions that advance learning. Teachers of all content areas can employ assessments that provide information about student learning throughout units of study as well as those more traditional final or summative assessments. Examples of formative assessments include the following:

- Student self-assessments
- Exit slips (brief informal written assessments that students complete at the end of class)
- Student reflection journals
- Examples of student work
- Short assessments with accompanying rubrics
- Anecdotal notes or notes from conferences (see below)

By using a variety of data sources to know our students as learners, we recognize their accomplishments and can accelerate their learning and achievement.

Conferring

"Tell me about your writing today," probes Jennifer as she kneels down to confer with one of her young writers.

> LUCIA: I am trying to show the story, not tell it.
> JENNIFER: What story are you trying to show? And what have you tried?
> LUCIA: Well, I don't want all of my journals to sound the same; you know "last night I did this and then this and then this." I want the story to be more like the ones we are reading in class.
> JENNIFER: Maybe, you could read over some of your favorites. I know that you liked the short pieces by Sandra Cisneros and the poetry book by Tupac Shakur. You may be able to find more ideas there. Those books are in the memoir area of our bookshelf.
> LUCIA: Oh yeah. I'll read the Tupac book again. Thanks Miss.
> JENNIFER: Okay, then I'll check back in with you tomorrow or the next day. But if you need anything just ask.

Jennifer's brief interaction with Lucia highlights some of the benefits of conferring. "Conferences work because they teach a habit of mind. They help students learn how to reflect on their own work, to review their own progress, to identify their own problems, set their own goals, and make plans and promises to themselves about steps they are going to take" (Zemelman et al., 1998, p. 200).

I consider conferring an essential component of instruction at any grade level, in any content area. I am currently working with Anne McManus, a high school art teacher from Loveland, Colorado. Anne has found that conferring with her students has instilled a sense of craft in them that has directly impacted their work in the studio. As she confers, she asks her students direct questions about their work ("Tell me which element of art you are working on?") and provides immediate feedback ("Have you had a chance to examine the work of Salvador Dali?" or "Have you tried using complimentary colors?"). Students often apply Anne's suggestions or questions to their paintings or drawings. Her support nudges students toward independence.

Secondary teachers may find conferring counterintuitive, since they were trained to be experts within their content areas and then to impart this knowledge to students; however, students still need individual contact that engages them with their learning. Conferences, or "conversations" as Anderson (2000) calls them, provide many benefits:

- Teachers build relationships with individual students.
- Teachers gather crucial information about students' strengths and needs.
- Teachers can tailor their instruction for individual learners.
- Students are empowered to articulate their strengths and needs.

- Students who are reluctant to participate in whole-class discussions for social, cultural, or language reasons are given voice.

If you sit down to work with a student and find yourself at a loss for words, consider asking the following questions:

1. What are you working on?
2. How is it going?
3. What do you plan to do next? (Zemelman et al., 1998, p. 200)

As you and your student are having this dialogue listen carefully as you gather information, select just one teaching point to share with this particular student, leave the student with a plan for how to practice, and later record and reflect upon the conversation.

Formative assessment and conferring allow teachers to meet students where they are developmentally and then to nudge them to greater understanding. This concept is often referred to as working in one's "zone of proximal development," a phrase that was coined by educational researcher and theorist Lev Vygotsky (1978). Simply put, if we talk to our students and reflect on what their work is telling us, we can support them to move forward as thinkers and learners.

ENGAGING CLASSROOM COMMUNITIES AND THE FUTURE

Walking the halls of today's urban secondary schools can feel like navigating the roughest of waters—high tides of adolescence-induced emotion or bleak Bermuda Triangles that suck students into nothingness. Yet it is imperative that teachers "teach as if we are surfing on the crest of the future's breaking wave" (Smith & Wilhelm, 2006, p. 187).

In this chapter, I offered a snapshot of a group of urban adolescents and their teachers riding that breaking wave: battling poverty, crime, the stresses of immigration, some of the lowest achievement scores in the state, a politicized school and district, and budget constraints. Jennifer Swinchart and Jill Dreier have shaped a classroom culture that reflects all that we hope for today's students: a sense of belonging, a dedication to academic rigor, and a strong net of unwavering support.

This type of engaging classroom community must become the norm rather than the exception for today's adolescents. Achievement data from this class suggests that pairing an engaging community with sound instructional practice does promote academic achievement for urban students and makes their right to literacy a reality.

HOW TO BEGIN

- Consider belonging, rigor, and support. In which areas do you excel and what would you like to refine? Then prioritize: How can you spend your energy?
- Get to know your students better. Use interest surveys, conferring, formative assessments, "noodling," and observations.

- Assess yourself on the dimensions of rigor. Which are developed in your own classroom practice?
- Set a goal for student conferences. Try to make individual contact with each of your students. Reflect on the data you collect.

LINGERING QUESTIONS

- At the secondary level, how do we create reforms that address classroom culture?
- What are the similarities and differences in terms of how belonging, rigor, and support play out in various content areas?

LEADERSHIP PERSPECTIVES

From Diane Lauer, former principal of Conrad Ball Middle School:

- *From rhetoric to reality.* Recently there has been a lot of talk about "rigor, relevance, and relationships." Jones paints a picture of what that looks like in a real classroom with real students. Consider how that picture compares to your department, school, or district vision. How do you know that you really know kids?
- *Risk.* In my years as a teacher and school leader, I have learned that kids won't take learning risks if they do not feel safe. And that means that learning for kids won't happen if we as teachers don't take the risk to change our teaching practices. What are you willing to risk?

From Garrett Phelan, principal of César Chávez Charter School (Capitol Hill campus):

- *Classroom environment.* If we cannot create classroom environments that promote risk taking, we cannot promote learning and authentic, meaningful success. How do you encourage discussion, protect time to confer with and coach students, and engage deeply in texts that yield authentic learning in the discipline? What is the physical environment of classrooms in your school: What is on the walls, and how are desks arranged? What is the intellectual environment: What is the focus of the lesson, how is time structured, and what are the students doing?
- *Support.* Support and scaffolding for secondary students can take many forms. We must always ask ourselves, "Does the support I'm giving students enable less-than-full effort and surface thinking? Or does it enable inquiry, thinking, literacy, and independence?" Only the latter truly empowers students.

RELATED READINGS

Michael Smith and Jeffrey Wilhelm's book *Reading Don't Fix No Chevys* (Smith & Wilhelm, 2002) discusses the importance of building relationships with students and staying connected with their interests.

Ron Ritchhart's book *Intellectual Character* (Ritchhart, 2002) goes into great depth regarding the importance of rigor.

Carl Anderson's book *How's It Going?* (Anderson, 2000) describes how to effectively confer with students.

Rick Wormeli's book *Fair Isn't Always Equal* (Wormeli, 2006) provides an eye-opening and forward-thinking view of the role of assessment in today's classrooms.

CHAPTER 10

Thinking, Not Shuffling: Expecting All Students to Use Their Minds Well

Wendy Ward Hoffer

IN THIS CHAPTER: Secondary students are too rarely engaged in meaningful work at school. Wendy Ward Hoffer offers a four-part framework teachers can use to help them plan so students are actually "thinking," rather than just shuffling through the school day.

KEY POINTS

- When we waste students' time expecting them to shuffle through the motions of school, we waste their minds.
- To create learning opportunities that engage students and culminate in worthy understandings, we must adjust four things: understanding goals, tasks, teaching stance, and assessments.
- Creating a classroom where thinking is central means planning not only what the teacher will do, but more important, how students will spend their time and energy.

If you spotted Miguel in the lunchroom dressed in black, shoes untied, you would probably expect him to punch you as fast as loan you a dime. But when you talk with him, you realize he is exceptional: He cites obscure facts about professional sports; he speaks two languages fluently; he taught himself to play the guitar.

I have known Miguel all his life. When he was in tenth grade, I asked him how high school was going. "OK," he said. When I asked him to say more, he explained, "We shuffle. We shuffle papers around on our desks. We shuffle books in our lockers. We shuffle from room to room. High school is *all* about shuffling." I was crestfallen.

As I visit schools and classrooms, I often look at the landscape through Miguel's eyes: Is this class about shuffling? Alarmingly, I often hear myself answering yes. Whenever I see students drudging through mundane tasks, filling in predictable worksheets, or listening to long lectures with minor opportunities to respond, I feel culpable as an adult. There are many Miguels in the room, capable of far more than we expect of them.

WHAT SHUFFLING LOOKS LIKE

Consider the following scene from Ms. Jones's algebra class:

PROBLEM OF THE DAY

Use the Table of Squares and Square Roots to complete:

1) 13^2 2) 30^2 3) 50^2

4) $\sqrt{169}$ 5) $\sqrt{900}$ 6) $\sqrt{2500}$

Each student has been given the "Table of Squares and Square Roots" on which to find the answers to this day's "warm-up." Students chat, put on makeup, draw, and otherwise busy themselves as Ms. Jones ricochets around the room fighting fires of distraction. When "work time" is over, Ms. Jones calls on students who raise their hands to volunteer their correct answers. She praises each and gives ample time for those who have not located the answers to copy them. Throughout the period, I picture Miguel sitting in the back, shoulders slumped, doing the minimum to get by and shuffle on down the hall.

Most of our students are trained in the tricks of performance. In a math classroom, they know how to hunt and copy, complete worksheets, perform calculations at the teacher's call, apply a formula immediately after receiving it. With passion for the subject and compassion for struggling students, many math teachers have gotten used to handing students proverbial mathematical fish—facts, procedures, formulae to memorize and apply—rather than teaching them how to fish: a square root's meaning, origins, importance, and how to calculate it. To Miguel's disappointment, the effort to make math palatable deprives him of opportunities to think.

As a staff developer for the Public Education & Business Coalition, I am struck by how hard teachers work to keep students on target to complete tasks. Often, for the sake of order or speed, we take the responsibility for mathematical understanding and thinking out of learners' hands. When we do this, mathematics becomes a spectator sport. This could be said of any content area where students' participation is reduced to listening, memorizing, and following directions.

For the welfare of our students, ourselves as teachers, our schools and our nation, our classes must be about more than shuffling. We must empower students—all students—as fishers in the sea of knowledge, equipped with the skills, modes of thinking, qualities of character and, above all, confidence to make meaning for themselves.

THE POWER OF EXPECTATIONS

Three things set us apart from other tool-using simians: upright posture, opposable thumbs, and our ability to think and reason at a high level.

What if we, capable of walking upright, were never expected to do so? Imagine children carried everywhere from birth, their parents buying ever-bigger strollers, pushing children around until they grew strong enough to use wheelchairs by themselves. At some point in those children's lives, if they chose to use their innate ability to walk, they would likely struggle tremendously. Muscles would have atrophied, and the neural connections required for this complex balancing task might never have been made.

But who would do that to a child? Everyone expects children to walk. We train them—first holding two hands, then only one—to balance on their feet. We prop them against the couch and beckon them from across the room. When they fall, we lift them up, brush them off, and expect them to try again and again, knowing that part of learning is to struggle, become frustrated, and persevere.

In the same way, no child is born with fully developed intellectual competencies; these skills must be learned, and are best learned through experience designed to promote understanding. As Katherine Merseth (1993) compels us, "'Teaching as telling' can no longer be the operative form of instruction in mathematics classrooms. Instead, multiple opportunities must be provided for students to engage with mathematics" (p. 533). This applies to all content areas.

The National Research Council's volume *How People Learn* (2000a) refers to a 1959 study by Wertheimer: Two groups were instructed how to find the area of a parallelogram, one by the understanding method, and the other by the rote method. While both groups demonstrated proficiency on initial assessments, the members of the group trained by the understanding method were able to transfer their learning to similar yet unique problems. The rote group, meanwhile, responded to novel, related tasks with the unfortunate disclaimer, "We haven't had that yet." These rote learners did not believe in their ability to think independently about this concept.

Just as a child must struggle to learn how to walk, she also must reach with her brain to learn the skills of thinking. The teacher's role is to support, not eliminate, this struggle. We must believe that each student—regardless of language abilities, cultural heritage, or socioeconomic status—is capable of mastering the thinking herself.

Here, then, is our own Problem of the Day: How?

PLANNING FOR THINKING

In their book *Understanding by Design*, Grant Wiggins and Jay McTighe (2005) discuss two major pitfalls, or "twin sins," common to many schools and classrooms: activity-based teaching and coverage-based teaching. Neither approach necessarily culminates in understanding. Instead, teachers end up either keeping students busy with ineffective activities or rushing through units or texts in an effort to finish the curriculum or book by year's end. Both approaches are exhausting for teachers and mind-numbing to students.

In my early years of teaching, I was afraid of students having free time. I thought busy meant learning, and spent a lot of time at the copier. Even with everything I had learned in graduate school, my class was all about shuffling. With pressures from all sides, I slipped into comfortable routines. It was not until I put understanding—instead of activities or coverage—at the crux of my curricular designs that things changed for me and my students.

As shown in Figure 10.1, four interdependent aspects of our planning can transform students' experiences away from shuffling: understanding goals, tasks, teach-

Figure 10.1. Changing Planning to Minimize Shuffling

> **Understanding goals:** Let go of coverage; stick to big ideas and power standards.
>
> **Tasks:** Let go of busywork in favor of tasks that promote understanding.
>
> **Teaching stance**: Let go of knowing everything; focus on drawing students out.
>
> **Assessment**: Let go of tallying points; focus on gathering data that document understanding.

ing stance, and assessment. Each proposal, taken separately, offers leverage toward shifting students' experience in our classes. Yet we see even more opportunity to make holistic changes when we look at the relationship between the four: No matter which corner we start in, a change in any of these essential elements requires a change in others (see Figure 10.2).

A change of task—for example, from a worksheet to a more thought-provoking project—requires a change in assessment, in most cases. When we let students figure out for themselves the difference between the graph of x^2 and the graph of 2^x, rather than simply memorize a rule, we invite creativity. To develop a rule of their

Figure 10.2. Holistic Change Pyramid

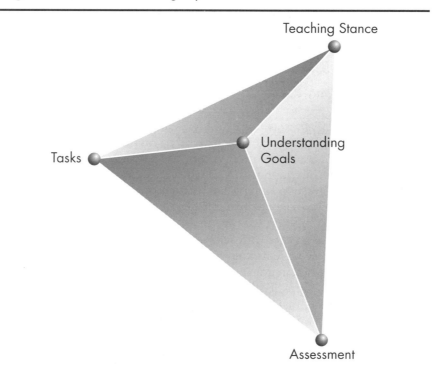

own, they will have to test, prove, and defend it in ways that require deeper assessment than a jiffy quiz.

The good news, then, is this: We do not need to change everything at once. We can start in any corner we like, try something new, and see where it takes us. In this chapter I look at each of the four aspects of planning to see how we can revise classroom practice to maximize thinking and minimize shuffling.

UNDERSTANDING GOALS: BIG IDEAS, NOT ISOLATED FACTS

Most states, districts, and schools are under continuous pressure to lengthen the list of standards and benchmarks students must meet. Hardworking teachers are stressed with expectations of coverage.

Take, for example, the "box and whisker plot." Despite taking AP calculus in high school, I never knew what this data display was until I began teaching middle school math. Suddenly the box and whisker plot found its way onto the Colorado state test and into our school's math curriculum. Students were drilled for weeks on the rudiments of finding and representing quartiles and outliers, rulers in hand.

While I have nothing against the box and whisker plot per se, it is one of a very long list of data displays that our students could memorize. Instead of going into each display in detail, we as teachers and curriculum developers would serve students far better by taking the long view: In our lives and in the future, there will be a growing number of ways to graphically represent information. What is important is that we understand the nature of graphic representations and the qualities of a just representation, and gain the skills to understand any form of data display we encounter. Given this stance, our instruction focuses less on a particular display and more on the transferable understanding to be gained from making sense of one. Teachers in every content area might ask:

> Do I focus on covering the details, or do I use them as examples to deepen students' understanding of the big ideas?

When we stop looking at standards as a checklist and start linking them to overarching concepts that define our content area, we provide learners a framework for future knowledge and ideas, contributing to their becoming lifelong learners.

Further, when we identify understanding goals and make them central to our planning, we begin to see tasks differently. For example, instead of Civil War activities we look for tasks that promote understanding of a big idea demonstrated by that content: racism, government, or identity. To teach for thinking starts with knowing what it is we want students to think about and understand.

Figure 10.3 provides a sampling of big ideas that could weave together numerous standards in each content area. Big ideas differ from standards: They are overarching, can apply to many content areas or topics, and require students to construct understanding. Choose your big idea from this list or invent your own, but be sure the big ideas you spend time on are encompassing and worthwhile.

Figure 10.3. What's the Big Idea?

MATH	SCIENCE	SOCIAL STUDIES	LANGUAGE ARTS	PERFORMING/ VISUAL ARTS
Problem solving	Energy	Civilization	Identity	Creativity
Logic	Evolution	Cultural diffusion	Perspective	Activism
Justification	Patterns of change	Innovation	Creativity	Culture
Communication			Voice	Point of view
Multiple representations	Scale and structure	Humans and the environment	Conflict	Evidence
Analysis	Stability	Values and beliefs	Symbolism	Representation
Communication	Systems and interactions	Economics	Conventions	Interpretation
		Political ideas and institutions	Literature as a mirror	Chronology
		Conflict and cooperation	Writing as a record of human experience	

Note: The author is grateful to Diana Froley deForest for her advice on the "big ideas" in the arts and to Jeremy Hoffer and Stevi Quate for theirs on language arts.

Sources: Math: National Council of Teachers of Mathematics, 2000. Science: California Department of Education, 1990. Social Studies: Michigan Department of Education, 2008. Language Arts: J. Hoffer, 2008; Quate, 2008. Performing/Visual Arts: DeForest, 2007.

TASKS FOR UNDERSTANDING, NOT BUSYNESS

As I work with teachers to use students' time to help them understand big ideas by making meaning of important content, many old pieces of paper fly into the recycling bin. Longtime favorite activities can be evaluated based on two questions:

- What will students be thinking about while experiencing this task?
- What will this task show me that students understand?

These questions shed new light on what is worthwhile.

Take the word-search activity, for example, a well-loved task capable of keeping children in their seats for up to 30 minutes. But what more will a seventh grader gain toward comprehending conceptual mathematical vocabulary by finding the letters for *variable* in a page of jumbled letters?

That was an easy one to let go of. Other time-wasters are often disguised as engaging hands-on activities, such as having students design marvelous foldables displaying unit vocabulary. One teacher's eighth graders became highly skilled at cutting and creasing construction paper to create doors revealing key definitions. In terms of understanding, though, this task was essentially an art project containing words copied from the textbook's glossary. How could this teacher root the task more deeply in the big ideas and understanding goals of the unit? She decided to change the project. She now asks students to focus their foldable on one concept and represent creatively how it relates to other important concepts from this unit and others. She also adjusted her grading system to reflect evidence of understanding, deemphasizing aesthetics.

By asking "What will students think about while experiencing this task?" and "What will this task show me that students understand?" and finding satisfactory answers, we can transform old-favorite tasks into meaningful learning experiences for all students:

- A research paper becomes a multigenre project.
- A math quiz becomes a reflection about what I do and don't understand so far.
- A science worksheet becomes an original investigation.

When we focus on the thinking and evidence of understanding, we also honor the gifts and challenges of English language learners who are not yet proficient in our language, yet have deep conceptual understanding. When we open the doors to multiple representations of knowledge, we honor the thinking of every learner, regardless of language ability.

With creative design, we can assign tasks that get kids thinking. Once we have designed an evocative task, our next job is to coach students to demonstrate their brilliance and understanding.

TEACHING STANCE: LISTENING, NOT LECTURING

In the old days, being a teacher meant knowing everything and standing at the front of the class delivering informational lectures. But in the very, very old days, to *educate* meant "to draw forth." In order to teach for understanding, we must return to the root meaning of education: Our job is to evoke understanding from our students through experiences and conversations.

Think about a time when you felt really smart: Was it when you were listening to someone explain something to you, or was it when you were able to figure something out for yourself? For me, it was the latter. I was 12 years old. The question was why some trees lose their leaves in the winter and others don't. I thought about it for a long time and then said "Every tree needs a way to deal with the snow!" My teacher liked this explanation; all of a sudden, I wanted to become a naturalist.

To create opportunities for all students to experience themselves as bright thinkers, we need to think of them as that. It is sad to hear frustrated teachers complain about students' "low abilities"; one teacher I observed described working with her bilingual class as "teaching a bunch of sticks." Only after many years of shuffling, I thought to myself, did this group of English language learners begin to behave like inanimate objects during school. No one expected more of them.

To draw every student out, we need to stop knowing and to start asking, to remember the child learning to walk. A stance of confidence in students' thinking, which we can demonstrate through a number of strategies shown in Figure 10.4, is essential before we can stop the shuffling.

When we begin from a stance of optimism about what our students are capable of, our classrooms become lively celebrations of thinking, and our job as assessors is transformed.

ASSESSMENT: ARCHAEOLOGY, NOT ACCOUNTING

Most teachers work hard to develop their own just grading systems reflective of each unit they teach, assigning points to all of the in-class tasks, worksheets, and homework assignments, as well as each quiz, test, and project. Often, we work to ensure that each unit adds up to a nice round number of potential points in the grade book.

This fall, many Denver public school teachers were shocked to learn that their tried and true grading systems are no longer acceptable: All middle school teachers have been required to switch to a new system of standards-based progress reports. Instead of documenting how many points students are earning in their classes, teachers are suddenly being expected to keep track of learners' progress toward standards. This progress is not indicated clearly with the grading systems previously used: 300 out of 300 probably means that the student understands most everything, while a mere 147 out of a possible 300 is harder to interpret; 147 could mean a student didn't understand, or it could mean he understood completely but felt lazy, or it could mean that the child understood some of the standards but not all. The score alone does not report what a learner is confused about or proficient at, or why.

 # SCORES ARENT THAT DETAILED

Figure 10.4. Teaching for Thinking

- Believe that all students are capable.
- Value thinking over coverage.
- Model your own thinking.
- Share thinking through reflective dialogue.
- Teach students to ask questions of one another and answer other students' questions.
- Honor a range of approaches and strategies.
- Focus on the thinking behind the problem solving more than the right answers (but those are important, too).
- Resist the urge to rescue; turn questions back to the learners.
- Create opportunities for small successes and build on those.
- Hold all students accountable to high expectations; give real consequences.
- Provide students authentic feedback on performances.

So, how do we know what students know? Let us visit together the classroom of Mrs. Jemez (pseudonym):

An algebra teacher who views herself as both a facilitator and a mathematics learner, Mrs. Jemez is working with students to help them understand the role of each variable in a linear equation, as well as how to make meaning of story problems. Today students are asked to find the equations of two lines described in a story problem. Pairs of students attempt the complex solution. After 10 minutes of work time, students share their ideas with the class. From a class of 30 pupils, seven distinct answers emerge. One by one, students come to the board, taking turns sketching the situation, explaining their thinking. The rest of the class listens and poses questions to the explaining students.

They work the problem several ways before arriving at an answer the majority agrees on. The group keeps discussing and explaining until all are sure that this is right, and they understand. Mrs. Jemez stops the discussion just before the bell and asks each student to turn over their notes and, on the back of that page, answer the following question, What do I understand now about the nature of linear equations? These written reflections serve as evidence of understanding.

When our goal is to teach for understanding, we must let go of assessment as an accounting task and look at it instead as an archaeological one. Our role is to gather evidence of all sorts—conversational and written, informal and formal—to document our own theories about a student's level of understanding. This can be a big and time-consuming leap, but one that Miguel and all of our students will appreciate. As they study math, or Latin, or geography, we study their understanding of it.

What do we look for as evidence of understanding? There are many opportunities for formative, ongoing, and summative assessment in all content areas:

- Oral explanations while conferring
- Explanations to peers during group work
- Contributions to class discussion
- Presentations of thinking
- Reflection writing
- Clearly reasoned written explanations
- Metacognition
- Questions

Gathering, organizing, storing, and sifting through notes and assessment data every term can be daunting to a teacher who sees more than 100 students each day. One easy record-keeping strategy is to create a rubric that identifies the learning targets of the entire unit. This rubric includes goals related to achievement, aptitude, effort, and attitude (Stiggins, Arter, J. Chappuis, & S. Chappuis, 2002, p. 412). Each area of the rubric provides space for students to be scored on a 5-point scale, with room for notes.

We can then make one copy of the rubric for each student in each period, keep those on a clip board, and take a few minutes during each class to gather data on the progress of a rotating handful of students. Using this method over the course of several weeks, we end the unit with a simple, one-page summary for each learner that provides anecdotal evidence of understanding.

These rubrics, coupled with other assessments, inform us about students' progress toward standards. While an initial investment of effort is required to put this system in place, once up and running, it provides an accessible, systematic way to document students' understanding.

PUTTING IT ALL TOGETHER: UNDERSTANDING GOALS, TASKS, TEACHING, AND ASSESSMENT

Understanding Goals: How Do We Formulate These?

Ask yourself, "Why am I doing this? What is this lesson actually about?" Instead of just writing "positive and negative numbers" as a daily objective, think more deeply:

Positive and negative numbers as an example of a counting system
Linear equations as a tool for solving problems
Order of operations as a mathematical convention, of which there are many

While these phrases may not seem too inspiring, the breakthrough is to consider what each little item on the list of benchmarks has to do with the bigger framework of mathematics. It helps students understand the context of what they are being asked to think about.

What About Tasks?

Some teachers balk at spending a whole period on one word problem as a colossal waste of time, but I see it differently. You can have students complete every problem in every lesson in the book, but to what end? Half the time they are confused and just write down some fake math to fill the page and get some points. What we do during class when we delve into a single word problem—not just any old problem, but a rich one—is tease out all of the possible areas of confusion, all of the missteps and misconceptions until we are all convinced we agree and are right. We must work to create a climate in our classrooms where there are no dumb questions, where students know how smart they are and how brave to ask questions. So the time we spend really understanding one problem together is a rich and deep learning experience. It is meaningful for them to watch one another, listen, ask. This is not a traditional use of time in a math classroom, but it is one of the most evocative tasks—and simple ones— for drawing out student understanding.

So many of us spend our planning time thinking about what we will do during the period, but we need to come at it from a different angle: Focus on what the *kids* will be doing. Plan hard to make sure that the time they are in class, they are doing something purposeful and useful. Ask yourself, "What is it like to be a student in my class?" Then plan from the student perspective.

Teaching Stance: Drawing Students Out

We have already been to college and earned our degrees. Now it is the students' turn. We do them a far greater service by listening than lecturing. Build their confidence, then ask a lot of questions to draw learners out. Some standard questions include:

- What are you thinking?
- Are you sure? Why?
- Could you explain it another way?
- What might you need to double-check?
- What questions do you have?

When we talk with students in this way, it keeps them in the driver's seat: They feel responsible for their own learning, for their own understanding.

Assessment: How Do We Know What They Know?

This is tricky. We cannot keep it all in our heads, so we need systems of documenting learners' understanding. One is through written work. We must demonstrate what we expect, the depth of thought and detail required for a quality reflection. We can also use a unit rubric for each student to help keep track of conversations, not everyone's every day, but a few each class. Get excited when the kids say smart and insightful things; celebrate and record those. It can be a time-consuming task, but well worth the effort. These rubrics are a simple but powerful record of student learning.

Our classes cannot, in the least, be about shuffling. Changes in students' participation and behavior will not happen overnight, or even in a month. Yet, with dedication and support, all students can learn to take responsibility for their own understanding—if we believe in them, if we coach them, if we let them.

HOW TO BEGIN

- Look at your class through students' eyes. Ask yourself, "Is there any shuffling going on in here? How can I reduce or eliminate that?"
- Pick one unit and one corner of the figure in Figure 10.2. Start there. Try one new thing, and observe the ripple effect this has on the rest of your students' experience.

LINGERING QUESTIONS

- Who benefits from schooling being reduced to shuffling?
- Where will the time and inspiration come from for teachers to overcome our own tendency to shuffle?

LEADERSHIP PERSPECTIVES

From Diane Lauer, former principal of Conrad Ball Middle School:

- *What do we really want for our students?* No one would say that they want shuffling for students. Yet Hoffer challenges us to ask ourselves, "What is it like to be a student in my class?" "What is it like for a student to move through classes in a day at our school?"

- *Professional development as shuffling?* How can we as a staff assess whether we are shuffling or not? How can we push ourselves as adult learners and leaders to be sure that we have meaningful goals, relevant tasks, and ways to assess our own progress?

From Garrett Phelan, principal of César Chávez Charter School (Capitol Hill campus):

- *Meaningful work.* We must look deeply at what we do in class—everything from the warm-up, to class exercises, to homework. Is every task we offer meaningful? Is the purpose to become more literate, a deeper thinker, and gain more understanding? Or is the purpose simply to maintain order and control? Do we as a faculty have the courage to "reexamine our own thinking, our own teaching?"
- *Fail better.* Samuel Beckett once said "Try again, fail again, fail better." Can we create powerful classroom environments in our school where good failing is honored? The goal, as Hoffer notes, is to "support, not eliminate, the struggle" to learn. Do students' brains ache as their muscles would after a good physical workout? If they are confused at times on their learning path, is that all right? Did they have to struggle to attain understanding, or was knowledge just given to them?

RELATED READINGS

Robert Marzano's book *Classroom Instruction That Works* (Marzano, 2001) details practical instructional strategies to facilitate thinking.

Grant Wiggins and Jay McTighe's book *Understanding by Design* (Wiggins & McTighe, 2005) offers a powerful template for planning and step-by-step guidance on teaching for understanding.

The National Research Council's book *How People Learn* (NRC, 2000a) describes the research base for best instructional practice.

Richard Stiggins's book *Student-Centered Classroom Assessment* (Stiggins, 1997) thoughtfully examines a range of assessment systems and tools designed to gauge student thinking and understanding.

CHAPTER 11

Independence Is the Greatest Gift I Can Give: Using the Gradual Release of Responsibility Framework

Jennifer Kirmes

IN THIS CHAPTER: Jennifer Kirmes, who teaches high school science, shares her own journey of how to use the Gradual Release of Responsibility (GRR) framework as a way to plan instruction in a way that helps students develop and internalize key skills. She describes how she uses the GRR framework to help students develop independence as learners, and addresses common concerns teachers have about whether and how to use GRR with secondary students.

KEY POINTS

- Developing students' independence should be central to secondary teachers' work.
- The Gradual Release of Responsibility framework helps middle and high school teachers deliberately and effectively plan toward this independence.
- Despite secondary teachers' belief that they already know this, or that secondary students don't need it, independence won't happen unless we plan for it.

In October of my first year of teaching, I assigned my 11th-grade chemistry students their first lab report. I planned it all out carefully. First, I wrote a rubric for the lab report, then I wrote a description of a chemistry lab report that outlined the sections of a lab report and the specifics of what each section should include. Finally, I found a lab report I had written as an 11th grader; students would familiarize themselves with the rubric by using it to assess my report.

The students seemed to like the lesson, especially grading my own high school writing. They understood the rubric so well, I thought; they would write great reports. Imagine my surprise when the reports were due and only 2 out of 35 students turned in the assignment.

First, I was angry. Then I was baffled. After a weekend of thinking about nothing else, I had my first big teacher "aha" moment: They had not written their reports because I had taught them *what* to do, but not *how* to do it.

HOW CAN I MAKE THEM NOT NEED ME?

Three years ago I began teaching while a Teach For America corps member, with a fresh-out-of-college passion to make my students into thinkers. After 5 weeks of intensive training, I was assigned to teach chemistry and physical science at César Chávez Charter School in Washington, D.C., which serves about 420 primarily low-income Latino and African American students. Of those 420 students, 70% qualify for free or reduced-price lunch, 99% are people of color, and about 6% are English language learners. In the chemistry class I described earlier, about 15% of my students had qualified for special education services and support.

I quickly fell in love with my students, but felt like I was working at least 100 times harder than they were. And I found that many more experienced teachers were feeling the same way. Evidently, developing independent thinkers was easier imagined than done.

Yet I knew the issue was not students' work ethic. Students have a right to effective instruction, teaching that supports them to master key content and skills while also fostering their independence as thinkers, readers, and writers. As a teacher, I believed it was my responsibility to design such instruction, and I wanted to know how.

The answer I found was the Gradual Release of Responsibility framework, which gives teachers a structured way to think about how to best support students in becoming independent thinkers. In this chapter, I describe the stages of GRR and the difference it made for me and continues to make for my students.

THE GRADUAL RELEASE OF RESPONSIBILITY FRAMEWORK

The GRR framework was first introduced by Pearson and Gallagher (1983) for use in literacy instruction; it has since become respected best practice in other disciplines. A Public Education & Business Coalition staff developer introduced me to GRR, which I now use as a key instructional framework in my daily, unit, and year-long planning to teach skills and processes ranging from solving quadratic equations to working effectively in groups, to—yes, at last—writing those lab reports.

The framework progresses through six stages of instruction that help lead students to independence. In the early stages, as they are exposed to a new skill or strategy, the students rely heavily on the teacher. In the middle stages, the teacher and students work collaboratively so students can experience success in a structured way. In the later stages, students are given opportunities to practice the skill independently. Thus responsibility for the new skill is gradually released from the teacher to the students, giving students ownership over their learning. The six stages are shown in Figure 11.1.

GRR is a natural way to teach and learn skills. For example, when my dad taught me to ride a bike he gave me direct instruction, pointing out what riders do:

Figure 11.1. Gradual Release of Teacher Responsibility Means Gradual Increase of Student Independence

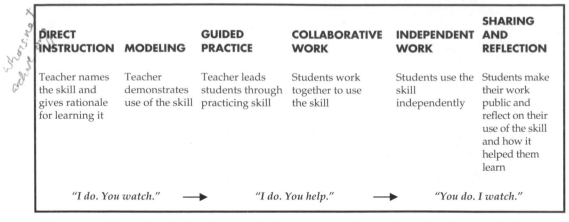

DIRECT INSTRUCTION	MODELING	GUIDED PRACTICE	COLLABORATIVE WORK	INDEPENDENT WORK	SHARING AND REFLECTION
Teacher names the skill and gives rationale for learning it	Teacher demonstrates use of the skill	Teacher leads students through practicing skill	Students work together to use the skill	Students use the skill independently	Students make their work public and reflect on their use of the skill and how it helped them learn

"I do. You watch." ⟶ *"I do. You help."* ⟶ *"You do. I watch."*

Note: Adapted from "Developing Expertise in Reading Comprehension," by P. D. Pearson, L. R. Roehler, J. A. Dole, and G. G. Duffy, 1992. In S. J. Samuels and A. E. Farstrup (Eds.), *What Research Has to Say About Reading Instruction* (pp. 145–200). Newark, DE: International Reading Association.

"See the boy on his bicycle, Jen? He's balancing himself." He showed me how to balance and steer. He guided me (with training wheels for support) and gave me collaborative work—he ran alongside me and steadied me as I found my balance. Eventually, he let go. But he kept watching. When I fell, he picked me up, encouraged me, and asked me to reflect—"What happened?"—so I would learn from my mistake. Big kids need GRR too because it lets them master and take ownership over skills even more important than bike riding.

In each of the next six sections, I discuss a stage of GRR, explaining what I did the first time I tried to teach my chemistry students how to write a lab report and what I did the next time when I was following the GRR framework. I also list key points about each stage's importance, appearance, and method.

STAGE 1: DIRECT INSTRUCTION—NAMING AND FRAMING

In Stage 1 the teacher gives students direct instruction, naming and defining the skill for the students and telling them why they are learning it.

In my initial attempt, I did give students a rubric that named for them what a successful, complete lab report looked like. But instead of giving them a rationale, all I did was repeatedly tell them this report would be worth 25% of their grade. I thought, wrongly, that the grade was a rationale. This threat did not motivate them; it just made them anxious and angry.

The second time around, I presented the lab report differently. I first told students that learning to write a lab report was the best thing they could do to prepare for college science courses. I told them that when I was in college, I wrote at least one lab report a week; if they wanted to be scientists, engineers, nurses, or doctors they would be following in my footsteps. I also assured them that we would take time to practice writing the report in class in order to help them become successful lab report writers.

When I told students what they were going to learn, why it was important, and how they were going to learn it, they were more motivated. They sat up straight, listened, and asked questions like "Are you sure we can really do it if we're not even in college yet? I tried hard last time and could not figure out what you wanted us to do."

WHY IT MATTERS

- Naming skills explicitly for students gives them useful academic vocabulary and helps them describe what they are trying to achieve.
- Framing the rationale helps motivate students.

WHAT IT LOOKS LIKE

- Connect the new skill to others the students have already mastered.
- Tell students how this new skill will help them learn or communicate knowledge in their content area.
- Give students an organizing mnemonic or metaphor to help them understand how the details you are explaining fit into the big picture.

TIPS TO MAKE IT WORK

- Activate students' prior knowledge to get them engaged.
- Keep your explanations or information to less than 5 minutes.
- When naming skills, use common language your school has agreed upon.

STAGE 2: MODELING—EXPERT THINKER AT WORK

In Stage 2 the teacher models, showing students how to use the new skill by actually demonstrating her use of it. Teacher and literacy expert Chris Tovani says that in this stage, teachers open their brains and make their "expert" thinking visible to students (Tovani, 2000). Modeling is essential: it shows kids *how*, rather than just telling them *what*. They understand what is expected of them and have something concrete to work toward.

In my first attempt at teaching lab reports, I did not yet understand the difference between actually modeling and just providing a finished model or example. I did give students a sample of a completed report. But I never modeled the *process*—the thinking and writing—used to produce that product.

On my second attempt, I showed students how I did every step of the lab report writing process. I started by putting up the assignment sheet, looking at it and saying, "Oh my gosh there is too much to look at on this page. I am completely overwhelmed! I'm going to do this one section at a time."

I covered up the rest of the sheet and started to read the instructions for the introduction: "Start by stating the name and experimental question for this experiment."

I paused, then said, "Shoot, I can't even remember what this experiment was called. Oh, but I have them written down on the handout with the procedures on it."

I riffled through a stack of papers that hopefully looked to my students like something they might pull out of their disastrous backpacks, grabbed the sheet, held it up victoriously, and said, "Here, everything I need is right on this sheet! The experiment was called 'investigating specific heat' and the experimental question was 'what is the relationship between specific heat and energy storage' so I guess I will write 'In the experiment called investigating specific heat we tried to answer the question: what is the relationship between specific heat and energy storage?'" As I spoke I wrote it down on a blank transparency so students could see all my thinking, as well as hear it.

In my early attempts, when I skipped the modeling and just told students what to do and sent them off, it was a nightmare—even my best students were off task or doing nothing.

This happens to us all. Some students don't understand the directions, so they can't start. Some students can't actually do independently what we've asked and need our assistance. Some students think they know what to do, but are wrong, and need to start over. All because we didn't *show* them how.

WHY IT MATTERS

- When students see a skill in action, they know what they are expected to do and how to get started.
- Watching the skill actually being performed helps struggling students gain the confidence to try it, offers English language learners a concrete mode of a process in action (as opposed to an abstract explanation), and gives exceptionally talented students a high expectation to work toward.

WHAT IT LOOKS LIKE

- Perform the skill at the highest level you would want your students to attain and clearly articulate your entire thought process.
- Have students note their questions or thoughts as you model.

TIPS TO MAKE IT WORK

- Stick to teacher modeling—don't let your students jump in! Students need this time to concentrate on learning how to perform a skill, so they have a more complete understanding of what to do when it is their turn.
- Keep modeling to under 10 minutes. Focus on just a few key processes.
- Give the time when you model a special feel. The students should be quiet and attentive. You might have to teach, practice, and reinforce these behaviors with younger students, but it will pay off in the end.

STAGE 3: GUIDED PRACTICE—TRYING IT OUT TOGETHER

During guided practice in Stage 3, the teacher supports students as they begin to experiment with the skill or strategy that was just modeled. This stage builds students' confidence and gives them a chance to check their own thinking against yours before they begin to experiment on their own. You also get to check your students' understanding.

During my first lab report attempt, I thought that having students read the assignment sheet aloud to their peers and giving them a couple of opportunities to ask questions was sufficient guided practice. Unfortunately, students weren't actually practicing anything, so they weren't actually learning anything.

The second time, when I taught students how to write an introduction, after the direct instruction and modeling, I invited my students to join me in the process.

> JENNIFER: Jonathan, please tell me where I might look to find out what the hypothesis was.
>
> JONATHAN: Well, last time you looked on that sheet.
>
> JENNIFER: What sheet?
>
> JONATHAN: The one that you found in that huge stack of papers, the one with the procedures and the title and the question on it.
>
> JENNIFER: Oh, this paper. Thanks, Jonathan, and Ronnisha, do you have this paper with you?
>
> RONNISHA: Yup.
>
> JENNIFER: Perfect, so could you tell me what our hypothesis was for this experiment?
>
> RONNISHA: My paper says, "If we test oil, water, and steel, then the substance with the highest specific heat—water—will also store the most energy.
>
> JENNIFER: Excellent, thank you, Ronnisha. Now for the writing. José, can you please tell me how to put that hypothesis into a sentence for our introduction?
>
> JOSÉ: Well, just write "our hypothesis was" and then write what Ronnisha said.

I probed more, and got José to tell me the entire hypothesis again. As he spoke, I wrote the second sentence of the introduction onto the overhead and asked the students to copy it down if they hadn't already done so.

WHY IT MATTERS

- Guided practice provides a low-stakes environment for students to practice together. Students build the confidence they will need to use the skill without direct teacher support.
- Solving problems together can build a culture of success in your classroom.

WHAT IT LOOKS LIKE

- Students help you use the skill in front of the whole class.
- You give students multiple chances to see and practice the new skill.

TIPS TO MAKE IT WORK

- Keep up the pace. Involve as many students as you can so your class doesn't check out.

- Use guided practice as a way to check for understanding. If a random sampling of students can demonstrate some ability to apply the skill, then they are ready for collaborative work.

STAGE 4: COLLABORATIVE WORK—NOW YOU SUPPORT EACH OTHER

Stage 4 represents a significant shift in responsibility for the new skill or strategy. Whereas in Stages 1–3, teachers do most of the work and the thinking, now students do. They practice the new skill in pairs or small groups as the teacher watches and takes opportunities to guide students' thinking process.

In my first lab report attempt, I thought I had addressed collaborative work. But my error was that I had students work collaboratively to *evaluate* my sample report using the rubric—a completely different skill. If I wanted them to learn to *write* lab reports, then that's the skill they should be practicing in their groups.

The second time around, I gave the groups 4 minutes to come up with the last sentence of the introduction. I asked for any last questions, and said I would be circulating if they needed anything during the work time.

As I walked around, I saw students rummaging through backpacks to find the assignment and heard them discovering that the last part of their introduction had to be a brief description of the experiment. They found the description on their lab sheets and turned it into the final sentence of their introduction.

The collaborative work stage let me check for understanding and push student thinking. As I circulated, I asked some of my less confident students to explain their process to me. How did they know what information to look for? Why did their lab report need an introduction? I also challenged my more advanced students to expand the description using what they remembered from doing the lab.

I find Stage 4 tremendously rewarding: I love watching students work together, since it lets me witness genuine productive learning, assess student progress, and choose next steps.

WHY IT MATTERS

- Students get another chance to see the skill modeled.
- Students get support from peers (Peregoy & Boyle, 2005).
- Strong students improve their understanding by explaining their use of the skill to peers.

WHAT IT LOOKS LIKE

- Assign students to collaborative work groups with a task to complete within a specific amount of time.
- Circulate, observe, confer, and give specific feedback.
- Differentiate. Give students individualized feedback.

TIPS TO MAKE IT WORK

- Consider students' academic and social skills in order to design effective work groups.

- Structure work so students talk about processes, not just answers.
- Use a timer, so you protect time for the independent practice that comes later.
- Check to be sure you are observing, not doing! If you have gone through the stages correctly, you should not answer many questions during collaborative work.

STAGE 5: INDEPENDENT WORK—WE MADE IT!

In Stage 5 students work individually to practice and demonstrate their mastery of the skill orally or in writing. While they work, the teacher circulates, assessing individuals' mastery or pushing next steps.

In my initial lab report attempt, I gave students what I thought was independent work time, but since I hadn't set up the expectation of silent, individual work, they used the time to goof off. I also expected much of the independent work to be done at home, which was unrealistic for their first-ever lab report.

When I have used GRR well, I look around my classroom during Stage 5 and see students madly writing or reading, applying the new strategy. When I retaught how to write lab reports, students had seen me model, had written the first sentence as a class, and had written the second sentence in collaborative groups. Only then did I ask each student to take 5 silent minutes to write the third sentence on their own. I said, "I appreciate how well you worked together. Now I need you to try this on your own." I circulated, supporting a student who had been absent the day of the modeling and pushing advanced students to use multiple detailed sentences.

WHY IT MATTERS

- Students will not do well on assessments if the assessment is the first time they have ever been asked to perform a skill on their own.
- When students practice skills on their own, they will take more ownership over them, will master them thoroughly, and will use them more authentically, transferring them to other areas of learning.

WHAT IT LOOKS LIKE

- Create a quiet, supportive environment where students feel confident and accountable for independent work.
- Engage all students in useful, meaningful work related to the skill being taught.
- Design work that will help students learn new content while practicing the newly acquired skill.

TIPS TO MAKE IT WORK

- Make sure your students understand that the reason for working quietly and independently is to give all students a chance to practice skills on their own in order to master them.
- Provide time for independent work in class. Don't assume that students have a quiet supportive place to do independent work elsewhere.

- Realize that "finishing" independent work will not look the same for every student; some may complete more work than others. The crucial thing is that every student get time to practice independently.

STAGE 6: SHARING AND REFLECTION—MAKING IT MEANINGFUL AND TRANSFERABLE

In this final stage students make their work public and reflect on how their use of the new skill helped them to understand new content. My PEBC staff developer described this as giving kids time to "zip up the backpack" for all the knowledge and skills I have crammed in. If they leave the class without zipping, or reflecting, everything falls out.

When students can name what they have learned and share it proudly, it signifies—not just for their peers and teacher, but for themselves—that the skill is now truly their own. Realizing this boosts their confidence and encourages them to use their new skill independently, flexibly, and strategically in other areas of learning. It inspires them to work hard to keep their success going.

The first time I assigned the lab reports and so few were turned in, I gave my students a questionnaire designed to make them feel guilty. I now realize that reflection should be designed to benefit students. The second go-round, after they had written independently their brief description of the lab, I asked students to reflect in writing on the following questions:

- What resources did you use?
- Do you think you could write all three sentences of the introduction on your own next time? Why or why not?
- How has your opinion of your ability to write lab reports changed since we started working on it together in class?

Students then shared one of their responses, most saying that they now believed they could write an introduction on their own, and that they felt better about it after practicing. Some students received applause from classmates!

After many months of work, when students completed an entire lab report independently, we reflected again. This time, I asked:

- Which section was the easiest for you to write, and why?
- Where did you struggle?
- What support would have helped?
- How will you get that support next time?

WHY IT MATTERS

- Giving students time to think about their learning helps them retain it.
- When students share their skill publicly, they gain confidence and can transfer the skill to new contexts.
- Shared success builds a supportive classroom culture.

WHAT IT LOOKS LIKE

- Students present their work to their classmates and are recognized for it.
- Students reflect about how the new skill helped them learn new content and how they might use it in the future.

TIPS TO MAKE IT WORK

- Don't skip this stage or cut it short.
- Have students reflect in a variety of ways: in writing and orally, in pairs and as a whole class, on their own work and on the work of others, on short-term and long-term objectives.
- Start each day by reflecting on what was learned and accomplished the day before.

QUESTIONS AND CONCERNS ABOUT USING GRR

Teachers who are considering using GRR in their classrooms or who have just started using it often have some general questions or nagging concerns about this framework. This is only to be expected when adopting a teaching practice that is new and different. In the sections below, I address the questions I have heard most often.

Isn't This What I Already Do?

You may be surprised how easy it is to forget a crucial stage if you don't think purposefully about each of the six. I know exceptional teachers who are still weak in one of the stages.

My own Achilles's heel is skipping modeling to go straight into guided practice. But because I am aware of that tendency, I plan so as to prevent it. Which stage do you do poorly or skip inadvertently? When you acknowledge your Achilles's heel and plan purposefully to compensate, you will feel empowered to lead your students to independent thinking and learning.

Isn't This Elementary?

Some teachers wonder: If I want my students to be ready for college, shouldn't I treat them like college students? If you treat your students like college students before they are ready, you are setting them up for failure. The best thing you can do to help your students prepare for college is help them build up their skills until they have a comprehensive repertoire of strategies they can use flexibly and independently.

What If I Don't Have Time for All This?

As one of our PEBC staff developers always reminds us, "Teaching is choosing." You may have to prioritize some content and skills over others, but what good are you doing if you teach 100 skills that none of your students can do independently next year?

What Skills Should I Target?

Since using the six stages of GRR requires very supportive and highly structured learning, use it only for skills that are most essential or transferable, ideally the ones that will help your students become better thinkers and learners in multiple content areas. And don't waste your time using GRR on things students can already do for themselves.

What If I Already Do This, but Students Still Don't Master the Skills?

Review Figure 11.1. Are you really addressing all six stages? If so, are you spending enough time on each? At which stage do you lose your students? How can you better support your students so they can be successful during this stage?

What If One of the Stages Doesn't Work for Me?

Play to your strengths and develop your weaknesses. For students to gain independence, they must progress through all of the stages. Think hardest about the stage you like the least. Observe how a colleague teaches it. Do your students need more support? Different expectations? More of one of the preceding stages?

TIME FRAMES FOR USING GRR IN INSTRUCTIONAL PLANNING

Teachers use GRR to give their students the academic skills that will help them think and learn independently. Some of these skills, like asking questions of a text, can be taught in a single lesson or a few lessons. Fitting a full GRR lesson into a 45- or 50-minute period requires moving students through the stages quickly and precisely. But it is doable if you hold yourself to the following time allotments:

- Direct instruction, 5 minutes
- Modeling, 5–10 minutes
- Guided practice, 5–10 minutes
- Collaborative work, 10 minutes
- Independent work, 15 minutes
- Reflection, 5 minutes

Other processes, like writing a 5-paragraph essay or collaborating with peers, are more complex and can take an entire unit or year to teach. GRR supports these more challenging behavioral and academic objectives as well.

For example, when I finally taught my students how to write effective lab reports, we did it over many months. Each time we did a lab activity, I focused our work on only one part of the report. In my discussion of the six stages, I've explained how I did this with introductions; I taught the other sections of the lab report similarly. It took until April or May for students to write lab reports completely independently. I will never forget the sheer joy I felt in June when I read their final lab reports: Every student submitted a report; every report contained all sections; and, best of all, every report demonstrated an understanding of the chemistry involved in the lab *and* of the process of writing a lab report.

IF THEY'RE NOT LEARNING, I'M NOT TEACHING

When I first learned about GRR, it seemed foolishly straightforward and possibly superfluous. But I have found that its simplicity is part of its beauty. Teachers already have the skills needed. There's nothing flashy or new. It makes sense. And it works.

GRR keeps me honest. It would have been easy for me to think that my students did not complete their lab reports that first time for reasons unrelated to my teaching. But using GRR, I have to ask myself if I've equipped students with everything they need in order to be successful:

- Have I told them what they are doing and why?
- Have I modeled it for them? Have I guided them through it a couple of times?
- Have they worked collaboratively?
- Have they practiced independently while I watch?
- Have I given them chances to reflect on their learning and share?

When I have done all of those things, I can feel confident that all of my students are ready to succeed independently.

HOW TO BEGIN

- Think about a lesson in which you taught a skill-based objective. Try to identify the six stages of GRR in that lesson.
- Plan a lesson using the six stages.
- Think about routines and structures you can build into your classroom that will support GRR.

LINGERING QUESTIONS

- What is a healthy balance of skills and content in a middle school or high school course?
- How can I use GRR to better meet the individual needs of each of my learners?
- How can I make sure I am teaching the skills that will help students become independent learners and thinkers?

LEADERSHIP PERSPECTIVES

From Diane Lauer, former principal of Conrad Ball Middle School:

- *Planning scaffolded instruction.* For so many secondary teachers, *scaffolding* can be a nebulous term. But when you put that idea in the GRR matrix, it becomes clearer how we can support our students at each stage as they progress toward independence. Often, secondary teachers want to go from modeling to independent work, rushing through the guided practice.

- *Learn from the specialists.* Performance-based instructors in classes like physical education, art, and music probably already use GRR intuitively and skillfully: Learn from them. GRR is a great leverage point to focus on as a whole staff. It is a topic that teachers in every content area can connect to, discuss, and point to in their lessons. I would encourage teachers to observe each other teach in the various stages of GRR to help them visualize and better understand the nuances of the model.

From Garrett Phelan, principal of César Chávez Charter School (Capitol Hill campus):

- *Rewarding professional work.* We have all heard the mantra "work smarter, not harder." Kirmes raises questions about the real work a teacher should be doing. Hard work will never disappear in our profession. But hard work that is unsuccessful or unsatisfying debilitates us, diminishes our sense of efficacy. GRR helps our hard work be smart: It lets us create the conditions that allow students to make meaning and reflect on their learning. That is rewarding work.
- *GRR for the high school graduate.* Each teacher should use GRR at a developmentally appropriate level for his or her students. But a high school should also look at GRR as a 4-year plan. When a student graduates, has he been mentored, apprenticed, and then set free as an independent thinker?

RELATED READINGS

Cris Tovani's book *I Read It, but I Don't Get It* (Tovani, 2000) illustrates strong modeling in a high school classroom. Particularly relevant for Stage 2 or if you want to see how GRR can be applied across a yearlong course.

David Conley's book *College Knowledge* (Conley, 2005) outlines content-specific skills successful high school graduates should have. Consider using GRR to teach these important skills.

Gravity Goldberg and Jennifer Serravallo's book *Conferring With Readers* (Goldberg & Serravallo, 2007) powerfully demonstrates how to support students well during the collaborative and independent work stages by providing a model for conferring that builds students' confidence and supports their skill development.

Suzanne Peregoy and Owen Boyle's book *Reading, Writing, and Learning in ESL* (Peregoy & Boyle, 2005) focuses in Chapter 3 on how group work can support English language learners, offering structures and strategies that will help all students learn how to learn through collaboration with peers.

CHAPTER 12

Time to Think: Using the Workshop Structure So Students Think and Teachers Listen

Samantha Bennett

IN THIS CHAPTER: In describing what makes literacy expert Cris Tovani's teaching different, Samantha Bennett, Tovani's instructional coach, synthesizes many of the themes in this volume. Bennett focuses on Tovani's use of the workshop model of instruction to help students learn that "thinking is the thing." She describes specific strategies Tovani uses to listen deeply to students, challenge their thinking, build their understanding, and foster their independence.

KEY POINTS

- The workshop model is a structure and routine that helps teachers focus on and foster student thinking.
- Teachers must define their work as listening to and researching students.
- To propel their thinking, students need authentic tasks, texts, and a "need to know."
- Conferring with each student lets teachers instruct, assess, and honor individual student's thinking.

"To find the core of a [classroom]," wrote Theodore Sizer and Nancy Sizer (1999), "look at the way the people in it spend their time—how they relate to each other, how they tangle with ideas. Look for the contradictions between words and practice, with the fewer the better. . . . Its hour by hour functioning is what is important. Judge the [classroom] not on what it says but on how it keeps" (p. 18). "Keeping" is about the maintaining and sustaining routines and patterns of teaching and learning, and Cris Tovani's secondary classroom keeps differently from most.

As you enter Cris's room, your eyes zoom around a space set up to support reading, writing, and talk. The back wall is filled floor to ceiling, side to side with books. A magazine rack overflows with current issues of *Skateboarder*, *O*, *People*, *JET*, *The New Yorker*, and *Sports Illustrated* magazines. Over the board are posted these guiding questions:

- How does fear distort reality?
- When would you be willing to sacrifice freedom for security?
- What does it take for an individual to rebel against authority?
- How does ignorance empower those in control?

On another wall, chart paper spills over with student writing—their questions, comments, connections. Desks are in groups of four, with just enough space for Cris to weave among them.

Cris's students "keep" differently. You see students in a group, huddling over a short newspaper article about self-immolation in Afghanistan. One student asks, "Why are the women treated so poorly? What did they do to deserve it?" Another student responds, "What *could* a woman do to deserve setting herself on fire?!" Another says, "How many people is it going to take before someone pays attention?" And then this: "I think it is courageous. It is the only way you can say no!"

Cris's instruction "keeps" differently. As you search for the teacher, you see she is on one knee, leaning into one of the groups. "That is amazing!" she exclaims. "I didn't even think about that when I read that passage. Shante, do you know what you just did? You did what good readers do! You made a connection to your own life that not only helped you understand, but by sharing it, you helped your entire group! Wow, I can't wait to share your thinking with the rest of the class."

Cris's *teaching* "keeps" differently. Each day, Cris deliberately plans her instruction around one enduring understanding: that reading, writing, and thinking helps students make meaning of, and gives them power in, the world. It is what she wants students to remember in 10 years, when the plots of novels have faded, the chemical compound for salt has dissolved, the formula for the slope of a line has slipped away. She wants them to remember that their engagement as thinking adults in the world is what matters most.

Cris Tovani herself "keeps" differently. As author of two best-selling books on adolescent literacy, *I Read It, but I Don't Get It* (2000) and *Do I Really Have to Teach Reading?* (2004), Cris could quit the classroom and bask in her stardom. Instead, she digs into learning with her struggling high school readers and writers each day. She also coaches teachers of English, social studies, math, and science, not only in her school, but around the nation, helping them help students learn more, do more, and perform better in school and beyond.

I became Cris's instructional coach through my work at the Public Education & Business Coalition. I get to be an extra set of eyes and ears in her high school English classes and in her demonstration lessons across the country. Her teaching synthesizes many of the principles and practices you have read about in this volume. She believes that young people can think more powerfully when a teacher shows them how, by making meaning from text and articulating their thoughts in talk and on paper. And she believes that their ability to make meaning will help students act more intelligently and courageously in the world.

The workshop model is the persistent pursuit that allows Cris to "keep" student learning at the forefront of her practice. The workshop model is the daily structure and routine that helps Cris practice these beliefs, building student understanding (described by Hoffer in Chapter 10) and using Gradual Release of Responsibility (described by Kirmes in Chapter 11) to promote student independence.

THE WORKSHOP MODEL: TIME FOR STUDENTS TO THINK

> *School is a place where young people go to watch old people work.*
> *—An (unfortunate) old adage*

When Cris is teaching, the classroom becomes a literal and figurative workshop, where students spend most of each class "doing the work" of learning: reading, writing, and talking about important content that will empower them to participate in, lead, and transform society.

The workshop model—the everyday pattern of Cris's instruction—has five essential parts:

1. *The opening structure.* Cris begins with a few minutes to welcome students and quickly assess their background knowledge of the topic.
2. *The minilesson.* Cris sets the purpose for both skill practice and knowledge acquisition.
3. *The work time.* Cris releases students to read and write. She confers to learn about how students are making meaning and how she can help them do it better today, while she plans her next steps for the debrief (today) and the minilesson tomorrow. This is real-time assessment driving instruction and purposeful differentiation, one student at a time.
4. *The "catch."* She pulls the group back together, adding another layer of instruction, if during work time she notices that student stamina is beginning to wane, that students complete the task in the minilesson, or that students are showing patterns of brilliance or of confusion that she wants to address with the entire group. This "catch" lets Cris label the thinking she heard in the first work time, or think-aloud with a more sophisticated text so students can continue to build their background knowledge. The key is that the "catch" is quick; she doesn't keep students for long, quickly releasing them again to the original task or an additional task. I use the analogy of fly-fishing—you have to throw students back into the water before they stop breathing and die!
5. *The debrief.* At the end of class, Cris gathers students to celebrate and synthesize the great thinking they did during the work time.

Figure 12.1 shows the cycle of a workshop in terms of classroom time.

Recently, Cris taught a demonstration lesson in Williston, North Dakota, in an eighth-grade American history class (two 46-minute periods over 2 days). They had just begun a unit on the thirteen original colonies. The students in this class were representative of the school population: about 33% qualified for free or reduced-price lunch, approximately 15% were people of color, and none were officially designated as English language learners.

THE OPENING STRUCTURE: SETTING THE PURPOSE
AND ASSESSING BACKGROUND KNOWLEDGE

Cris begins, "So, Mr. C. was sharing with me that you were studying the American Colonies. As I started thinking about how our country was formed, a couple of

Figure 12.1. Workshop as a Daily Cyclical Structure

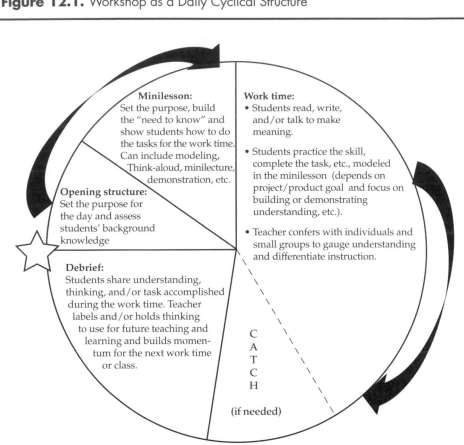

questions popped into my head: What does it mean to be an American? and How did the original colonists shape what we believe today? I think they are good questions, because they don't necessarily have one right answer. Please jot down on that sticky note in front of you what you think it means to be an American. I'm going to come around and talk to you as you write. Get to work."

This took just one minute, and already most students have their pencils going, brainstorming a list. As they write, Cris walks around and talks to individual students. She says to one, "Wow. That is a huge idea. Can you talk to me more about that? That is so important. Add that to your paper so you can remember it later." Students continue to brainstorm on the sticky notes for 4 more minutes, and then Cris calls their attention up front to the overhead.

She says, "OK, what did you come up with?" On the overhead, she writes their responses:

- Not to be ruled
- To be free
- To be treated equally
- To further peace in the rest of the world

- To have rights
- To be whatever you want to be when you grow up

Armed with some clues about what students already know about the topic, Cris dives into the minilesson:

THE MINILESSON: SHOWING STUDENTS HOW TO BUILD BACKGROUND KNOWLEDGE OF CONTENT BY MAKING MEANING FROM TEXT

Cris continues, "OK, put your names on those sticky notes. We are going to bring these back at the end of our 2 days together. We have a little bit of studying to do first, and I want you to see how much smarter you get over the next 92 minutes we'll spend together. I found another piece of text that is going to help us get smarter about our guiding questions, What does it mean to be an American? and How did the colonists shape what we believe today?"

Cris goes on, "This text is from a book called *A History of US: Making Thirteen Colonies* (Hakim, 2005). She writes about history kind of like the *National Enquirer*. She puts lots of juicy stories into it. I'm going to read you a little bit."

Cris reads the first paragraph and then stops to think aloud, "Let's annotate the text here. When we add our questions and connections on the side of the text, it helps us remember our thinking and we can come back and use it later when we are looking for support for the arguments in our essays. That way, we don't need to reread the whole thing. I'm going to write a few questions I have next to the text: 'A market for people? Slaves and women? Why did the colonists have to buy wives? Were wives like slaves? This makes me think that people had to be tough to survive here.' I'm also wondering if this thinking might help me figure out something important about the colonists' lives? I need to read some more.

"Now it is your turn. Go to the chunks that look interesting to you, but here is the key: We are trying to figure out how the original colonists shaped our beliefs about what it means to be an American. As you read, annotate the text, just like we did here. It can be a connection or a question, or anything that pops into your head when you read. I'm going to come around and talk to you about what you're thinking."

THE WORK TIME: STUDENTS READ, WRITE, AND TALK TO THINK

With that 12-minute minilesson, Cris arms students with a reason to read and releases them to do so for 15 minutes straight. As they read, Cris circulates, going first to students who aren't annotating, to help them find an entry point—a place to dig in, make meaning, and write to hold their thinking.

She approaches a young man who is staring glassy-eyed at the page. Cris says, "Are you stuck? Where are you going to start? You don't know? OK. Make a little chunk mark here. (She draws a line after the first paragraph.) And one here, and one here. OK, choose *one* of those chunks to read, then write down what it makes you think. There is no wrong answer. Write down what you think. It might be something you want to add to your definition of what it means to be an American. Give it a try and I'll be back in a few minutes to see your thinking."

With that individualized attention and specific direction to read "one chunk," he gets right to work. I imagine him thinking, "OK, I can read one chunk and write something down. This crazy lady thinks I can do it and I'm pretty sure she is going to come back and check, so I guess I'll try."

Cris approaches another student, looks over his shoulder, reads his annotation and says,

> That's such a smart question, "Why do they get to win the land if the Native Americans were already there?"—Yeah! Do you know anything about what land ownership was like in England? Could just anyone own land? No. You had to be pretty rich. Good, add that. That is one of those things I'm thinking is still with us today. Write that down. That will help you write a response to our guiding question. Great job. Keep going.

Cris confers to build relationships and to get to know students so she can differentiate instruction—one student at a time, just in time.

THE DEBRIEF: TIME TO SYNTHESIZE THINKING

After 15 minutes, Cris calls the class back together: "OK, I know not everyone has finished the article, so I'm just going to read the last few paragraphs out loud and ask you to hold one more piece of thinking." She reads aloud, and then continues:

> Everyone pair up. I want you to share your thinking, share some of your annotations. See if you can get smarter by talking to someone else. If they wrote something that makes sense to you, add it to your paper. Remember, we are trying to figure out how the colonists influenced our beliefs about what it means to be an American today.

The students talk while Cris circulates and listens in, adding comments and complimenting students who are sharing. Just before the bell rings, she says,

> We'll start tomorrow by sharing some of the amazing comments I heard while I was listening to you talk. Please leave your articles on the table so I can give you credit for your thinking today. I can't wait to dive back into this with you tomorrow. Thank you for your thinking.

WHO IS DOING THE WORK?: THE FIRST FORTY-SIX MINUTES

As Cris's coach, my main role is to observe carefully, to label, synthesize, and share with her what I noticed and wondered as she was teaching. Because Cris believes that whoever is doing the reading, writing, and talking is doing the thinking, I always chart the actual time, in minutes, of teacher talk vs. time for students to think and work. Figure 12.2 shows my notes about use of time during the lesson and the implications for student learning. Twenty-eight minutes were protected for student thinking. Clearly, the students are doing the work in this classroom. But, the

Figure 12.2. Workshop Time Chart

	ACTIVITY	PURPOSE	TEACHER TALKS (min.)	STUDENTS READ, WRITE, TALK (min.)
9:27-9:37	*Opening structure:* What does it mean to be an American? ❑ Question ❑ Students respond on sticky notes ❑ Cris confers with individual students ❑ Cris records students' thinking	Sets purpose of lessons Elicits student thinking Reinforces that student thinking matters most Makes student thinking permanent and public, so that the teacher and students can revisit it later	4	6
9:37-9:49	*Minilesson:* Think aloud	Models how Cris makes meaning as a reader Shows students how to annotate and talk back to the text, ask questions, make connections, and synthesize thinking Labels nonfiction text structures Sets purpose for reading Asks students to label teacher's thinking as she reads	12	
9:49-10:04	*Work time:* ❑ Students read and annotate ❑ Cris confers with individual students	Reading = thinking Writing = thinking Listening and probing for more = teaching	0	15
10:04-10:06	*Catch:* ❑ Cris reads last chunk aloud ❑ Cris asks students to record, or "hold," their thinking one last time	Bringing closure to article Reading aloud for students who didn't get to the end	2	0
10:06-10:13	*Release:* Students pair up to share thinking	Talking = thinking	0	7
Total			18	28

implications for Cris's work outside the classroom are huge. How does Cris plan for the use of time in a workshop?

PLANNING FOR STUDENTS TO DO THE WORK: FIGURING OUT WHY

When most teachers sit down to plan, they usually ask themselves, "What am *I* going to do tomorrow?" When Cris plans, she asks herself, "What are the *students* going to do tomorrow?"

This is a paradigm shift. Instead of thinking, "What is going to come out of *my* mouth tomorrow?" teachers have to think, "What do I want to come out of *students'* mouths tomorrow? What 'text' (article, photograph, diagram, cartoon, chart, quote, and so on) can I offer to get them reading, writing, and talking to think?"

First, Cris has to get clear on what she expects them to know (guided and informed by state and local standards, district assessments, and so on). She must prioritize standards and also must articulate something that standards and curricula generally lack: why the content is worth knowing. This is crucial for student engagement and motivation. Cris reflected:

> When the teacher asked me to do a demo lesson on the colonies, the first question I asked myself was, "Why do eighth graders need to know about the American Colonies? Why does this matter?" First, I was thinking "What does it mean to be an American?" There are so many pieces to this, and then ideas for text started bubbling up and more questions emerged. . . . "What did those colonists do that is still here today?" . . . I had to build the need to know, that is why the questions are so important. . . . So, I Googled in "What does it mean to be an American?" and thousands of documents popped up! I could build a whole 9-week unit around those big, juicy questions and find lots . . . of text to help students build their understanding. (Interview, September 25, 2007).

So, how did Cris structure the second day to help students continue to build their background knowledge and demonstrate understanding?

CONNECTING ONE DAY TO THE NEXT: THE OPENING STRUCTURE AND MINILESSON ON DAY TWO

On Day 2, Cris begins, "Last night I did a little homework. So many of you asked or wrote about freedom yesterday, and that made me think about what it means to be free and what it means to be a patriot. I Googled in the words *patriotic quotes.* Here is the thinking of some famous Americans: Harry Truman was a president, Jackie Robinson was the first Black professional baseball player, Thomas Wolfe was a Southern writer. Pick two or three of the quotes to read. If one strikes you as interesting, circle it. Just like yesterday, add some of your thinking to the quote if it strikes you." She pauses to let students do this.

"Last night, I also read through your annotations and I want to share how smart you are. Here are some things you wrote that will help you begin your essay today on what is means to be an American."

Cris puts up an overhead titled "Smart Thinking from Yesterday." She continues, "So here are a few things you wrote":

> Why did the English colonists have more rights than other Europeans who came here? (John)

> What does pluralistic and veto mean? (Scott, Eli, and Jim)

> Why would colonists have less freedom in a New World? (Eli and Sarah)

Why do people who move to America have more rights than people in Europe? (Kenzie)

Why do French only invite Catholics into their colonies? (Carrie)

Why doesn't everyone have the same freedom? (Lonnie)

"Wow. That list is a great start. I can tell we are getting smarter about this big question of what it means to be an American. I want to give you some more things to think about today before we dive into the writing. I brought two different articles today to help you. One is an essay from a newspaper writer. He addresses the same question I'm going to ask you to write about today: What does it mean to be an American? He is writing this right after 9/11, so you know it will be filled with lots of emotion.

"The other choice is from a Frenchman named Crevecoeur on what it means to be an American too, but from a historical perspective. If any of you are up for a challenge today, you might be interested in this text. Just like yesterday, our purpose for reading is to get more information about what it means to be an American. Do some more reading and annotating today, and then we'll dive into writing an essay. I'll be circulating so I can hear your thinking."

On Day 2, the opening structure and minilesson took only 4 minutes, most of which was used to highlight student thinking from the day before. Because of the time she took yesterday, to think aloud and show students how to annotate, the only "teacher talk" today was Cris introducing the quotes and the explanation of the text choices.

THE WORK TIME: GOING DEEPER WITH THE CONTENT, ONE STUDENT AT A TIME

Cris releases the students to read and begins conferring. She reads a student's annotations and comments, "I see you are underlining a few sentences here. Great. Can you tell me why you are underlining them?"

The student replies, "I think they are important."

Cris responds,

Great! I agree with you, I think that sentence is really important too, but I'm going to give you a challenge. Can you add to the side here *why* you think it is important? Then you can use that for your writing later today, and you don't have to reread the whole thing and do that thinking all over again. I'm excited to see what you come up with. Keep going.

Then Cris moves on to another student.

The student shares, "I think it is important that the rights are written down somewhere. It is kind of like our rules in class, since Mr. C. has them posted, we can't say we didn't know."

"Great! Write that. That is at the crux of our government. When we know our rights, no one can take them away. Amazing. Keep going."

Cris confers with students for 10 more minutes. One by one she helps students make meaning, record their thinking, and build their background knowledge—on vocabulary, primary documents (the Federalist Papers, Constitution, and Bill of Rights) and the rule of law. As she confers, she sees that students have enough annotations to begin their essays. But she knows from experience that students may need to talk about their thinking before they write. So she asks them to pair up and share their annotations and how they might start their essays about what it means to be an American.

After listening to students' conversations for 9 minutes, Cris decides students are ready to write. She calls them back together for a "catch."

THE "CATCH" AND "RELEASE": CRIS MODELS HER OWN WRITING AND GIVES STUDENTS TIME TO WRITE

Cris wants to show students how to synthesize their thinking—from their reading, their annotations, and their conversations—and begin to write an essay about what it means to be an American.

She begins, "Now it is time to start organizing your thoughts into an essay. Listening to your thinking over the past 2 days and talking to you has really influenced my thinking about this question. Many of you wrote yesterday that being an American means that we fight for what is right. I'm going to begin my essay with a quote about that: 'Throughout our history, and still today, the most effective way to love our country is to fight like [heck] to change it.' (Kazin, 2008)." She thinks aloud as she writes on the overhead:

> At first, this quote disturbed me. Now that I've thought about it, I realize how important it is for Americans to participate in their government. To be an American means to work hard to make the USA better. I think a true American is brave and willing to do what is right even when it isn't easy. Like the colonists did.

Cris wraps up her minilesson saying,

> I'm going to stop there, to give you time to write, but I know I'll need some examples about the Colonists fighting for what they thought was right. I'm going to have to go back into the texts we've read to support my argument.
>
> We only have about 10 minutes to write, so just get down your initial thoughts about what it means to be an American. See if you can fill a half-sheet of paper in the next 10 minutes. If you want, you can start your essay with one of the quotes you circled today. Get to work.

The "catch" took about 4 minutes, but it set students up powerfully for their next chunk of work time. Cris both told them what she wanted them to do and showed them how. She modeled her choice of a quote to begin her essay, tied it to her opinion, and then showed them that her next step needed to be supporting her argument with evidence from the text.

Students wrote for 10 minutes (the "release"); then Cris brought them back in time for one student to share the start of her essay, which functioned as the debrief.

Cris ended Day 2 with, "Wow! Thank you so much for your thinking today. I can't wait to read these essays. Please leave them on your desk so I can pour over them tonight."

The flow of this 46 minutes of instruction differed from Day 1—only 9 minutes of teacher talk and 37 minutes of students reading, writing, and talking. Because Cris used the day before to build the need to know and introduce a big question (What does it mean to be an American?) and an important task (the essay) she was able to release the students to do the work for a longer period of time on Day 2.

WHAT THE STUDENTS WROTE

So, what impact did 92 minutes of scaffolded reading, writing, and talk have on the students' understanding?

At the opening of class on Day 1 David wrote on his sticky note that being an American meant "To be able to have stuff that is yours." At the end of Day 2 he wrote,

> I think it means to have freedom like to go to school to get an education, to have a religion you want and not one you are forced have. In America you can work hard to get what you want. In America you can choose what to be, you don't get told. Americans fight for what is right and to right the wrongs that you see. That's what I think it means to be an American.

His paragraph on Day 2 still shows a fairly basic understanding, but if you read closely, he demonstrates one of the founding beliefs of the American colonists that lingers today—that you can work hard here and choose what you want to be. That is a big idea that began with the American colonists.

On Day 1 Allison wrote, "It means having freedom and rights. We have rules, but they let us have a free life. We are able to have different beliefs. To be treated equally."

On Day 2 she expands, using the words of Harry S. Truman. She opens with his quote, "You know that being an American is more than a matter of where your parents came from. It is a belief that all men are created free and equal and that everyone deserves an even break." She continues in her own words:

> There is that strong word again, *belief*. Being an American means having our own beliefs and not being forced to believe in one certain thing only. We have the choice of our religion, of who our role models are, of what we dream. Being an American lets us have a good education. The choice of what we want to do in life and the right to vote. We have to participate to make a difference.

She used a quote to support her thinking, and the word *choice* resonates in her writing, giving so much for her teacher to tie more content to, for example, What choices did the colonists have in this new land? I can imagine some great texts to inspire her thinking tied to that question.

After a week or two of continuing to study the lives of the colonists and revising these essays, students' writing would be worthy of publication in any op-ed column in any newspaper in America. Why these values and beliefs have endured, and why we fight for them, is a topic every thinking adult in America is concerned about right now.

WHY DOES THE WORKSHOP MODEL MATTER?

Using the workshop model matters because it is a daily agreement to focus on what matters most: student thinking. Workshop can help students gain agency and urgency in their learning.

When the focus of class is what comes out of students' mouths instead of the teacher's, it will eventually change students' worlds. When you structure your class time in the way you've seen Cris Tovani do here, students will gain the courage and the risk-taking habits of mind to become the reading, writing, speaking-out kind of citizens we need to have succeed in and lead our world.

For the workshop model to work, it can't just be about the use of instructional time. We need to plan differently—to give students a reason to read and write, and an authentic, real-world task.

As Suzanne Plaut writes in the introduction to this book, "Education is meaningless if it does not actually increase the student's ability . . . to make sense of and engage with the world. . . . literacy enables students to have a voice, take a stand, and make a difference."

Our students need us. Be intentional. Know *why* you are doing everything you do. Structure time for students to read, write, and talk; ask them to do important work. Your work in planning for their work is essential. Every teacher plays a role. Play.

HOW TO BEGIN

- When planning, ask: "What will my students do tomorrow?" and then, "What information or modeling do they need from me to do it?"
- Be intentional: Use time for students to do the work. Invite a colleague into your classroom to time the amount of teacher talk vs. student reading, writing, and talking.
- Use GRR (see Chapter 11) and show students *how*. Try doing your own assignments, and use your steps as the basis for minilessons.
- Be able to answer these questions about any content you teach: "Why do students need to know this? How will knowing this make them a better adult? What do I want them to remember 10 years from now?" Align your instruction and assignments to your goals for understanding.
- Spend less time grading papers and more time documenting students' thinking.

LINGERING QUESTIONS

- What does understanding really look like?
- How much evidence is enough? How do I *really* know what my students know and are able to do?

- Is it possible for secondary teachers to know 120 students deeply?
- If we focus on knowing students as deeply as we know our content, what are the implications for the school structure, content demands, and curriculum design?

LEADERSHIP PERSPECTIVES

From Diane Lauer, former principal of Conrad Ball Middle School:

- *Responsive planning.* Not only does Tovani use class time differently from most teachers, she also plans differently. She monitors the learning of the class and changes the shape of what they will do tomorrow based on what happened today. This is a *big* shift for a lot of teachers who plan in advance (as they were taught to do) and have tons of worksheets, labs, or activities ready for kids. How does seeing Tovani's teaching (and planning) shift your paradigm about what and how to plan?
- *Foundational frameworks.* It wasn't until teachers at my school started visiting PEBC lab classrooms that we began to truly understand the instructional shift involved in the use of the workshop model and GRR. I think that these frameworks are bigger and more foundational than the thinking strategies; you see a lot of movement in student achievement when teachers start to use these structures.

From Garrett Phelan, principal of César Chávez Charter School (Capitol Hill campus):

- *Who is doing the work?* When I walk through our building to observe, I often ask myself, "Who is doing the work of thinking in these classrooms?" If it is the teachers, might we in some way be usurping students' civil rights? Do we have the patience to let them develop literacy and thinking?
- *Standards are not the enemy.* We see how Tovani works with history standards in a meaningful way. Standards do not have to be our enemy; they can be the stimulus for us to create essential questions and enduring understandings. This requires synthesis. As teachers, we must ask, "What underlies the standards? What big question might be implied? Why am I teaching this?" At our school we have sought to embrace the standards and not fight them, so we can focus on the real work of protecting the right to literacy of all students.

RELATED READINGS

Samantha Bennett's book *That Workshop Book* (Bennett, 2007) describes thinking strategies and the workshop model in K–8 literacy classrooms.

Debbie Miller's book *Reading with Meaning* (Miller, 2002) is a compelling story of implementing the workshop model with first graders. A must-read for any secondary teacher who says, "My kids can't sit still for more than 15 minutes."

Ron Ritchhart's book *Intellectual Character* (Ritchhart, 2002) offers an incredible blend of theory, research, and stories of powerful middle school teachers. Every time I reread this book, my thinking about thinking changes.

Grant Wiggins and Jay McTighe's book *Understanding by Design* (Wiggins & McTighe, 2005) helps teachers set curriculum priorities and focus on students' "need-to-know." A great step-by-step guide to designing empowering curriculum.

The National Research Council's book *Engaging Schools* (NRC, 2004) calls attention to the social context in which learning takes place and explores how to structure schools to maximize student motivation and engagement.

Reflecting on Part III

- Consider patterns across the four chapters in Part III. How do the authors define the role of teachers and of students in the learning process?
- At your school, which of the principles or practices described in Part III are already in place? How might your faculty build upon those strengths?
- These authors state or imply that secondary teachers must spend their time differently. How do you choose to spend time with your students? What type of "talk" and "tasks" do you ask students to do?
- How well do your school's assessment policies and practices align with what your faculty says you value most?
- What connections do you see between the general frameworks described in Part III and the beliefs and practices described in Part II?
- Consider this text as a whole. What *assumptions* do this group of authors hold? What do you *agree* with in the text? What do you want to *argue* with in the text? What parts of the text do you want to *aspire* to? (Gray, 2005)
- As you consider this entire text and your discussions of it, how has your view of your work been clarified, challenged, or changed?
- What is one specific action you, your department, grade level, or faculty will commit to?
- How can your colleagues support one another and hold each other accountable to protect all students' literacy rights?
- What would success look like?

LEADERSHIP PERSPECTIVES

From Diane Lauer, former principal of Conrad Ball Middle School:

- *Common language.* The only way to create synergy in your building is to have a common language. That's why teachers like to talk about kids so much: It's what they have in common. "I have him in math, and you have him in art, and he's a pain." Until we have a common language and a vision, we are not going to have powerful instructional conversations. If we have that common language, we have a clear picture of where we are going and can make connections across content and skills and even the process by which we scaffold learning. When we are all doing this together, then we can help each other. What common language has this volume offered your faculty?
- *A shift in how we plan.* Teachers typically plan "Here are all the things kids need to know and be able to do" as a kind of grocery list. These four authors tell us ways that teachers might plan differently. If I really want a student to under-

stand a concept like "civil rights," what are the leverage points? How do we embed the skills in the content? If I am really thinking about students being literate, then my key questions (which should impact the way I plan) should always be: What skills does a human need to be literate in my content? What does it really mean to think scientifically or artistically or like a historian? Do I really understand that for myself? And can I infuse that professional level of what that thinking needs to be like in the lessons I design and in the way I use time?

From Garrett Phelan, principal of César Chávez Charter School (Capitol Hill campus):

- *Paradigm shift.* If we approached teaching as a guarantee and a commitment to the right to think, how would we shift our ideas of teaching? If you read closely and accepted the challenges of this text, what would you let go of? What would you revise? What new things would you adopt? Could we let go of control and being center stage? Could we as teachers observe, coach, and listen more?
- *The school schedule.* What sort of school schedule allows for inquiry, thinking, practicing, and reflecting? How far are we as a staff willing to go to promote literacy? What are we willing to give up?
- *Students' rights.* Rights always have to be fought for, defended, and protected. What would it look like in your classroom to fight for, defend, and protect the civil rights of your students to think and be literate in your discipline? A right is not more freedom, but more responsibility. A classroom with a literacy foundation is a classroom supporting young people to be more responsible for themselves, others, and their community.

Implications of Adolescent Literacy Rights and Future Directions

Suzanne Plaut

Literacy is a currency that buys students access, opportunity, and power in our democratic society. As Kofi Annan stated poignantly in a speech launching the United Nations Literacy Decade, "Literacy is the key to unlocking the cage of human misery; the key to delivering the potential of every human being; the key to opening up a future of freedom and hope" (Annan, 2007).

We entrust teachers with the crucial work of turning these keys. Every secondary teacher can and should help students develop the literacy skills needed to build content understanding and to become increasingly independent as learners. Teachers themselves also need support as they learn and apply new instructional practices. And secondary schools' systems and structures must change, toward a culture that values and expects participation of all its members.

Adolescents have a right to much more than the sad scenes that Hoffer (Chapter 10) and Woods (Chapter 1) describe: students shuffling compliantly through the school day, or feeling shut down by teachers who either do not foster or who actively discourage students' desire to think and express themselves.

At PEBC, we believe that *all* students are capable of understanding and independent thinking, and have the right to the type of literacy that leads to both.

Specifically, we believe the following research-supported principles:

- *Literacy involves students actively making meaning of, with, and through text.* Adolescents need the skills to help them comprehend a wide variety of texts, and to interpret, critique, and evaluate texts (Allington, 2001; McLaughlin & DeVoogd, 2004; Weaver, 2002).
- *Students will become increasingly independent thinkers, readers, and writers by using the strategies of proficient readers and by being metacognitive.* They should be able to self-assess; name their learning process, strengths, and needs; reflect on their growth; set goals; and advocate for their learning needs (Flavell, 1985; Pearson et al., 1992; Perkins, 1995).
- *Strong literacy skills and comprehension of content are interdependent and mutually reinforcing.* Content-area teachers can integrate literacy in service of their goals, as an integral part of their curriculum (Geenleaf, Brown, & Littman, 2004; International Reading Association, 2004; Wineburg, 2001).

- *Learning is social*. Students learn best when the classroom culture supports peer sharing and questioning (NRC, 2000a; Sturtevant et al., 2006; Vygotsky, 1978).

TEACHERS AS GUIDES TO ACCESS AND POWER

In every classroom described in this book, these beliefs manifest in practice. Teachers guide students to the knowledge, strategies, and stance of competent and confident learners. As shown in Part I, when faculty embrace explicit comprehension strategy instruction (described in Chapter 1), students learn to notice, name, and claim the strategies (shown in Chapter 2), and thus become empowered. And as students are guided in how to apply these literacy skills—in their content-area classes (Chapter 3) and in the world (Chapter 4)—they see the relevance of their learning.

The authors in Part I show us how students can use literacy to claim their citizenship rights here and now: whether by challenging censorship in their school newspaper, by taking an advocacy role in a neighborhood building project, or simply by continuing to question the status quo. A recent study by an organization called Rock the Vote found that 80% of voters younger than 30 who cast ballots in the 2008 "Super Tuesday" primaries attended college (see Cornish, 2008). Yet literacy buys students more than just the facility to analyze political issues enough to cast a vote. It buys them access to work stability, opportunity for economic wealth, and with this the power to engage in our democracy not only as voters but also as advocates, critics, organizers, or candidates.

All secondary teachers can help develop this literacy currency. Content-area teachers can intentionally link their teaching to the literacy strategies that support the cognitive "core" of their academic discipline. The teachers described in Part II do just that: help students grapple with difficult problems in mathematics, give students the real intellectual work of inquiring scientists and analytical historians, and guide students to becoming both "data-literate" and self-directed while mastering language arts standards. These teachers value not only literacy, but authenticity: students have time to do real thinking about issues of real substance. Further, students are empowered to produce new knowledge rather than to just be passive consumers.

All of these teachers are, in some sense, educating students to participate in a democracy. As Gerardo Muñoz states (see Chapter 7), "It's about civil rights . . . you are a member of society, you have a voice, and you need to use it." We see youth like his student, Carrie (the self-described feminist) learning to "speak out": She now challenges her classmates' sexist comments or patriarchal assumptions. And she has carried the skills she gained in Gerardo's class to her other classes and out into the world. She has the power to advocate for the greater social good.

As shown by the authors in Part III, teachers across all content areas can embrace common language and instructional practices to empower students. Students learn to think best when they learn in community (Chapter 9) yet also develop independence (Chapter 11). This happens when instruction is designed so that the tasks, time, and talk all align to place student thinking and learning at the center of daily class activities (Chapters 10 and 12).

The shifts we advocate in teaching and learning parallel shifts that are happening in our economy as a whole. Two renowned economists, Murnane and Levy (1996), describe the "principles for educating children to thrive in a changing economy"—specifically the "new basic skills" that American workers need. These include "hard skills" such as math, problem solving, and reading; and "soft skills" such as "the ability to work in groups and to make effective oral and written presentations" (p. 9). Clearly, literacy is integral to these skills. And such skills greatly increase a citizen's chance to have economic stability, opportunities at work (including upward mobility), and an ability to advocate for oneself, one's family, and the greater good.

EFFECTIVE INSTRUCTION DOES NOT HAPPEN IN ISOLATION

We realize that secondary teachers' and students' work does not occur in a vacuum. Focusing on "adolescent literacy" or even on "best-practice instruction" is necessary, but insufficient. Many students—due to transience, poor instruction, teacher turnover, or a myriad of other factors—already are underprepared and disengaged when they enter high school. This is in large part due to challenges at the systems level.

Even if a school's faculty shares this book's and PEBC's vision and core instructional practices, policies at the district, state, and national level also must actively support literacy goals. If students' "thinking muscles" are to fully develop, assessment policies and practices must address more than just mastery of discrete facts or skills. What is measured becomes what is valued and thus what is taught. We must get our incentives right: assessing genuine thinking and evaluating authentic learning. To achieve this alignment in service of our goals for students, we must address these fundamental priorities:

- Districts need to design and fund school structures that align with our vision of teaching and learning put forth in this volume, in which student thinking is at the center.
- Districts and schools need to provide ongoing professional development opportunities that improve teachers' daily work with students.

SCHOOL SYSTEMS AND STRUCTURES

A school leader once told me, "If you want to know a school's values, look at its budget, schedule, and staffing assignments." For teachers to succeed in the practices we advocate, school resources must be targeted toward the dual priorities of student and teacher learning.

School leaders can design schedules so students have large blocks of time to read, write, talk, and think. Students should not rush to seven different classes each day, without time to synthesize or reflect. Struggling students should receive intensive and targeted support. Classes should be staffed with sufficient and qualified instructors (Elmore, 2000; Honan, Childress, & King, 2004).

Schools must allocate time and funds so teachers can meet regularly to plan and assess student learning. Similarly, staff need time and support to communicate with parents and the community about student learning.

In many secondary schools where PEBC consults, the administration has re-organized staff assignments. Up to five teachers (from all content areas) receive intensive training in instructional and coaching skills. They then teach half time and spend the rest of their day directly supporting colleagues.

Middle and high school principals need training to guide teachers as they learn how to support students' literacy rights. And principals' jobs must be restructured so they also have the time needed to support teachers in this work.

However, *all* adults in a school share the responsibility for the school's goals, processes, and outcomes. Leadership must be "distributed," rather than residing solely with the principal (Elmore, 2000; Spillane, Halverson, & Diamond, 2001). For example, in PEBC project schools, the professional development plan is over-seen by a school-based leadership team that includes teacher representatives. This team helps articulate and guide the school's mission. School administrators provide the necessary time, money, and expertise to train and support teachers as school leaders.

Creating and supporting effective schools is complex work. It requires a com-prehensive approach, long-range planning, and consistent focus. There is no "quick fix." We must channel time and energy in ways that produce real results for stu-dents. And we must have structures in place to sustain improvement (Fullan, 2003).

PROFESSIONAL DEVELOPMENT

As Linda Darling-Hammond, a national expert in teacher education, states, "Put simply, expert teachers are the most fundamental resource for improving educa-tion" (Darling-Hammond, 2008). If we truly hope to develop such expertise, policy makers, school leaders, teachers, and community members must reconceptualize teaching as a true profession with its own rigorous standards and requirements for ongoing learning.

Such a reconceptualization is based on the fundamental belief that teachers have a right to learn and to work in a school structure that supports learning. If teachers are to help students to access learning and power, then schools must do the same for teachers. At PEBC, we specifically believe the following:

- *Teaching requires an inquiry stance.* Effective teachers become increasingly reflective about what they are doing, why they are doing it, how it affects students, and what they could be doing differently. They can analyze and articulate their approach and can continue to question and refine (Weinbaum et al., 2004).
- *Teachers benefit from the same types of learning experiences that benefit students.* School leadership must set clear purposes for adult learning, carve out ample time, and address the diverse range of teachers' needs, interests, and knowl-edge base. Teachers need time to reflect on what they are learning and to address both what it means for their work with students and how to apply those insights (Roy & Hord, 2003).
- *Teacher learning helps teachers become school leaders.* When teachers' intellec-tual abilities, and motivation to learn and teach are honored, they not only

refine their own instruction but begin to influence colleagues in developing shared priorities for students.

"Job-embedded" professional development best embodies the above beliefs: teachers learn during the day, on site, rather than at conferences or through "in-services" (Roy & Hord, 2003). This learning can take many forms. For example, PEBC helps teachers implement peer-learning labs, in which colleagues observe each other teach and have very structured conversations about evidence of student learning. Or teachers who teach the same course can be given release time to design units and key learning activities.

Central to any teacher learning is the analysis of relevant and timely data about student learning and achievement. Leadership must schedule regular, sufficient, protected time for teachers to look at student work and analyze quantitative data in order to identify students' strengths and gaps. Such analysis is more likely than abstract conversation to actually impact teacher practice.

In many countries such professional development is already the norm. Japan is renowned for its "lesson study": A group of teachers designs a lesson; one teacher teaches it while colleagues observe; then they all analyze the lesson and collectively refine it. In Finland new teachers are given 20 hours each week to work with colleagues and observe more experienced teachers. And Singapore has developed three career ladders for teachers, to develop mentors, curriculum specialists, and future principals (Darling-Hammond, 2008).

The United States can learn from these countries. Teachers, like students, have the right to think, and the right to learn in a culture of thinking. Policies that enable teachers to function as true professionals are highly correlated with higher levels of student achievement. We ought not to underestimate teachers' power: In many respects, they play the most significant role in ensuring the health of our democracy.

WHAT WE STRIVE FOR

Deborah Meier reminds us that "the goal is educating, and that means knowing what we're educating *for*. Purpose must be decided upon" (2002, p. 161).

Ted Sizer (1997) offers a compelling response to the question of purpose: "Schools are to provoke young people to grow up intellectually, to think hard and resourcefully and imaginatively about important things." "Important things" certainly include key concepts in every content area. Yet when students are truly literate, they also then are free to decide what *they* think is important. Being a thinker means not only understanding what issues are on the ballot and casting a vote, but being thoughtful and articulate enough to raise new issues and redefine the discourse.

The 1989 Convention on the Rights of the Child recognized literacy (not just education) as a right. The 1975 Persepolis Declaration goes so far as to claim literacy as a fundamental human right which is "recognized as a mechanism for the pursuit of other human rights" (UNESCO, 2008).

Literacy has long been linked to power. In his 1845 autobiography, Frederick Douglass describes his realization that learning to read was "the pathway from slavery to freedom" (quoted in Sisco, n.d.). And today, individuals who lack the ability to comprehend, analyze, interpret, and critique texts are generally denied influence.

The cost of inaction is even greater for our society as a whole. Our world desperately needs thinkers, youth who can reason, analyze, and create. Secondary schools can and must be at the vanguard of a social movement that asserts—and secures—literacy as a civil right for all students.

References

Allington, R. L. (2001). *What really matters for struggling readers: Designing researched-based programs.* New York: Addison-Wesley.

Anderson, C. (2000). *How's it going? A practical guide to conferring with student writers.* Portsmouth, NH: Heinemann.

Annan, K. (2007). United Nations Literacy Decade, 2003–2012. *Literacy as freedom.* Retrieved Feb 26, 2008, from http://portal.unesco.org/education/admin/ev.php?URL_ID=13919&URL_DO=DO_TOPIC

Arendt, H. (1961). The crisis in education. In *Between past and future* (p. 192). New York: Penguin.

Bay-Williams, J., & Herrera, S. (2007). Is "just good teaching" enough to support English language learners?: Insights from sociocultural learning theory. In W. G. Matrin & M. E. Strutchens (Eds.), *The learning of mathematics: Sixty-ninth Yearbook of the National Council of Teachers of Mathematics* (pp. 43–63). Reston, VA: National Council of Teachers of Mathematics.

Beane, J. (2005). *A reason to teach: Creating classrooms of dignity and hope.* Portsmouth, NH: Heinemann.

Beck, I. L., McKeown, M. G., & Kucan, L. (2002). *Bringing words to life: Robust vocabulary instruction.* New York: Guilford Press.

Bennett, S. (2007). *That workshop book: New systems and structures for classrooms that read, write, and think.* Portsmouth, NH: Heinemann.

Bereiter, C., & Bird, M. (1985). Use of thinking aloud in identification and teaching of reading comprehension strategies. *Cognition and Instruction, 2,* 131–156.

Bradbury, R. (1953). *Fahrenheit 451.* New York: Ballentine Books.

Brown v. Board of Education, 347 U.S. 483 (1954).

Brown, H. D. (2000). *Principles of language learning and teaching* (4th ed.). New York: Addison Wesley Longman.

Cai, J., Lane, S., & Jakabcsin, M. S. (1996). The role of open-ended tasks and holistic scoring rubrics: Assessing students' mathematical reasoning and communication. In P. Elliott & M. Kenney (Eds.), *Communications in mathematics, K–12 and beyond: 1996 Yearbook of the National Council of Teachers of Mathematics* (pp. 137–145). Reston, VA: National Council of Teachers of Mathematics.

California Department of Education. (1990). *Science framework for California public schools: K–12.* Sacramento, CA.

Cambourne, B. (1995). Toward an educationally relevant theory of literacy learning: Twenty years of inquiry. *The Reading Teacher, 49*(3), 182–190.

Capps, R., Fix, M., Murray, J., Ost, J., Passel, J. S., & Herwontoro, S. (2005). *The new demography of America's schools: Immigration and the No Child Left Behind act.* Washington, DC: Urban Institute.

Close, E. (2005). *Conversations support literacy learning and achievement, K–12: Research findings from CELA.* Retrieved May 23, 2008, from http://www.ala.org/ala/aaslpubsandjournals/kqweb/kqarchieves/volume30/303Close.cfm

Colorado Critical Friends Group. (2002). *Working together to improve student learning* (S. Quate, Compiler). Denver, CO: Author.

Colorado model content standards for language arts. (2005). Retrieved May 21, 2008, from http://www.cde.state.co.us/cdeassess/documents/OSA/standards/math.html

Colorado model content standards for mathematics. (2005). Retrieved January 5, 2008, from www.cde.state.co.us/cdeassess/documents/OSA/standards/math.html

Conley, D. T. (2005). *College knowledge: What it really takes for students to succeed and what we can do to get them ready.* San Francisco: Jossey-Bass.

Connally, E. (2000). *Functions modeling change.* New York: Wiley.

Conrad, L. L., Matthews, M., Zimmerman, C., & Allen, P. A. (2008). *Put thinking to the test.* Portsmouth, ME: Stenhouse.

Cornell University Law School. (2005). Civil rights. *Legal information institute.* Retrieved

October 11, 2005, from http://www.law
.cornell.edu/topics/civil_rights.html

Cornish, A. (2008). Non-college kids outsiders
to rising "youth vote." *NPR.* Retrieved February 26, 2008, from http://www.npr.org/
templates/story/story.php?storyId=
71944288

Costa, A., & Kallick, B. (2004). Launching self-
directed learners. *Educational Leadership, 62,*
51–57.

Daniels, H., & Zemelman, S. (2004). *Subjects matter: Every teacher's guide to content-area reading.* Portsmouth, NH: Heinemann.

Darling-Hammond, L. (2008, February 25). How
they do it abroad. *Time Magazine, 171*(8), 34.

de Lange, J. (2003). Mathematics for literacy. In
B. L. Madison & L. A. Steen (Eds.), *Quantitative literacy: Why numeracy matters for schools
and colleges* (pp. 75–89). Princeton, NJ: National Council on Education and the Disciplines. Also available at: http://www.maa
.org/ql/pgs75_89.pdf

Delpit, L. (1995). *Other people's children: Cultural
conflict in the classroom.* New York: New Press.

Dewey, J. (1938). *Experience and education.* New
York: Macmillan.

Didion, J. (1976, December 5). Why I write. *New
York Times Magazine,* p. 2.

Elmore, R. F. (2000). *Building a new structure for
school leadership.* Washington, DC: Albert
Shanker Institute.

Elsasser, N., & John-Steiner, V. (1987). An inter-
actionist approach to advancing literacy. In
I. Shor (Ed.), *Freire for the classroom: A source-
book for liberatory teaching* (pp. 45–62). Portsmouth, NH: Boyton/Cook. (Original work
published 1977)

Fisher, M. T. (2008). Catching butterflies. *English
Education, 40*(2), 94–100.

Fisher, D., & Frey, N. (2007). *Checking for understanding: Formative assessment techniques for your
classroom.* Alexandria, VA: Association for
Supervision and Curriculum Development.

Finn, P. J. (1999). *Literacy with an attitude: Educating
working-class children in their own self-interest.*
Albany: State University of New York Press.

Flavell, J. H. (1985). *Cognitive development* (2nd
ed.). Englewood Cliffs, NJ: Prentice Hall.

Freire, P., & Macedo, D. P. (1987). *Literacy:
Reading the word and the world.* Westport, CT:
Greenwood.

Fullan, M. (2003). *The moral imperative of school leadership.* Thousand Oaks, CA: Corwin Press.

Gay, G. (1994). *A synthesis of scholarship in multicultural education.* Oak Brook, IL: North Central Regional Educational Laboratory.

Gay, G. (2002). Preparing for culturally responsive
teaching. *Journal of Teacher Education, 53*(2),
106–116.

Geenleaf, C., Brown, W., & Littman, C. (2004).
Apprenticing urban youth to science literacy.
In D. S. Strickland & D. E. Alvermann (Eds.),
*Bridging the literacy achievement gap, grades 4–
12* (pp. 200–226). New York: Teachers Col-
lege Press.

Gere, A., Fairbanks, C., Howes, A., Roop, L., &
Schaafsma, D. (1992). *Language and reflection:
An integrated approach to teaching English.* New
York: Macmillan.

Glasser, W. (1992). *The quality school teacher.* New
York: Harper Collins.

Goldberg, G., & Serravallo, J. (2007). *Conferring with
readers: Supporting each student's growth and independence.* Portsmouth, NH: Heinemann.

Graves, D. H. (2001). *The energy to teach.* Portsmouth, NH: Heinemann.

Gray, J. (2005). *4 A's text protocol.* Retrieved May
16, 2008, from http://www.nsrfharmony.org/
protocol/search.html

Greene, S. (Ed.). (2008). *Literacy as a civil right:
Reclaiming social justice in literacy teaching and
learning.* New York: Peter Lang.

Guthrie, J. T., Wigfield, A., Barbosa, P., Perence-
vich, K. C., Taboada, A., Davis, M. H., et al.
(2004). Increasing reading comprehension and
engagement through concept-oriented reading instruction. *Journal of Educational Psychology, 93*(3), 403–423.

Hakim, J. (2005). *A history of US:* Book 2. *Making
thirteen colonies.* New York: Oxford University Press.

Hand, B., Wallace, C., & Yang, E. (2004). Using
a science writing heuristic to enhance learning outcomes from laboratory activities in
seventh-grade science: Quantitative and
qualitative aspects. Research report. *International Journal of Science Education, 26*(2), 131–
149.

Harris, T. L., & Hodges, R. E. (Eds.). (1995). *The
literacy dictionary: The vocabulary of reading and
writing.* Newark, DE: International Reading
Association.

Helfand, D., & Blume, H. (2008, January 2). Left out, students want a voice in reform. *Los Angeles Times*, p. 8.

Hernández, A. (2003). Making content instruction accessible for English language learners. In G. G. Garcia (Ed.), *English learners: Reaching the highest level of English literacy*. Newark, DE: International Reading Association.

Hillocks, G. J. (1986). *Research on written composition: New directions for teaching*. Urbana, IL: ERIC Clearinghouse on Reading and Communication Skills, and the National Conference on Research in English.

Hirsh, E. D. (2004, February 24). Many Americans can read but can't comprehend. *USA Today*. Retrieved December 5, 2007, from http://www.usatoday.com/news/opinion/editorials/2004-02-24-hirsch-edit_x.htm

Holt, L. (1965). *The summer that didn't end*. New York: Morrow.

Honan, J. P., Childress, S., & King, C. (2004). *Aligning resources to improve student achievement: San Diego City Schools*. Boston: Harvard Business School Publishing.

Hyde, A. (2006). *Comprehending math*. Portsmouth, NH: Heinemann.

Hyde, A. (2007). Mathematics and cognition. *Educational Leadership, 65*(3), 43–47.

International Reading Association. (2004). *The role and qualifications of the reading coach in the United States: A position statement of the International Reading Association*. Washington, DC: International Reading Association.

Joftus, F. (2002). *Every child a graduate: A framework for an excellent education for all middle and high school students*. Washington DC: Alliance for Excellent Education.

Johnson, K. R., & Raynolds, R. (2006). *Ancient Denvers: Scenes from the past 300 million years of the Colorado Front Range*. Golden, CO: Fulcrum.

Kamil, M. L. (2003). *Adolescents and literacy: Reading for the 21st century*. Washington, DC: Alliance for Excellent Education.

Kazin, M. (2002, Fall). A patriotic left. *Dissent*. Retrieved January 6, 2008, from http://dissentmagazine.org/article/?article=560

Keene, E. O. (2008). *To understand: New horizons in reading comprehension*. Portsmouth, NH: Heinemann.

Keene, E. O., & Zimmerman, S. (1997). *Mosaic of thought: Teaching comprehension in a reader's workshop*. Portsmouth, NH: Heinemann.

Keene, E. O., & Zimmerman, S. (2007). *Mosaic of thought: The power of comprehension strategy* (2nd ed.). Portsmouth, NH: Heinemann.

Kenney, J. M. (2005). *Literacy strategies for improving mathematics instruction*. Alexandria, VA: Association of Supervision and Curriculum Development.

Kleinfeld, J. (1975). Effective teachers of Eskimo and Indian students. *School Review, 83*, 301–304.

Larson, L. (2003). *The complete Far Side: Vol. 1. 1980–1994*. Kansas City, MO: Andrews McMeel.

Lipman, P. (2004). *High stakes education: Inequality, globalization, and urban school reform*. New York: RoutledgeFalmer.

Lopate, T. (1975). *Being with children*. New York: Simon and Schuster.

Marzano, R. (2001). *Classroom instruction that works*. Alexandria, VA: Association for Supervision and Curriculum Development.

Maton, A., Hopkins, J., Johnson, S., Labart, D., Warner, M. Q., & Wright, J. D. (1994). *Evolution: Change over time* (Teacher's ed.). Prentice Hall Science. Englewood Cliffs, NJ: Prentice Hall.

McKeown, M. G. (1985). The acquisition of word meaning from context by children of high and low ability. *Reading Research Quarterly, 20*(4), 482–496.

McKeown, R. G., & Gentilucci, J. L. (2007). Think aloud strategy: Metacognitive development and monitoring comprehension in the middle school second-language classroom. *Journal of Adolescent & Adult Literacy, 51*(2), 138–147.

McLaughlin, M., & DeVoogd, G. (2004). Critical literacy as comprehension: Expanding reader response. *Journal of Adolescent & Adult Literacy, 48*(1), 52–62.

Meier, D. (2002). *The power of their ideas: Lessons for America from a small school in Harlem*. Boston: Beacon Press.

Merseth, K. (1993). How old is your shepherd? An essay about mathematics education. *Phi Delta Kappan, 74*, 548–554.

Michigan Department of Education. (n.d.). *The social studies history themes project*. Retrieved January 3, 2008, from http://www.michiganepic.org/historythemes/

Miller, D. (2002). *Reading with meaning: Teaching*

comprehension in the primary grades. Portland, ME: Stenhouse.

Moffett, J. (1966). *Teaching the universe of discourse.* Boston: Houghton Mifflin.

Montaigne, M. (1965). Of the education of children. In *The complete essays of Montaigne* (D. Frame, Trans.). Stanford, CA: Stanford University Press. (Original work published 1580)

Murnane, R. J., & Levy, F. (1996). *Teaching the new basic skills: Principles for educating children to thrive in a changing economy.* New York: Free Press.

National Assessment of Educational Progress (NAEP). (2007). *The nation's report card: Reading 2007.* Retrieved May 22, 2008, from http://nces.ed.gov/nationsreportcard/pdf/main2007/2007496_3.pdf

National Council of Teachers of Mathematics. (2000). *Principles and standards for school mathematics.* Reston, VA: Author.

National Reading Panel. (2001). *Put reading first: The research building blocks for teaching children to read.* Rockville, MD: National Institute of Child Health and Human Development.

National Research Council (NRC). (2000a). *How people learn: Brain, mind, experience, and school* (Expanded ed.). Washington, DC: National Academy Press.

National Research Council (NRC). (2000b). *Inquiry and the National Science Education Standards: A guide for teaching and learning.* Washington, DC: National Academy Press.

National Research Council (NRC). (2004). *Engaging schools: Fostering high school students' motivation to learn.* Washington, DC: National Academies Press.

Nieto, S. (2001). What keeps teachers going? and other thoughts on the future of public education. *Equity and Excellence in Education, 34*(1), pp. 6–15.

Nieto, S. (2006). *Teaching for social justice in schools: Stories of courage and corazon.* Paper presented at National Teachers of English Assembly for Research, Chicago, IL.

No Child Left Behind Act of 2001 (NCLB). 107th Congress 115 (2001).

Nystrand, M., Gamoran, A., Kachur, R., & Predergrast, C. (1997). *Opening dialogue.* New York: Teachers College Press.

Padrón, Y., Waxman, H., & Rivera, H. (2002). *Educating Hispanic students: Obstacles and av-*

enues to improved academic achievement. Santa Cruz, CA: Center for Research on Education, Diversity & Excellence.

Pearson, P. D., & Gallagher, M. (1983). *The instruction of reading comprehension.* Champaign: University of Illinois, Center for the Study of Reading.

Pearson, P. D., Roehler, L. R., Dole, J. A., & Duffy, G. G. (1992). Developing expertise in reading comprehension. In S. J. Samuels & A. E. Farstrup (Eds.), *What research has to say to the teachers of reading* (2nd ed., pp. 145–199). Newark, DE: International Reading Association.

Peregoy, S. F., & Boyle, O. F. (2005). *Reading, writing, and learning in ESL: A resource book for K–12 teachers* (4th ed.). Boston: Pearson/Allyn & Bacon.

Perkins, D. (1995). *Smart schools: Better thinking and learning for every child.* New York: Free Press.

Ritchhart, R. (2002). *Intellectual character: What it is, why it matters, and how to get it.* San Francisco: Jossey-Bass.

Roy, P., & Hord, S. (2003). *Moving NSDC's staff development standards into practice: Innovation configuration* (Vol. 1). Oxford, OH: National Staff Development Council.

Salinas, J. (2000, February 21–26). *The effectiveness of minority teachers on minority student success.* Paper presented at meeting of National Association of African American Studies and National Association of Hispanic and Latino Studies, Houston, TX.

Schmeck, R. R. (1988). Individual differences and learning strategies. In C. E. Weinstein, E. T. Goetz, & P. A. Alexander (Eds.), *Learning and study strategies: Issues in assessment, instruction, and evaluation* (pp. 171–191). San Diego, CA: Academic Press.

Schmoker, M. (2006). *Results now: How we can achieve unprecedented improvements in teaching and learning.* Alexandria, VA: Association for Supervision and Curriculum Development.

Schoenbach, R., Braunger, J., Greenleaf, C., & Litman, C. (2003). Apprenticing adolescents to reading in subject-area classrooms. *Phi Delta Kappan, 85*(2), 133–138.

Schoenbach, R., Geenleaf, C., Cziko, C., & Hurwitz, L. (1999). *Reading for understanding: A guide to improving reading in middle and high school classrooms.* San Francisco: Jossey-Bass.

Schultz, K. (2003). *Listening: A framework for teach-*

ing across differences. New York: Teachers College Press.

Schuster, L., & Anderson, N. C. (2005). *Good questions for math teaching: Why ask them and what to ask.* Sausalito, CA: Math Solutions Publications.

Shulman, L. S. (1986). Those who understand: Knowledge growth in teaching. *Educational Researcher, 57*(2), 4–14.

Sisco, L. (n.d.). *"Writing in the spaces left": Literacy as a process of becoming in the narratives of Frederick Douglass.* Retrieved February 20, 2008, from http://www.indiana.edu/~ovid99/douglass.html

Sizer, T. (1997, November 24). *Keynote speech.* Paper presented at the 10th annual fall forum of the Coalition of Essential Schools, San Francisco, CA.

Sizer, T., & Sizer, N. (1999). *The students are watching.* Boston: Beacon Press.

Smith, M. W., & Wilhelm, J. D. (2002). *Reading don't fix no Chevys: Literacy in the lives of young men.* Portsmouth, NH: Heinemann.

Smith, M. W., & Wilhelm, J. D. (2006). *Going with the flow: How to engage boys (and girls) in their literacy learning.* Portsmouth, NH: Heinemann.

Spillane, J. P., Halverson, R., & Diamond, J. B. (2001). Investigating school leadership practice: A distributed perspective. *Educational Researcher, 30*(3), 23–28.

Stiggins, R. J. (1997). *Student-centered classroom assessment* (2nd ed.). Upper Saddle River, NJ: Merrill.

Stiggins, R. J., Arter, J., Chappuis, J., & Chappuis, S. (2002). *Classroom assessment for students learning: Doing it right—using it well.* Portland, OR: Assessment Training Institute.

Strickland, D. S., & Alvermann, D. E. (Eds.). (2004). *Bridging the literacy achievement gap, grades 4–12.* New York: Teachers College Press.

Sturtevant, E. G., Boyd, F. B., Brozo, W. G., Hinchman, K. A., Moore, D. W., & Alvermann, D. E. (2006). *Principled practices for adolescent literacy: A framework for instruction and policy.* Mahwah, NJ: Erlbaum.

Thomas, M. (2004). *Write about math: The test connection, grade 7.* Columbus, OH: McGraw-Hill.

Toulmin, S. E. (1958). *The uses of argument.* Cambridge, England: Cambridge University Press.

Tovani, C. (2000). *I read it, but I don't get it: Comprehension strategies for adolescent readers.* Portland, ME: Stenhouse.

Tovani, C. (2004). *Do I really have to teach reading? Content comprehension, grades 6–12.* Portland, ME: Stenhouse.

Tucker, M. (2007). *Tough choices or tough times: The report of the New Commission on the Skills of the American Workforce.* San Francisco: National Center on Education and the Economy.

UNESCO. (2008). Why literacy matters. *Education for all: Global monitoring report.* Retrieved February 24, 2008, from http://portal.unesco.org/education/en/ev.php-URL_ID=43048&URL_DO=DO_TOPIC&URL_ SECTION= 201.html

U.S. Department of Education. (2007). *Office for Civil Rights: Overview of the agency.* Retrieved November 11, 2007, from http://www.ed.gov/about/offices/list/ocr/index.html

Vygotsky, L. S. (1978). *Mind in society: The development of higher psychological processes.* Cambridge, MA: Harvard University Press.

Weaver, C. (2002). *Reading process and practice* (3rd ed.). Portsmouth, NH: Heinemann.

Weinbaum, A., Allen, D., Blythe, T., Simon, K., Siedel, S., & Rubin, C. (2004). *Teaching as inquiry: Asking hard questions to improve practice and student achievement.* New York: Teachers College Press.

Wenden, A. L. (1985). Learner strategies. *TESOL (Teaching English to Speakers of Other Languages) Newsletter, 19,* 1–7.

Wiggins, G., & McTighe, J. (1998). *Understanding by design.* Alexandria, VA: Association for Supervision and Curriculum Development.

Wiggins, G., & McTighe, J. (2005). *Understanding by design* (2nd ed.). Alexandria, VA: Association for Supervision and Curriculum Development.

Wilhelm, J., Baker, T., & Dube, J. (2001). *Strategic reading: Guiding students to lifelong literacy, 6–12.* Portsmouth, NH: Heinemann.

Wineburg, S. (2001). *Historical thinking and other unnatural acts: Charting the future of teaching the past.* Philadelphia: Temple University Press.

Wormeli, R. (2006). *Fair isn't always equal: Assessing & grading in the differentiated classroom.* Portland, ME: Stenhouse.

Yolen, J. (1992). *Encounter.* San Diego, CA: Harcourt Brace Jovanovich.

Yore, L. D., Bisanz, G. L., & Hand, B. M. (2003).

Examining the literacy component of science literacy: 25 years of language arts and science research. *International Journal of Science Education, 25*(6), 689–725.

Zemelman, S., Daniels, H., & Hyde, A. (1998). *Best practice: New standards for teaching and* *learning in America's schools.* Portsmouth, NH: Heinemann.

Zola, J. (2003, April 30). *Scored discussion in social studies.* Paper presented at the Colorado State Social Studies Conference, Littleton, Colorado.

About the Editor and the Contributors

Samantha Bennett, MA, a former middle school teacher, is an instructional coach at the Rocky Mountain School of Expeditionary Learning in Denver, Colorado. She is the author of *That Workshop Book: New Systems and Structures for Classrooms That Read, Write, and Think* and works at schools around the country to help teachers harness the energy to teach and learn.

Jeff Cazier taught science and now works as an instructional coach at Prairie Middle School in Aurora, Colorado. He has 19 years of experience teaching middle school, serves as a PEBC National Lab host and cofacilitates PEBC's Science Institutes. He has been featured in the Association for Supervision and Curricum Development's video *Classroom Instruction That Works*.

Lesli Cochran, MA, teaches language arts at Conrad Ball Middle School in Loveland, Colorado. She has taught for 8 years and serves as a PEBC National Lab host. She has served at the district level as the Middle School Language Arts Curriculum Coordinator, is a member of the Colorado Association of Middle Level Educators, and has presented at the National Schools to Watch conference.

Wendy Ward Hoffer holds an MA in education from Stanford University and earned National Board Certification while teaching middle school math and science. Currently a PEBC staff developer in urban middle schools and a coleader of PEBC Science Institutes, she is writing a book (forthcoming from Heinemann) for science teachers about how to prioritize student thinking.

Michelle Morris Jones, MA, is a PEBC staff developer. She coaches teachers and leaders in secondary schools, serves as an adjunct professor in the Boettcher Teachers Program (preparing urban teachers), and facilitates seminars on teacher leadership. Previously, she taught literacy in elementary and middle schools in predominately urban settings.

Jennifer Kirmes, MAT, is a mentor teacher at César Chávez Charter School in Washington, D.C. In her role as mentor, she teaches physics and earth science classes while also working to support and develop other teachers in the science department. She is a Teach for America alumna.

Moker Klaus-Quinlan is a PEBC staff developer who works with secondary educators. She has taught Grades 4–8 and has earned National Board Certification. She holds a BA in environmental studies and a master's degree in education, with an emphasis on literacy.

Dagmar Koesling, MEd, MALD, is a math teacher and curriculum developer at Fenway High School, an urban public school in Boston. She is a teacher-educator for the Boston Teacher Residency (BTR) program and teaches the math methods course for BTR middle and high school preservice teachers. She has also served as a consultant to math departments of several small schools.

Marjorie Larner, MEd, is a former PEBC staff developer, teacher, and administrator who works as a coach, and designer of professional development for districts, universities, publishers, and nonprofit organizations. Her collaborators on the chapter in this volume were Susan Marion and her students Maile Gove, Ana Gutierrez, Orlinda Ramirez, and Warren Swiney from the Denver Center for International Studies, where Larner coaches through the Asia Society's International Studies Schools Network. Larner's publications include *Pathways: Charting a Course for Professional Learning* and *Tools for Leaders: Indispensable Graphic Organizers, Protocols, and Planning Guidelines for Working and Learning Together.*

Diane Lauer is a former principal of Conrad Ball Middle School and current director of instructional coaches for the Thompson School District in Loveland, Colorado (where PEBC has consulted since 2002). She has presented regionally and nationally on various school reform efforts and is the state director of the Colorado Trailblazer Schools to Watch program and a member of the National Forum to Accelerate Middle Grades Reform. She has been published in the *Journal of Staff Development.*

Joanna Leeds has a master's degree in school leadership from the Harvard Graduate School of Education. She currently works in kindergarten and first-grade classrooms in Charlottesville, Virginia, pushing students to develop critical skills. She is a former teacher and PEBC staff developer. She has also worked as an instructional coach with the Colorado Small Schools Initiative and the Institute for Educational Equity.

Paula Miller is a PEBC staff developer with a master's degree in reading. She has 26 years experience in education as a teacher of middle and high school language arts and reading, a district and state agency staff developer, and a campus and district administrator. She has written articles for *Educational Leadership, Voices in the Middle,* and *Classroom Leadership.*

Garrett Phelan is the principal of the Capitol Hill campus of César Chávez Charter School, where PEBC consulted from 2005–2008. A teacher for 30 years, he received his secondary teaching credential from the American Montessori Society and holds a BS in psychology from Central Connecticut State University.

Suzanne Plaut (Editor) is Vice President of Education at the Public Education & Business Coalition. She received her EdD from the Harvard Graduate School of Education, where she also served on the editorial board of the *Harvard Educational Review.* She has also served as a university supervisor for preservice teachers and as director of literacy and literacy specialist in several of Boston Public Schools.

Jennifer Swinehart taught for 4 years at Bruce Randolph Middle School where she was a language arts teacher, literacy coach, and PEBC National Lab host. She also facilitated literacy curriculum trainings in Los Angeles and Baltimore. Jennifer now teaches middle school language arts at the International School in Manila, Philippines, and is earning her masters degree in multidisciplinary studies.

Baynard Woods, PhD, is the chair of the History Department and a mentor teacher at César Chávez Charter School in Washington, D.C.

Angela Zehner earned her master's degree in the education of diverse learners. She taught math and was an instructional content coach for Prairie Middle School in Aurora, Colorado, where she is now an assistant principal. She has 18 years of teaching experience and served as a PEBC National Lab host.

Index